THE ACTIVIST'S HANDBOOK
HOW TO FIGHT BACK IN YOUR COMMUNITY

LEARN HOW TO: RESTORE FREEDOM, TAKE THE OFFENSIVE, CHANGE THE DEBATE, & HOLD ELECTED OFFICIALS RESPONSIBLE

American Policy Center

Many of the enclosed documents, and the links to other research documents mentioned in articles, can be found in the Activist Training Tool Kit located on the American Policy Center web page:

www.americanpolicy.org/tools
password: apc1225

TABLE OF CONTENTS

Part One

Taking the Offense for Liberty...1

Freedom Pod/Planting the Seeds of Freedom..................1

Green New Deal - The Mask of Agenda 21.....................2

Agenda 2030 Goals..3

In Local Government...7

Betrayal by the National Association of Realtors..............9

How to Improve Our PR & Change the Debate...............13

How to Counter These Powerful Forces..........................14

Legislative Action...18

Taking Offense to Restore Liberty....................................19

How to Control the Action...20

Citizen Ninja! - 8 Rules for Successful Activism...............21

How to Organize..23

How to Research..25

City Survey, Getting to Know Your Community 27

How to Write Effective Letters..30

Tools for Making Private Property the Center of Your

Efforts 32

Resolutions 33

How to Use Resolutions...34

Candidates Promise to Protect Property Rights...............35

Facilitated Meetings, Consensus, and the

Delphi Technique..38

State Legislative Action 44

The Five Bill Package to Launch a Revolution..................44

The Silver Bullet for Victory..46

Can We Take Back our Election Proces?..........................50

Why Don't Elected Representatives and their Agents Respond to Citizens?...53

Civil Rights Act Section 1983..53

Battles Fought...58

Worldwide Private Property Rights Movement................63

Private Property and the Eradication of Poverty..............65

Part Two

The Forces Behind Agenda 21 & Green New Deal............71

Non-Governmental Organizations NGOs........................75

Hiding Their Agenda in NewSpeak...................................78

Programs of Agenda 21 & Green New Deal.....................79

Form-based Codes..79

Affirmatively Furthering Fair Housing.............................80

Urban Growth...82

International Building Codes..83

Complete Streets...84

What Works Cities..85

Transition...85

Wildlands Project..87

Conservation Easements..88

Endangered Species Act...94

National Heritage Areas...96

Agriculture..104

Regionalism...108

The Transect..109

Attacks on Private Property...111

Banning Zoning for Single-family Homes.......................111

Eminent Domain...112

Rent Control on Landlords...114

Alternative Energy..115

A21/GND in Schools and Churches................................130

School Reform = Indoctrination......................................131

Green Invasion of Christian Churches............................132

What Do I Mean By a Freedom Pod?..............................136

Agenda 21 to Green New Deal...139

The Growing Threat of Smart Meters.............................146

Handouts..148

Meet ICLEI...161

Coordination..166

American Planning Association 183

Sample Bills to Protect Property Rights..........................193

PART 1 – HOW TO FIGHT BACK
TAKING THE OFFENSE FOR LIBERTY

1. Introduction:

"The first lesson of economics is scarcity; there is never enough of anything to fully satisfy all those who want it. The first lesson of politics is to disregard the first lesson of economics." Economist Thomas Sowell

There is a determined force in the world dedicated to an agenda designed to "reorganize human society." Those are their words. To achieve that agenda they intend to change our economic system away from free markets and into powerful government control of production, development, and food production as they remove individual choice through a one-size fits all blueprint for human action they have labeled "Sustainable."

While the plan is global in origin and scope, it is being systematically imposed through local, county, and state government under the excuse of environmental protection. The forces behind the agenda are rich, politically powerful, and well organized. They dodge, duck and weave through any organized opposition, and use any crisis as a new tool to keep moving forward. The recent Coronavirus is a prime example of that. Where massive, draconian measures were used by government at every level to contain the spread of the virus, now Sustainable policy proponents see an opportunity to use many of the same "emergency" tactics under the threat of a declared environmental crisis to rush their agenda into place.

As a result of the emergency measures taken for the virus and the new threat of a push for government to keep those emergency measures in place to combat an unproven environmental crisis, American citizens must learn bold, determined tactics and political skills to preserve and protect Constitutionally-protected rights and personal liberties now threatened like never before in the nation's history.

This action kit is designed to provide history, background, and training to help concerned citizen understand the threat, its origins, the players behind it, their policies and tactics, and how to effectively combat it by taking the offence to restore and defend liberty.

PLANTING THE SEEDS OF FREEDOM
TURNING YOUR COMMUNITY INTO A FREEDOM POD
TO PROTECT PRIVATE PROPERTY, FREE ENTERPRISE AND INDIVIDUAL CHOICE

by Tom DeWeese

The Green New Deal is the latest and most effective tool of choice to force massive policy changes to our national system under the excuse of climate crisis. Now the forces behind this agenda are working through state legislatures and city councils to rush it all into place.

That is why the American Policy Center has focused this Action Kit to teach activists to take direct action at the local and state level. Other training programs focus on running Presidential and Congressional campaigns, but this Action Kit training program is based on the fact that successful local action moves up as others observe the benefits and how it was accomplished. Soon it will reach the state legislative level where keen legislators can make it state law, which can then spread to other states. Eventually such a movement moves into Congress because successful legislators will move into Congressional positions. Then the whole country is affected by the success that perhaps started in your community. It rarely works the other way around because of the massive influence of special interests at the federal level. In short, we need to sneak up on them one level at a time, one freedom pod at a time.

GREEN NEW DEAL IS AGENDA 21
THE GROWING DRIVE TO MAKE IT LAW

by Tom DeWeese

For more than 30 years I've worn a tinfoil hat because I, and a few others, were able to read between the lines of the UN's Agenda 21. Then, last year when the global forces used a nitwit bartender to launch their Green New Deal, the Republican Party laughed, but immediately I could see exactly what was happening. It was Agenda 21 all over again, but this time on steroids.

Well, get ready because they are about to launch an all-out drive to impose the Green New Deal at every level of American government. Their inspiration for this new game plan is from the lessons they've learned from the Coronavirus lock-down. Fear is the key. The new urgency will be climate change using the pandemic tactics

Ironically, the policy designated to save us all from this very old, but renewed crisis is their thirty year old solution – Agenda 21, now renamed the Green New Deal.

First, let's make one fact very clear. The Green New Deal *IS* Agenda 21, most recently labeled the 2030 Agenda. There is no difference and if Congressional Republicans like Senator Mitch McConnell and national Conservative leadership in Washington, DC had listened to my warnings over the years they would know that. In fact, we could have killed this insanity when it first infested national policy under Bill Clinton's Administration. Instead, they were dumbfounded and amused when an unknown bartended from New York suddenly laid down the gauntlet that now threatens to remove and replace our very system of government and economy.

Let me prove my case. First, let's review what the Green New Deal actually calls for. According to a report by a major proponent, the Green Party US: the plan is a "four part program for moving America quickly out of crisis into a secure, sustainable future." They label these four points as the "Four Pillars" of the Green New Deal.

1. **The Economic Bill of Rights, Consists of** the "right to full employment and ending unemployment by guaranteeing a job at a living wage in a safe workplace, empowered by labor unions; single-payer Medicare for all, tuition-free education from pre-school to college and the right to affordable housing. This last part comes with the creation of a federal bank that will solve distressed mortgages (through taxes, of course), and expand public housing. Payment of those taxes will be distributed in proportion to ability to pay.

2. A Green Transition, Here's where the tax money really ramps up to pay for investment in green business through grants and low-interest loans. The GND even determines how any money made in this investment is to be spent and into whose pocket any new wealth goes as it says the money will not go into the pockets of rich, absentee investors. So, goodbye stock market. Of course, the plan calls for redirecting investment into wind and solar, away from fossil fuels, enforce sustainable agriculture and forestry. Of coursed, there will be full employment for green jobs, mass transit, bikeways and pedestrian traffic rather than cars, and "regional food systems." That means no need for shipping goods by truck or air.

3. Real Financial Reform, Actually, this is one part of the Green new Deal that is not all together nuts. Ron Paul would even approve of some of it, especially the part that calls for getting rid of the Federal Reserve and breaking up the banking monopoly. But again, they target private investors, without which the only way to provide financial needs would be through government. That solution means tax dollars through the creation of public-owned banks that function as non-profit utilities. So, as these "real financial reforms" are implemented, it will be interesting to watch which powerful political leader will then rise up to control the entire money supply for their own personal agenda.

4. A Functioning Democracy, One sentence in the Green Party's report says it all, "Just as we are replacing the old economy with a new one, we need a new politics to restore the promise of American democracy." Of course, there never was any such promise because America is not a democracy. We are a Republic. That means the majority does not rule. The rights and property of a minority are protected, no matter what the majority on any given day may lust after. Simply adhering to the Constitution as written would fix all of the violations they outline in the Green New Deal, including guaranteeing voter rights. The Green New Deal calls for the creation of a "Corporation for Economic Democracy, a new federal corporation to provide publicity, training, education, and direct financing for cooperative development and for democratic reforms to make government agencies, private associations, and business enterprises more participatory." Specifically, it's a federal propaganda and economic-control machine, otherwise known as communism.

So, this is the grand plan for the reorganization of the United States of America. Its proponents insist that this is the plan to convert the entire U.S. economy to renewable energy within 12 years, while also sparking a massive burst of job-creation and technological innovation." Congressional Republicans have stated the plan is dead on arrival and is not to be taken seriously. Yet, take note of how many of these so-called solutions were actually used in the national shutdown under the cornonavirus panic.

Now, let's look at the 17 goals that were laid down in 2015 for the 2030 Agenda, which was simply a reworking of 1992's Agenda 21, basically providing more detail.

AGENDA 2030 GOALS

Goal 1. End poverty in all its forms everywhere. The only answer the plan offers for eliminating poverty is redistribution of wealth. The document calls for "equal rights to economic resources." That means government is claiming an absolute power to take away anything that belongs to you to give to whomever it deems more deserving. That is government-sanctioned theft. *(GND pillar 1?)*

Goal 2. End hunger, achieve food security and improve nutrition and promote sustainable agriculture. UN documents go into great detail on controlling food supplies. They detail enforcing "sustainable farming tactics" which have been proven to force up the cost of food production while decreasing yield. It is basically the old Soviet practice of farm control that turned the breadbasket of the world into non-productive wasteland. *(GND Pillar 2?)*

Goal 3. Ensure healthy lives and promote well-being of all at all ages. This means cradle to grave control over how and where we live and what we are permitted to eat. The healthy lives they promote means basically forcing us out of our cars and into walking and riding bikes as we are relocated into controlled high rise apartment buildings sanctioned by government. *(GND Pillar 2?)*

Goal 4. Ensure inclusive and equitable quality education and promote lifelong learning opportunities for all. We have long known that lifelong learning is the means to continually apply behavior modification practices to assure we maintain the desired attitudes, values and beliefs to live in a global village. *(GND pillar 1?)*

Goal 5. Achieve gender equality and empower all women and girls. The rainbow flag flies as we ignore Shariah law and its war on women. *(GND Pillar 4?)*

Goal 6. Ensure availability and sustainable management of water and sanitation. Ask California how sustainable water control is working for them as these policies have torn down water systems and dams to "free the rivers." *(GND Pillars 1&2?)*

Goal 7. Ensure access to affordable, reliable, sustainable and modern energy for all. Seriously? Their solution is to ban oil and enforce wind and solar power. *(GND Pillars 1&2?)*

Goal 8. Promote sustained, inclusive and sustainable economic growth, full and productive employment and decent work for all. And who decides what is "productive" or "decent" work? Do we leave it to the bureaucrats to decide? *(GND Pillar 2?*

Goal 9. Build resilient infrastructure, promote inclusive and sustainable industrialization and foster innovation. No real industry can remain in business under a government-managed economy with its shifting rules and constant increase in taxes. Government doesn't create industry or prosperity. *(GND Pillar 2?)*

Goal 10. Reduce inequality within and among countries. This is another form of redistribution of wealth that forces industries from first world to third world nations. How's that working for you America, with China making nearly everything, including our medicines? *(GND Pillar 4?)*

Goal 11. Make cities and human settlements inclusive, safe, resilient and sustainable. This is Smart Growth which promises a utopia of families and neighbors playing and working together, riding bikes, walking to work in stress free communities. It really means the end of private property rights, single-family homes, and replace those with stack and pack high rises where residents are over-taxed and over-regulated, rents are high and individual thoughts and actions are viewed as a threat to the "well-ordered society."*(GND Pillar 1?)*

Goal 12. Ensure sustainable consumption and production patterns. What more is there to say? Control from the top down. We are witnessing this firsthand now under the name of a pandemic emergency. *(GND Pillar 2?)*

Goal 13. Take urgent action to combat climate change and its impacts. Here it is! The root of the entire plan buried down near the end. Climate Change. How many scientific reports do real scientists have to present to show this is the greatest scam ever devised to conjure up a reason for government to control every aspect of our lives? *(GND Pillar 2?)*

Goal 14. Conserve and sustainably use the oceans, seas and marine resources for sustainable development. Control the water, control society. This one is really aimed at destroying the oil industry in order to enforce wind and solar power. *(GND Pillar 2?)*

Goal 15. Protect, restore and promote sustainable use of terrestrial ecosystems, sustainably manage forests, combat desertification, and halt and reverse land degradation and halt biodiversity loss. Have you been watching the news as the greatest fires in history are destroying millions of acres of forests? Why is this happening? Because of sustainable forest management that refuses to allow the removal of dead trees (fuel for very hot fires) from the forest floor. *(GND Pillar 2?)*

Goal 16. Promote peaceful and inclusive societies for sustainable development, provide access to justice for all and build effective, accountable and inclusive institutions at all levels. This is Social Justice which really means social engineering. *(GND Pillar 3?)*

Goal 17. Strengthen the means of implementation and revitalize the global partnership for sustainable development. This means the re-boot of Agenda 21, because that was the original "global partnership." *(GND Pillar 4?)*

In 1992 they told us that Agenda 21 was just a suggestion. Today, after experiencing the "wrenching transformation" of our society that Al Gore called for, we know it was much more than that. And we have suffered the consequences as government at every level has grown out of control, property rights have all but disappeared, the middle class is disappearing, and the world is in turmoil.

Now the power elite, which prey on the poor and helpless, are determined to finish the job. They are fast moving toward the goal of eliminating individual nation states, controlling individual actions and wiping private property ownership from the face of the Earth. Their goal is to make us all "equal" in the same chains to assure none of us can disrupt their well-ordered utopian nightmare.

*Agenda 21/GND side by side (it's the same policy)

 B. How the Sustainable forces intend to use Pandemic fear tactics to impose GND policy on local and state levels.

We watched as Nancy Pelosi and her team attempted to stack the emergency economic legislation with major parts of the Green New Deal. Now, as the crisis begins to subside and people are looking forward to getting their lives back to normal, the forces behind the Green New Deal are preparing to push even harder to put it into law, especially on the local level.

Once the current threat passes the Sustainable forces are going to rush into the void in a drive to keep much of these emergency powers in place. While most of us were kept in place at home, the GND forces were busy making place for our future.

They are determined to keep many of the massive controls in place. Free enterprise, individual choice, and private property ownership are the main targets.

During the nationwide shutdown I was able to intercept several of their plans. Here are just a few of the messages the radical promoters of the Green New Deal were issuing on how to use the Coronavirus tactics to promote their green agenda.

- "Global Green New Deal supporters Urge World Leaders to Learn from Coronavirus to tackle Climate Crisis."

- "The Coronavirus pandemic makes what we've already known clear: we need a Green New Deal to stop climate change, provide desperately needed jobs, and halt future mass pandemics."

- Time to switch to Game B – a globally-cooperative humanity worth its name…The plan has a name: a Green New Deal."

- New York Congresswoman Alexandria Ocasio-Cortez, the chief sponsor of the Green New Deal, is using the coronavirus panic to attack the property rights of landlords, saying "people shouldn't be making money off of just owning property." She is targeting landlords because by destroying them it will force all housing to be government housing – just as called for in the Green New Deal.

- Governor of California said the coronavirus crisis is "an opportunity to advance a more progressive agenda."

- A force called "Security and Sustainability Forum" held a series of Internet Townhalls during the pandemic to meet with local elected officials and to train activists to push this agenda.

- An environmental activist and Democrat candidate for the state Senate in Colorado, Arn Menconi, said, "Coronavirus has proved we can afford the Green New Deal…"

- The World Economic Forum (WEF), which works hand-in-hand with the World Health Organization (WHO) and the United Nations, is urging various governments to focus on "flattening the Climate Curve in the Post-COVID world."

- "This is a golden opportunity to retool our economies for the planet that we are living on, not the unlimited, infinitely stable one we wish we had. It is time to invest in resilient and sustainable infrastructure to build a new green economy…" Patrick Verkooijen, CEO, Global Center for Adaptation – a UN NGO.

The fact is, the global forces that have been behind the battle over "climate change" have learned that the threat of global warming is a tired, worn-out issue that most of the world has grown weary of hearing about and is now ignoring. The panic created by the cornonavirus pandemic has energized these forces. And they intend to keep that energy going to enforce the Green New Deal by using the tactics they've learned in the panic. Can it be anymore obvious what the Globalist Left has in mind for the freedoms of the United States?

Exposing the NGO forces operating behind the scenes (they only have power because your elected officials give it to them)

IN LOCAL GOVERNMENT

City Councils and County Commissions are the best places to organize to stop the Sustainable invasion. This is where you may have a personal relationship with an elected representative and where you can have the most influence. But you must not try to exercise that opposition alone. This is where your coalition must be organized, educated about the issues, and prepared with a goal and a plan to achieve it.

Have you ever wondered why your elected officials always seem to be susceptible and even eager to impose these plans? Have you wondered why they refuse to listen to your opposition? Well, for the answer, you need to fully understand and see the true makeup of your local government. It's not just the five or seven council members or county commissioners. And it's also more than just the NGOs and the planners.

Of course there are the typical NGOs like the Sierra Club and a host of others representing individual issues like bike lanes, land trusts, energy and water issues, historic preservation, and housing development, for example. Each brings their own well-worn plan and the application for the individual grants to see them enforced. And of course there are several different planning groups like the American Planning Association. However there is another line of heavy influence standing behind all of these layers of your hidden government. People who run for our local and state offices are not necessarily evil or wrongheaded. In many cases they are just good people who want to serve their community. However, when we elected our city councils, county commissions, mayors, legislators and governors, almost every community does a strange thing with these new, eager leaders. We send them off to indoctrination centers. Of course, they aren't officially called that. Here are some examples.

U.S. Conference of Mayors: Elect a new mayor and send him/her off to this national meeting where he/she can meet with other mayors and share and gain ideas for the community. That's a good idea, right? After all, this is an official government organization where our mayor should be.

Well, the U.S. Conference of Mayors is actually a 501(c)(3) private organization whose member cities are those with populations over 30,000. In 1996 they made the UN's Kyoto Global Warming Treaty a centerpiece of the Conference's agenda – calling on all cities to use the provisions of the treaty to reduce their carbon footprint. In addition, the Conference of Mayors has accepted the UN's Earth Charter as a guideline for policy decisions.

National Association of Counties: A private, 501(c)(3) organization, County Commissioners are sent here where 50 state affiliates represent more than half of the counties in America. Together with the U.S. Conference of Mayors, the Association of Counties established the Joint Center for Sustainable Communities and then provided the framework for Bill Clinton's Presidential Council on Sustainable Development.

National League of Cities: a private 501(c)(3) organization, the League of Cities represents more than 1,400 dues-paying communities. The League supports gun control, and opposes any kind of restrictions on state governments' takings of private land.

National Conference of State Legislatures: A 501(c)(3) private organization which works to ensure that federal programs operate hand-in-hand with state programs, making sure that federal programs are implemented into state policy in a seamless or harmonized manner – making it easier to argue that such polices are state rather than federal – its all local!

Council of State Governments: a private 501(c)(3) organization. The Council promotes worldwide "sustainable" zoning and such uniform state codes and regulatory systems, providing model statues for legislatures.

National Governors Association: A private 501(c)(3) organization that advocates Smart Growth, more government benefits for illegals, worked to block workfare requirements for welfare benefits and supports taxing the Internet.

These are the organizations to which we send our newly elected officials to learn about the proper role of government. As they listen to speaker after speaker we find that these are most likely the NGOs and planners, sharing program ideas and building the dream, all leading to Sustainable Development. The officials are even given sample legislation to take home. When they arrive home, the officials are met with representatives from the same NGO groups ready to help them put the policies in place. And, of course, they are armed with the grants to fund it all. Eventually, your elected representatives begin to believe this is all the proper role of government. So when local activists come in to oppose such plans, their immediate reaction (supported by the NGOs) is that you are fringe nuts to be ignored.

All of this is backed by these "official" leagues and associations that are obviously "official branches of government." So if they say it's the right thing to do, obviously it is! There's just one problem with that impression. All of these groups are 501(c)(3) private organizations. They are NOT governmental or mandatory. They have private agendas and membership by your community or attendance by your elected officials is not mandatory. The only reason these organizations, including the NGOs and planners, have any influence or power in your community is because your elected officials give it to them. Begin a campaign to end your community's or state's membership in these private organizations, and above all, work to stop your officials from attending their indoctrination meetings.

Knowing that your elected officials are under this kind of pressure and influence, how do you combat it? Of course, the local level is where the NGOs and planners mass behind your officials. Here they supply the tools, the training, and the money to make it all happen. A little research will reveal who the NGOs are. But before you attempt to go after them, be sure to organize your committee that is responsible for attending all of the council sessions as well as the planning meetings. Take note of who is in attendance. This will give you insight into the NGOs and planners. It will be obvious that several people in the room don't appear to be local, yet they seem to wield strong influence. You may see your local officials deferring to them during the meetings. These may be planners, NGO representatives, or perhaps even federal agents from HUD, EPA or DOT. Study them and find out who they are. You need to know who and what is to be your opposition.

The first order of business in your fight is to stop the local government from taking the federal grants. The NGOs are pushing them hard behind closed doors. Your voice will seem out of place and a bit crazy to your officials. Why not take the "free" money? This is where your research team will become vital. They can provide research to show why it isn't "free." It's vital that elected officials be made aware of the implications and the hidden strings attached to the grants. Plan your attacks accordingly.

PRIVATE PROPERTY RIGHTS AND SOCIALISM DO NOT MIX
BETRAYAL BY THE NATIONAL ASSOCIATION OF REALTORS

The National Association of Realtors (NAR) is the main stream organization in which nearly every real estate agent in the nation belongs as a means to keep up with the latest ideas and trends in the property selling industry. NAR members are the professionals that all of us look to for the best approach to buy and sell our homes. One of NAR's mottos is "protecting the American dream of home ownership". And they claim to protect property rights.

Would it then surprise you that NAR is a major promoter of a plan that actually results in the destruction of private property rights? NAR documents show the Association is working to advocate the policy of Smart Growth for local community development.
Urban planners promote Smart Growth policies because they adhere to the dogma that urban sprawl (development projects) are a danger to the environment, increasing pollution and housing costs, creating more driving time, and shopping stress. In addition, say planners, such "urban sprawl" uses up more natural resources and reduces open space.

In response, Smart Growth advocates promote policies to encourage individuals to live in denser population communities that take up smaller tracts of land per housing unit. Such communities also advocate that residents rely more on walking, biking, or public transportation than on cars. Smart Growth plans call for mixing retail and other commercial facilities with residential units. The point is to eliminate the need to commute to jobs or shopping. Everything will be right there in your neighborhood. Most recently, Smart Growth policies are pushing to include federal Section Eight Housing projects and the elimination of single-family home zoning protections.

Yet, the National Association of Realtors paints a delightful, positive picture of a Smart Growth future in its documents: "*Our members don't just sell homes, they sell neighborhoods.*" By promoting Smart Growth, NAR says it's working to "*create a range of housing opportunities and choices.*" "*Providing quality housing for people of all income levels is an integral component in any smart growth neighborhood. Housing diversity in terms of type and cost provides a healthy, diverse community. By using smart growth approaches to create a wider range of housing choices, municipalities can reduce the environmental costs of auto-dependent development, use their infrastructure resources more efficiently, ensure better balance of jobs, and housing, and generate a strong foundation of support for neighborhood transit, commercial centers and other services.*" So says NAR Smart Growth promotional materials.

Rail trails, walkable communities, complete streets, to help build "strong communities" are all part of the grand NAR vision for America's glorious future. It's the vision of utopia – a beautiful, well-controlled community of high-rises where shopping and jobs are within biking or walking distance or a quick ride on a quaint trolley. Wind turbines turn lazily in the background to supply all energy needs. There are no dirty smokes stacks, no cars, no parking problems, no grid lock, no sprawl. According to the vision, everyone is living in complete harmony.

Through professionally-facilitated meetings and surveys that have been created to deliver a pre-determined outcome, planners and NAR tell us that 84% of residents believe their communities are getting worse and so are "demanding" such planning be done to improve things. Under that excuse, NAR is just working hard *through the smart growth strategies to help create the neighborhoods consumers are demanding.*" And to make it all happen, they are passing out NAR Smart Growth Action Grants to realtor groups all over the nation. Where do such ideas originate and who is NAR working with to create such a policy? Well, to begin with, NAR is a member of the Smart Growth Network. It is joined with such organizations as the U.S. Environmental Protection Agency (EPA), National Resources Defense Council, American Farmland Trust, Rails to Trails Conservancy, and even the State of Maryland, among others. Now there's a crew from which any promoter of private property rights should run as fast as possible.

Just for the record, the National Resources Defense Council (NRDC), founded in 1970, was created by a grant from the Ford Foundation to be an environmental law firm. Their favorite tactic is to aggressively sue American industry and state governments to force compliance with radical environmental regulations, costing thousands of jobs and millions of dollars in lost revenues.

The American Farmland Trust's method of "preserving" family farms is acquisition and control of development rights, essentially controlling the farms and how they operate. Rails to Trails Conservancy is infamous for taking property that was leased to now defunct rail roads and turning the right of ways into bike and hiking paths. The only problem is, those pathways are in many cases still owned by the property owners, or their heirs, who leased them to the railroads. Basically the trails are simply stolen from the property owners. These are pretty strange bed-fellows for NAR, which claims to be working for property owners.

But, there is more. Throughout the NAR literature on Smart Growth, it continually quotes the United Nation's World Commission on Environment and Development, better known as the Brundtland Commission. It was named after its chairman, Gro Harlem Brundtland, Vice President of the World Socialist party. The Commission's officials report was called "*Our Common Future.*" That report coined the term "Sustainable Development.

The Brundtland Commission was preceded by a series of UN conferences that led to the findings and suggested policies for development of human society outlined in "*Our Common Future.*" One such meeting, Habitat I, held in 1976 in Vancouver declared in its official report, "*Land cannot be treated as an ordinary asset, controlled by individuals and subject to the pressures and inefficiencies of the market. Private land ownership is also a principle instrument of accumulation and concentration of wealth, therefore contributes to social injustice.*" Wait a minute! Isn't that the very definition of sales of real estate? Aren't home buyers basically individuals seeking to earn wealth from the equity that will be gained by the purchase of the property? Isn't that the very pitch every single realtor in the nation uses to encourage us to buy a home? Why, then would NAR bother to hang around with, and promote, policies created by such people?

Two major documents to come out of the UN after the Brundtland Commission, were Agenda 21 and the UN Biodiversity Assessment. That Assessment listed what was considered to be "not sustainable" in the brave new world being created for us. These include, "ski runs, grazing of livestock, plowing of soil, building of fences, industry, single-family homes, paved and tarred roads, logging activities, dams and reservoirs, power line construction, and economic systems that fail to set proper value on the environment." They of course meant Capitalism. Again, how do Realtors justify promoting policies that oppose single family homes and a free market through which to sell them?

The fact is, Smart Growth policies simply don't work. Irrefutable evidence now shows that urban planning actually creates the very problems Smart Growth is supposed to fix. The most notable result of implementation of Smart Growth policies is the destruction of American civil liberties and freedom of choice, and the elimination of private property rights. In fact, in 2012, the American Planning Association actually did a study of smart growth policies and concluded that they don't work. But there is money in those polices – grant money. And so the drive for Smart Growth goes on, nearly unabated.

Across the nation the drum beat can be heard in nearly every community through vast new "visioning plans" of various names and titles – usually followed by the numbers 20/50. That's by design, because most are being implemented by the same planners, fueled by the same grant programs, and aided by the same NGO private groups.

Smart Growth planners promote their schemes by insisting that Americans live the wrong way. And they use land-use regulations to impose on others what they insist is the right way to live. Listen to the sales pitch. In Omaha, Nebraska, the goal of its plan called Heartland 2050, according to its promoters, is to develop a strategic "vision" for the region's development over the next 30 years to assure "proper growth." This massive plan will lay the ground rules for transportation, housing, jobs, property/land use, education, and even health care. What does all of that mean? It means they intend to put a line around the communities involved and declare little or no growth outside that line. That means the focus for future housing will be for high-density neighborhoods living in high-rise housing. It means that the use of private cars will be discouraged in favor of public transportation. How is that done? Several ways including higher taxes on cars and on gasoline – and some states are now beginning to tax the miles you drive each year.

Heartland 2050 includes the program called the "Complete Street." That is an edict that cars must share the road with bicycles and pedestrian traffic. . It calls for "Traffic Calming," which means large speed bumps placed in the center of residential streets that make it very unpleasant to drive over.
In San Francisco new residential apartment buildings have no parking lots. Again, that's part of the design to reduce the resident's ability to drive their cars and instead use bikes and public transportation, including light rail trains, for trips around town.
So, how will all of these new planning schemes affect you? Are you going to be happy? Will life in your community improve? Well, the best evidence to help predict the future is to look where all of this has already been tried. Portland, Oregon was announced as the poster child for Smart Growth policy. There it has been fully implemented. You can take an airplane over Portland and actually see the Smart Growth boundary line around the city. On one side is vast, dense development. On the other side is nothing but open land.
Each of these plans focus on "density" of the population. What do you think will happen when you stop any kind of urban growth and, instead, demand that all development takes place in a certain contained area? Populations grow and so does the density of the population.

During the twenty years since Portland began its Smart Growth policy, the population has grown by 80%, yet the urban growth boundary has barley expanded. Now Portland has declared a housing shortage crisis. So, the planners keep upping the density requirements for housing. To increase urban densities, the planners turned dozens of neighborhoods of single-family homes into apartments and high-rise condos, that get higher, with ever- smaller living space. Then they gave tax breaks, below-market land sales and other subsidies to developers who built the high rises. That meant that traditional neighborhoods were invaded by high rise developments. Meanwhile, if you own a vacant lot, you could not build a single-family house on it – you would have to build a row house or apartment. In some cases, the restrictions are so tight, if your house burned down you could not rebuild a single family home on the property.

The center of the plan was the light rail train system. The desirable homes (according to the planners) were those built along the rail line. This would assure rider ship, they claimed. Whoops. Independent studies reveal that the people living in them don't ride public transit any more significantly than residents in single-family neighborhoods.

The result of Portland's grand plan is that increased density destroyed the entire livable atmosphere of the community. Congestion is worse, housing and consumer costs are higher, and urban services, including fire, police, and schools, have declined as the city took money from these programs to subsidize high-density developers.

The planners of Omaha's Heartland 2050 are excited that it is receiving grants for the federal department of Housing and Urban Development (HUD). HUD was one of the major participants in the UN Habitat Meetings and in the implementation of Agenda 21.

Moreover, the Obama Administration created the plan called Affirmatively Affirming Fair Housing (AFFH) through HUD in which neighborhoods would now be tested for diversity and if there aren't enough minorities or low-income residents living in them, HUD will force the input of more minorities in such neighborhoods. AFFH is still in force, even under the Trump Administration, but there are now efforts to disband it. Smart Growth, Sustainable Development, Agenda 21 policies has been spread throughout the nation by the strings attached to HUD and EPA and other federal grants. It's the Kool-Aid that spreads the poison.
If all of the smart growth plans are fully implemented, as advocated by the APA and supported by the National Association of Realtores, density in American cities will be as much as three times higher than is currently in New York City.

People seek to escape cities because they are expensive, inefficient, crime- ridden, drug- infested, over- taxed, over- regulated, cesspools. Living space is cramped, over priced and undersized. Some studies have shown that people forced to live in such an atmosphere are less healthy and more dependent on government.
Why would an organization like the National Association of Realtors jump on the band wagon to support such an anti-people, anti-private-property policy? How can such a policy be defended by an organization that says it advocates private property ownership and healthy communities?
If one could install a video camera at the door of every new home built in a suburban neighborhood to record the moment a family walked into their newly-purchased single-family home, they would record happy faces. Here a family has the room to expand and grow, on their own terms where there is a safe place for their children to play in their own yard. Isn't that the very image the nation's realtors promote?
Of course, Smart Growth urban planners would be quick to say such development encourages strip malls and costs communities more tax dollars. The fact is, those new commercial establishments not only provide goods and services for those new neighborhoods, they also provide jobs and generate tax revenues. That's how economies are built.

Smart Growth is pure socialism and it has never worked anywhere it has ever been tried. It destroys the economy. It devastates the poor. Building costs skyrocket. Housing shortages rise and freedom of choice falls. Through Smart Growth policies, government makes every decision for every life choice for every person. Is that really what America's realtors want to promote?
NAR claims it speaks for all Realtors. If so, then it's past time for America's Realtors to stop turning a blind eye to the policies being promoted by their national association. Because, in time, as more Smart Growth policies are forced into place, there will be less and less private property for realtor's to sell.
Realtors – for your own survival- it's time to start working to restore the very policy that created American wealth- private property ownership. It's time to say no to the socialism of the National Association of Realtors.

HOW TO IMPROVE OUR PR & CHANGE THE DEBATE

Concerning the battle to bring truth to the Climate Change debate, the majority of the people in our movement are highly educated and intellectual. Of course many are scientists. We have a deeply rooted belief in individual accomplishments and interests. We dislike and distrust government. We would rather have a tooth pulled than deal with a government bureaucrat. Many of us are fully focused on government at the federal level while ignoring it at the state and local levels.

As a result, many of us fail to understand that reporters and congressmen don't understand science, let alone economics and philosophy or a grasp of history. Nor does the average citizen. We wrongly assume that all we need to do to counter known mistakes and misinformation from the climate alarmists is to simply write a scholarly paper disproving it and set the record straight. It doesn't work because few will understand it, fewer still will ever attempt to read it. Emotions tend to decide debates rather than facts. In short, we badly over estimate the knowledge and intelligence and attention span of the average citizen and government official whom we are trying to convince.

Above all, we must realize the fight over climate change isn't a scientific debate, rather it's a drive for transforming the global political structure. The most powerful tool to achieve that end is the contrived threat of Environmental Armageddon. Many are familiar with the quote from Christiana Figueres (Executive Secretary, the UN Framework Convention on Climate Change). *"This is the first time in the history of mankind that we are setting ourselves the task of intentionally, within a defined period of time, to change the economic development model that has been reigning for at least 150 years, since the industrial revolution."* Now add to that quote from author Ted Trainer, writing in a document titled "Transition to a Sustainable and Just World." *"What then is the most effective transition strategy? The essential aim is not to fight against consumer – capitalist society, but to build the alternative to it."* And finally there is this very honest and to the point observation by Paul Watson (co-founder of Greenpeace). *"It doesn't matter what is true. It only matters what people believe is true."*

This is why much of our lobbying efforts and local activism are so ineffective. We are fighting the wrong battle, ignoring the true combatants. The recommended book, *The Business of America is Lobbying* states that, of the 100 top lobbying organizations, 95 are business related. While that statistic may be true of registered lobbying groups, it also misses a major reality of life inside government and the key to why we lose nearly every battle. That statistic ignores the hundreds of non-governmental NGO groups, the massive foundations like the Nature Conservancy, Sierra Club, Audubon Society, Pew Charitable Trust, Rockefeller Foundation, Ford Foundation, Packard, Merck, Heinz, MacArthur Foundation, W. Alton Jones, Natural Resources Defense Council, Environmental Defense Fund, World Wildlife Fund, World Watch Institute, and on and on.

These sources of funds and research papers feed a vast matrix of resources that pour their climate change message into the media. For example, the Pew Charitable Trust gave $300,000 to the Public Media Center to put their message into major newspapers, policy makers, and opinion makers and science journals. There are countless examples of such activities to control the message, involving millions of dollars. Our side has no such effort.

In addition, these same groups pour activists into the halls of government at every level, federal, state, and local. Elected officials are surrounded by them. They sponsor seminars for them to spread their message. They supply data, training, computer programs, and even their own people as staffers for the government offices. They provide everything the officials need including the grants to put their policies in place. Eventually, in such an atmosphere, even the most dedicated and honest official becomes convinced of the NGO position. Our side provides nothing even close to this onslaught. Then, when we try to present our counter-scientific evidence to them they simply reject it as radical and false (especially as the NGOs whisper in their ears that we are all nuts or lackeys of big business). If officials don't vote the way of the NGOs, there is a massive activist system in place to alert their people who, then, begin to apply pressure to change the officials' minds, or to eventually throw them out of office. In other words, the Climate Change/Sustainable forces make sure elected officials will feel pain for taking such actions negative to their agenda. However, if they ignore us, the officials feel absolutely no consequences. So, whom would you follow? Us or them?

Meanwhile public education has become a major tool in creating the perfect global village citizens who don't ask questions or doubt the propaganda in which they are drowning. That's because the same NGOs, foundations, and federal grant programs are feeding the education system. Check out the Eden Institute, a United Nations NGO which advocates a program called "Globally Acceptable Truth." Say's the Institute, "*the reason we have wars, poverty, and strife in the world is because there is too much knowledge.*" So, Eden says their mission is to provide the information that is necessary so the average people won't need to worry about making decisions in such a massive deluge of information. In reality, Globally Acceptable Truth is the actual curriculum of the public education system which no longer teaches academics, but, instead focuses on behavior modification. Teachers, textbooks, and classroom assignments all provide the exact same message with no opposing positions. The result is that the schools have become factories churning out those who readily accept their positions. Our side rarely has a chance to even have a speaker at a school, and if we do try to send one in, they are met with near riots for daring to bring a different opinion to the campus. Now you know the reason why.

These then are the powerful, well-funded, well prepared forces that we face in trying to get our message to the public. And it's why we fail. What, then, is the solution?

HOW DO WE COUNTER SUCH POWERFUL FORCES

First we must set our goals. What do we really want? Once decided, our every action must be to achieve that goal. Set your goal – plan your work – work your plan.

I would assume that what we want is truth in science. We also want honest government that operates inside the restraints of the Constitution that recognizes all individual's choice, property rights protection, and elected representation that protects the natural rights of every citizen. We want the ability to publish and speak our position on climate change, private property, free enterprise, and limited government, fully believing that if truth is at the center of the argument, the scare tactic will be exposed and defeated. The challenge lies in how that is to be accomplished.

Emotion Vs Intellect: One of our greatest challenges comes from the fact that it's difficult for educated people to deal with ignorance and misdirection in an argument. As Dr. Thomas Sowell said, "*It is usually futile to try to talk facts and analysis to people who are enjoying a sense of moral superiority in their ignorance.*"

As stated before, we attempt to argue scientific fact while the other side focuses on emotion and fear – "The Earth is warming, the seas levels are rising." "We have only 12 years before the world ends!" Someone must do something! Knowing full well that these are lies makes it hard to even engage. But that message is pouring from government, the media, and the education system and must be countered.

The first way to do that is to engage in some emotionalism ourselves. For example, what if we pulled away a bit from the specific issue of Climate Change and, instead, focused on some of the policies that are being enforced in its name – or in the overall name of Environmentalism? After all, Climate Change is the most effective tool to enforce Environmentalism. Environmentalism is the chosen tool to create the need for global governance. Global governance is the ultimate goal for it all, which means a drive to eliminate national sovereignty, leading to the destruction of our system of government and the free enterprise system. Promoters of radical environmentalism under the label of Sustainable Development have made many statements to confirm that fact.

What if we begin to clearly present the dire pictures of such a "sustainable" world? Let me give you three examples of such a future under the sustainable edicts (the consequences of Climate Change scare tactics).

1. California has declared that within the next ten years energy will come strictly from solar and wind power – for the protection of the planet. We all know that these sources of power don't work. We need to begin to paint the dire picture of the consequences of such misguided policy. There will be mandatory curfews for energy use, forcing all businesses, including local stores and major manufacturing to cease operation at night. Streetlights and traffic signals will be shut off, making it dangerous to venture out at night. The elevators in the "sustainable" stack and pack, high rise apartments will cease to work, as all personal computers will be inoperable, not to mention the millions of birds that will die in the turbine blades. Such is the future as a result of California's edict. Could we not gain public attention by issuing warnings to the people of California? Would this not lead to possible interview opportunities in the media? This is one of the various ways we could include such details in our articles. And as we have their attention from these dire warnings, we can slip in our message that Climate Change is the excuse for this disaster, yet there is no science to support it. People are going to be forced to suffer with no factual need for it. These are our facts – promoted by emotion. Do you want to add more emotion that the average American will relate to? Then use the very clear image of the national shut down and the threat of starvation and economic collapse just experienced in the name of the COVID19 virus. The Green New Deal policies being advocated will lead to the same result!

2. In Miami, Florida an elderly couple on a fixed income planted a tree in their front yard several years ago. Over the time the tree became diseased with termites and worms, and it became a danger to utility lines if it were to fall. So they family hired a licensed tree-trimming service to take it down. But according to Miami city code they needed a permit to take down the tree. They were fined $1000. In addition, the city demanded that the family provide a plan to plant 24 new trees or pay the city $1000 per tree that wasn't planted. The money was to go to the non-profit, private NGO Tree Trust Fund. It didn't matter that there wasn't enough room to plant that many trees, or any number even close to that. They offered to plant five trees. The city environmental department refused to waive or reduce the penalty. This was an environmental issue. They had damaged the "urban forest" by taking down the tree and they are going to pay. Again, it's an excuse about saving the planet. This example clearly shows the result of absolute power of government, working in collusion with the NGOs in the background. Again, under the excuse of Climate Change and sustainable environmental policy, reason is thrown out, tyrannical government is in place, and people are suffering. There are hundreds of such examples that can be used to display the control and lack of reason and fact by zealots in the name of saving the planet. Many law-abiding Americans have gone to jail over such issues, or had their property confiscated. In each case we would be able to slip in the negative image of such policy created without scientific basis.

3. The American beef industry has been taken over by the World Wildlife Fund (WWF) which has created the Global Sustainable Beef Roundtable. The goal is to force cattle growers to conform to massive regulations in

the name of "biodiversity." The WWF is one of the most powerful and most radical environmental groups in the world. They spread the lie that polar bears are disappearing because of Climate Change. They run ads on television dramatically showing the bears clinging to the last piece of melting ice before they drown. Of course it's all a lie. Polar bear populations are very healthy and the polar icecap is not melting. Yet these lies are rarely challenged. Now, WWF has taken over the beef industry even though they openly advocate ending beef consumption. In a recent report they said "*Meat consumption is devastating some of the world's most valuable and vulnerable regions, due to the vast amount of land needed to produce animal feed.*" They went on to insist that to "*save the Earth it is demanded that we change human consumption habits away from beef.*" Yet, here they are, in control of the beef industry. What better position could they be in to destroy it? They advocate that the land used to graze cattle could feed more people by using it to grow wheat and soy. In other words, they are in emergency mode as if there is a food crisis. Their policies, of course, will create that food crisis as they systematically attack our food supply. Meanwhile, Tyson Foods is teaming up with the Environmental Defense Fund to develop and employ the same dire regulations on other food supplies. This is, again, all in the name of protecting the Earth from Climate Change. Again, as a result of the COVID 19 lockdown, the over-controlled American agriculture industry broke down because of these policies and green control. It would be quite effective, and I believe easy to expose this destruction of our food supply and freedom of choice and promote the negative image of the environmental movement that seeks to control us all.

The point of each of these examples is the opportunity to mix emotion with our facts as we make our point. It will help in creating the negative image of the very movement to which we have been losing the climate change debate. Challenge the issue in the terms of right and wrong. Pull at the heart strings over the suffering of normal citizens who are victimized by uncaring, unreasonable, out of control government. This is how we change the debate and put them on the defensive as people start seeing them as tyrannical, and dangerous to their culture, freedom of choice, and economic well-being.

We have a wide array of resources in those who have dedicated themselves to this fight. Some excel in research and others naturally rush to the front lines and never waiver when the need arrives. We have some incredible elected representatives fighting hard to hold the line in our city councils, county commissions and state legislatures, though unfortunately, they are usually outnumbered. There are fantastic radio programs, locally and nationally, ready to carry the message. And we have a scattered few legal foundations and firms desperately working to defend us. Of course, I think we can all agree that lack of a strong legal force is perhaps our greatest weakness as a movement.

All of these resources, working together as a coordinated team, could make a major difference. We need to establish a network where ideas and talents can be shared. We can establish a website where reports of successful battles, contact information, sample legislation, and insight can be shared. We can establish training webinars featuring the very best leaders of our movement. And we can share joint media messages and legal teams. We can bring it altogether in a unified effort to counter those Green New Deal/Agenda 21 forces that now seem so formidable.

Preparing for the media we can create a speakers bureau. Everyone has a different talent and knowledge. Some are very scholarly. Others are better suited for activism and spreading the emotional side of the message. There are lists of some of the largest and most influential media outlets. Let us prepare media packets that bring out the emotional message, challenging the Greens at their own game. The packets can be created to that purpose, getting the attention of the program hosts and producers. We are offering something new from our side that will intrigue them. Watch for developments in the news and create an Emergency Response Team to issue an immediate news release with our response.

Take advantage of the large network of radio shows that daily spread our message. They are supporters of our positions. And pro-freedom radio shows actually outnumber the other side. It is possible to coordinate a strong message through all of them at the same time by issuing articles and news releases for which they will be happy to open their programs for interviews.

The instant the climate Chicken Littles publish a new outrageous report we should issue a debate challenge. We should, in advance, make a deal with a major news outlet, that if we do issue such a challenge they will be willing to carry the debate live. That would scare the other side to death! They have always refused to debate our positions. Instead they resort to name calling and arrogantly refuse to be in the same room with us, but we must now pressure them to come out of hiding. Announced to the nation that we are ready, right now to counter what they just said. When they refuse, then we have a new opportunity to hit the media circuit. The point is to be aggressive and never take our foot off their neck.

Openly attack those scientific journals that are refusing to publish our articles. We all know there is money and pressure being applied to shut off the ability to get our message out. Be relentless in exposing it. Just as we can use emotion to expose how dangerous and wrong the policies are on the local level, we can use the same tactic to expose these compliant scientific media outlets. What would *Science* do if we were to publish an in-depth report on how and why they are keeping out anything that disproves the theory of climate change? Expose the grants they have taken from sources that want our message locked out. Perhaps a report exposing their editors' links to some of these leftist sources would add pressure to our argument. If they deny such a charge then you have the perfect opportunity to shove an article in front of them and challenge them to print it. The main point is that we have to stop being so polite. Get nasty. Truth and freedom depend on it.

Here's a fun exercise in debunking our opponents. Each week, or each month, issue an article that exposes the massive force we are opposing. Make it the "**Group of the Week**" and reveal how much money they have, where it comes from, and how they use it. Which politicians pack their pockets with the money? Have their positions been disproved? What have been the results of policies they have promoted or pushed through? We must begin to discredit these forces at every level so they have a difficult time getting into places of power and influence. I've had experience with this. A few years ago my organization, American Policy Center, took on the International Council for Local Environmental Initiatives (ICLEI). They are one of the most powerful NGOs in the world with the goal of implementing Sustainable Development in every city on the planet. 650 American cities were paying them dues to bring in training, computer programs, grants, etc. We began to target them, exposing their real goals and exposing that tax dollars were going into their coffers to enforce those goals. Within a year we had succeeded in getting over 150 American cities to rescind their memberships. Later, the head of ICLIE USA told a colleague of mine that they were terrified of us and didn't know how to stop us because they couldn't get new American cities to join them. That should be our goal for every one of the NGOs now pushing Climate Change and Environmental/Sustainable policy.

And here's another valuable tool we can use to help change the debate. In each community, let us **establish a grading system of local government's protection of freedom.** Review new laws and regulations and rate them on how they protect or diminish freedom. On a scale of one to ten, review and report on the actions of your city council or county commission. Be sure to name the sponsors of such legislation, and list how each member of the council voted. Make them own their actions. If it was bad law, make sure everyone in town knows who is responsible. One suggestion would be to produce a copy of the legislation and place a picture of the sponsor/sponsors at the top. It's their bill! And include a detailed review, emphasizing why it is a danger to freedom. Perhaps, if possible, list the potential victims, such as those who will lose their homes through eminent domain, for example. Pass the document out to people attending public meetings, to the news media, and place them on store counters. If you are really organized, pass them outdoor to door throughout the community. Do this on a regular basis and you will get their attention. With strong impact they may just starting coming to you with their legislative ideas first, before introducing them, to make sure they aren't going to suffer public embarrassment from your efforts. That's what victory looks like!

LEGISLATIVE ACTION

I believe too many of us focus only on federal agencies and Congress for action. However, my experience shows we have a chance to make major steps forward in state legislatures and even city and county government. These are the places where most of the Sustainable policy is being implemented. That's a direct result of the hidden forces of the NGOs which surround local officials and pressure them to take the federal grants that have been written to enforce the sustainable policies written under the excuse of Climate Change. The grants are the cancer. This pressure can be countered.

Let me give you an example of what such a force could do. Today we have good people in many state legislatures who understand the problem. However they are just a few against the mighty force of Sustainable Development. How do they stand a chance of making a difference?

Let's say there are just three legislators in your state who stand against the current. However, by networking through our efforts, they meet similarly dedicated members from other states. Let's say they find three others in each of ten states. They network and discuss, eventually creating strong legislative ideas, perhaps a way to reclaim their state's rightful sovereignty over federal overreach, thus controlling the enforcement of Climate Change policy in their state. Alone they don't stand a chance of passing it in their respective legislatures.

However, here's how they implement this plan: On the same day, at the exact same time, in all ten states, these ten legislative teams introduce the exact same bill and hold ten separate news conferences (one in each state) to announce it. They are immediately supported by our network of activists in each state. Our network of radio shows begin to push the legislation by featuring both the legislators and local activists carrying the message. Meanwhile the legal team announces their legal support.

Do you think such a coordinated effort might just catch on and overwhelm the roadblocks? If such legislation could be passed in just two or three states we will have created an effective movement and more states will take up the cause. **(details on this tactic to follow in this manual)**

In conclusion, the way we present our case, both in the media and through legislation, must be aggressive and on a level that draws in the average citizens. Our movement needs to stop being so polite. It's time to go on the attack, expose our opponents, find new tactics that appeal to the emotions and sense of right and wrong of the general public, and organize. Do you know that in poll after poll the American public continually list Climate Change as the least of their concerns? Build on that. The people are ready to hear our new aggressive tactic. They may well cheer us on as they say "finally!" The consequences of losing this fight are too horrible to consider.

So, we've explained the issues, why they are dangerous, and why we have been losing. Now we have to show what needs to be done to change the debate and begin to push back and restore our freedoms. But how do we actually network, organize and begin to take action? So let's get into some details.

TAKING THE OFFENSE TO RESTORE LIBERTY
(Putting government back in the Constitutional bottle)

Where do these programs on the state and local level come from? How do they spread across the nation in such unison, and how do we combat them? In short, there is a dedicated and determined army of Non-governmental organizations (NGOs) working with local, state and federal officials, helping communities to apply for grants, and providing complete programs to be enacted. Many of these organizations helped to write Agenda 21 at the United Nations level, and then worked with Bill Clinton's President's Council for Sustainable Development to create the policies and even write the grant programs. All of these programs are theirs to begin with, so they know well the details and how to promote them. To combat them at the state and local level, we must also know those details and prepare an effective plan. What do we do?

The issue of Sustainable Development, and its new incarnation through the Green New Deal, affects every aspect of our lives. Nothing is left untouched by these tyrannical policies. When Agenda 21 was introduced at the United Nations Earth Summit in 1992, it was described as a "comprehensive blueprint for the reorganization of human society." That is the greatest attack ever devised on the sovereignty of our nation and the Constitution that was created to protect our natural rights.

Since nothing is left untouched and every right is under attack, it's understandable that people get confused and frustrated when trying to protect our rights. Gun rights, religion, freedom of speech, education, healthcare, energy use, personal privacy, and much more are all under attack. Concerned citizens start down one road to fight a policy, and then another right is attacked. This is done to divide us and weaken our ability to organize effectively. So, what do we do?

As we have fought this agenda over the past 30 years, one certain truth has emerged. Agenda 21/Sustainable Development policies cannot be enforced if private property rights are protected. That's why the American Policy Center has worked to put a laser focus on the protection of property rights as the most effective way to fight back. If you can affect policy that secures private property from the eminent domain bulldozers, the rules that prevent how you are allowed to use your own property (both personal and business use), and even guarding against the creation of massive licensing for every possible use of the property, then you will create your community to be a "Freedom Pod" in the middle of the sustainable assault that is taking over the nation.

To achieve that goal, the first step is to have a clear definition of property rights so you have a platform to stand on. People talk about property rights, but rarely know how to define what they mean. By 1997, as the sustainable policies were being rushed forward through every level of government, the challenges to private property protection were growing rapidly in the courts. Judges became hard-pressed to deal with many of these challenges because they actually lacked a good definition of what private property ownership really is. To deal with the situation that year, Washington State Supreme Court Justice Richard B. Sanders wrote a "Fifth Amendment" treatise to finally define property rights. His definition is especially useful in our fight against Sustainable Development policy because that is the exact policy he was addressing as he wrote his definition. That's why we recommend Justice Sanders' definition for your cause. Here it is: ***Property in a thing consists not merely in its ownership and possession, but in the unrestricted right of use, enjoyment, and disposal. Anything which destroys any of the elements of property, to that extent, destroys the property itself. The substantial value of property lies in its use. If the right of use be denied, the value of the property is annihilated and ownership is rendered a barren right.***

It's helpful for your credibility to have as your source a quote from a supreme court justice. Of course, the minute you offer a definition of private property that contains the words "unrestricted right of use," the Sustainablists heads will explode. Our experience I using this definition over the years has been almost comical. Immediately the attack will begin, and almost universally the exact same example is used to attack this word, "unrestricted." Here is what you will most certainly be told; "If you have 'unrestricted' use of property someone will put a smelly old pig farm next door to you!!!!" It must certainly be the most horrible thing they can think of! One personal thought is that it would be much worse if they eliminated single family home zoning protections so they could put low-income federal high rises next door to you, therefore destroying your property values. That is exactly what is now happening in cities across the nation under sustainable polices and regulations.

However, here is a better response to the attack against the word "unrestricted." Since the beginning of human settlements there have always been "nuisance" laws to protect the rights of property owners from things that affect individual property rights. In those circumstances, if your neighbor does something that affects your property, such as a bright light shining in your bedroom window, a loud noise blasting at all hours, or a terrible smell, then your first step is to talk with your neighbor and explain the problem. If your neighbor is a good person they would instantly understand and react by eliminating the problem. That is neighbor to neighbor taking care of the situation with no need for courts. If, however, your neighbor refuses to solve it then you have the right to go to court and file a nuisance complaint and let the court decide. The problem with Sustainable policies is that they are all one-size-fits-all policies, created by an uninvolved board or committee following international, national, or regional regulations that very little, if anything, to do with you or your property. That's not freedom of choice, or the right of unrestricted use. It's the root of tyranny. So that is why we suggest you fight the battle against sustainable polices focused on protecting property rights. However, if you prefer to take on the fight through other issues (and those certainly are vitally important too) you can use similar tactics by focusing on local use Vs the Sustainable "international" edicts.

Let's begin by stating some very simple, but well known, and effective guidelines:

RULES FOR ACTIVISTS
HOW TO CONTROL THE ACTION

1. *"Power is not only what you have, but what the enemy thinks you have."*
Power is derived from 2 main sources – money and people. "Have-nots" must build power from flesh and blood.

2. *"Never go outside the expertise of your people."* It results in confusion, fear and retreat. Feeling secure adds to the backbone of anyone.

3. *"Whenever possible, go outside the expertise of the enemy."* Look for ways to increase insecurity, anxiety and uncertainty.

4. *"Make the enemy live up to its own book of rules."* If the rule is that every letter gets a reply, send 30,000 letters. You can kill them with this because no one can possibly obey all of their own rules.

5. *"Ridicule is man's most potent weapon."* There is no defense it's irrational. It's infuriating. It also works as a key pressure point to force the enemy into concessions."

6. *"A good tactic is one your people enjoy."* They'll keep doing it without urging and come back to do more. They're doing their thing, and will even suggest better ones.

7. *"A tactic that drags onto long becomes a drag."* Don't become old news.

8. *"Keep the pressure on. Never let up."* Keep trying new things to keep the opposition off balance. As the opposition masters one approach, hit them from the flank with something new.

9. *"The threat is usually more terrifying than the thing itself."* Imagination and ego can dream up many more consequences than any activist.

10. *"The major premise for tactics is the development of operations that will maintain a constant pressure upon the opposition."* It is this unceasing pressure that results in the reactions from the opposition that are essential for the success of the campaign.

11. *"If you push a negative hard enough, it will push through and become a positive."* Violence from the other side can win the public to your side because the public sympathizes with the underdog.

12. *"The price of a successful attack is a constructive alternative."* Never let the enemy score points because you're caught without a solution to the problem.

13. *"Pick the target, freeze it, personalize it, and polarize it."* Cut off the support network and isolate the target from sympathy. Go after people and not institutions; people hurt faster than institutions.

8 RULES FOR SUCCESSFUL ACTIVISM
BECOME A CITIZEN NINJA!

Rule # 1. Training Optimizes Success
If you decide to take public action, first do not act alone. That is a sure way to be ignored by your opposition. Second, make sure those who want to help you know how. Hold training sessions to help them understand their role in achieving your goals. Find their strengths and build on them, for example, people who enjoy researching should be encouraged and guided to get into the details. Their information will be invaluable.

Rule # 2. Effective Activism Inspires Others
Effective activism leads to habitual and enjoyable civic participation. When you are effective you become a role model for others who want to emulate similar achievement.

Rule #3 Create Credentials
From the outside, Non Governmental Organizations may seem like they are large organizations, when often only as few as one to five people run them. Yet they gain power with elected officials from their image. You can do this too. Organizing your band of local activists into small coalitions can effectively encourage public participation and can give the impression that you represent a large coalition of citizens. That creates credentials for your efforts that can be powerful and productive.

Rule # 4 Hold 'Em Accountable
Hold individuals, organizations and government agencies accountable for their set of rules and standards. If a politician promises to be accessible to he public or an agency is bound by laws of transparency, it's up to us to point the finger and expose their wrong doing. For example, a certain city councilman was responsible for a regulation that had severely damaged a major industry. The revenues from that industry were now plummeting and that was causing a drop in jobs and tax income the city needed to survive. Local activists

shared with me a graph showing the drop in revenue. I suggested they put the councilman's picture on the graph. It was action - make him own it.

Rule # 5 Avoid Ruts and Stagnation

Organizations change leadership frequently which alters dynamics and policies. Stay current and relevant. Consistently evaluate your approach and adjust your strategy and tactics when your efforts begin stagnating. One of the first rules in organizing should be to write down your positions and your goals. This is important because as you become successful, you will have the attention of your opposition. Many times they are well connected and will use their influence and power to attempt to steer your organization off course. Perhaps a local official will suddenly appear at one of your meetings and begin to promise help, but then you find that help has led you in the wrong direction. Perhaps your leadership has sold out. Having your original purpose and goals clearly written will give you a powerful tool to regain control of your mission.

Rule #6 Pressure Tactics

Regular and persistent contact with public servants keeps the pressure on them to respond to your requests. Typically, regular citizens give up quickly when they do not succeed right away. Many government agencies and organizations intentionally frustrate citizens so they will give up. Always follow-up and stick with it. In addition, keep in mind that the NGO's are constantly in the officials face, pushing, giving them programs, money and encouragement,. They are at every meeting. We are not. So it is vital that those officials become familiar with you as well. If you can get some of them to talk with you regularly you may be able to answer questions and give them a means to stand up to the pressures of the NGOs.

Rule #7 Shift Public Opinion

Goal number one – change the debate. Make the case that the proposed policies create victims – not solutions. Show who the true victims are. Expose those pushing the bad policy. Most NGO groups have a record of similar actions they have taken in other communities. Research that information and present it to the community. Make them the outsider "carpetbagger."

Rule # 8 Propose Solutions

We all know the old adage: "If you're not part of the solution, you're part of the problem." Opposing an idea, plan, or agenda is good civic participation, but the message is more powerful if it is supported with either practical alternatives or facts that debunk the claims made by the opposition. As you go public with your fight, challenge their plans by exposing these facts --

- How the plan will harm the local economy

- Expose how Public Private Partnerships (PPPs) are full of risk for the city

- How it will increase the cost of property ownership (perhaps for private landlords) and destroy single family home ownership

- How it will change the culture/atmosphere of our town

- How it will adversely affect zoning

- Demand three bids for acquisition of any smart city programs

- Expose any financial conflict of interest (developers, PPPs, NGOs)

- Take your message to the public by organizing an impromptu town hall meeting for citizens. Present your findings and demand answers. This will help you build your movement.

Number one goal – stop your officials from taking federal grants. These are the Trojan Horse that brings in federal controls over local decisions for your community. Explain to your officials that the grants will diminish their roles and influence in conducting city business, as they were elected to do.

Become a Citizen Ninja: Activist Mary Baker has created a full program called Citizen Ninja. It's full training program for activists. Learn more at www.themarybaker.com

HERE ARE JUST A FEW SUGGESTIONS ON BECOMING AN EFFECTIVE CITIZEN NINJA

1. **Conquer Your Fear** Taking a public stand can be an intimidating thing. This is where most people come to a screeching halt. Speaking in public? No way! To overcome that fear think about what your are really scared of what is your perceived danger? Is there any danger? What do you see as your personal weaknesses? Mental preparation and practice leads to success.

2. **Be Assertive.** Self-assertion is a requirement for securing freedom within our Republic. Without action by you, the citizen, to hold our elected officials and public servants accountable there can be no outcome of "liberty and justice for all."

3. **Peg Your Audience.** Ignore those who oppose you. Nothing you do or say will change their mind. They have an agenda. Focus your energy or those who are uninformed or perhaps misinformed. That's how you begin to change the debate and build your movement.

4. **Ask a Question.** Pick your topic, know the answer to your question, be assertive with your knowledge, Peg your audience, Educate directly and indirectly, know your facts, Challenge false claims, expose misleading or omitted information, and educate the audience around you.

5. **Make a Statement.** This is where you can effectively use social media. Get your statement out there on FaceBook, Twitter, start an email list, make videos for You Tube. This is how you build a movement to support your position.

6. **Neutralize Your Opponent.** Use your knowledge, confound them with facts and common sense, and don't be afraid to use emotion. Don't hold back as you let people know why your opponent is wrong. Keep pounding away.

HOW TO ORGANIZE

1. Every Public Movement Needs a Team

The first rule for organizing opposition, or to promote policy is to not attempt to act alone. You don't need a majority, only a dedicated few, each performing specific tasks. Create a name for your organization and titles for officers and spokespeople.

First, **the Researchers.** This can be a team of two or three people who love to spend time going following the path down lots of rabbit holes. Find the documents, the grant programs, and the forces behind them. Very important- in the beginning stage of your research and early organizing **Do this quietly**. Don't issue press releases about what you are doing. You may have to ask questions that raise eyebrows, but don't make a target of yourself. Stay out of the way as much as possible at this stage.

Second**, the Watchers.** This is a team of three or four who will volunteer to attend every public meeting. If possible, they will record those meetings. They will take notes of what is said and who said it. Who are the main movers and shakes of the policy? On almost every city council, county commission or planning board there is one who is pushing the hardest. Find that person and then observe who they regularly associate with. Does that person stand to benefit personally from the plan? In addition, by regularly attending these public meetings, the team will begin to know all the players, the NGO representatives, the planners, and other interested parties. They will also learn if there is elected officials on the council that will support your side. The team must share this information with the researchers to look further into it.

Third, **the Strategist.** The leader, perhaps two or three people, who take the information from the researchers and watchers and decide how best to use it. The Strategist needs to do research too, know the policies, history, and why it is so dangerous. Plan the mission for the group. Why are you opposing these policies, who will be hurt by them, what is the solution, who do you need to help support your mission, and how to approach them. Above all, what will victory look like?

Fourth, **the Agitators.** These are the people who will be the spokespersons to address the public meetings and perhaps meet regularly with the elected officials. Keep in their face, be friendly if possible, but let those opposing officials know they will not go away. There should be at least five in this team. No one shoulder stand and address the committee alone. Usually the public only gets a couple of minutes to address the officials in a public meeting. The team should coordinate their presentations to assure they get in all of their points, one spokesman at a time. Create the impression that there is major opposition. The point in all of this is to make the issue public. Take away their ability to hide the details from the public.

Fifth, **the Victims.** You are opposing these policies for a reason. Someone is going to be hurt by them. If the policies being opposed are about community development or Sustainable Development Smart Growth plans, then most likely there are specific neighborhoods that will be affected by the plan. What impact will the plan have on those neighborhoods? Will it include the taking of property or homes, or businesses by eminent domain? If so, go to the owners of that property and inform them of the plan. Chances are they don't know. This is how you build your movement! Perhaps if the plan goes through they will lose their family investment or livelihood under the bull dozers. Their hopes and dreams for their future will be gone. These victims then become the poster child for your campaign to stop these policies. Tell their story. Emotions very often trump the official-sounding program that most people simply ignore. The most effect action you can take would be to have these victims address the council with their story. Keep using them as your example as to why this policy is very bad for the city.

Sixth **the Media Team.** A team of two or three who will stay inconstant touch with the media, through personal contact, news releases, and letters to the editor. In fact, the more letters you can generate, perhaps from a wide variety of people, the better. The team can help people write such letters. Try to establish a personal relationship with the editor or the beat reporter. If possible, provide some opinion articles about your position for the editorial page. It is a matter of fact that most local papers side with the other side. That's because they depend on the office holders and officials to get their news. If the beat reporter writes a negative story they will probably lose access to that office, which makes their job harder. In addition they will probably not be invited to the annual Christmas party. So they tend to ignore real stories by citizen activists. Instead they will print the official position of the government and label your movement as radical. This is why is vital that the media team take the groups news releases to the city council meetings and pass them out to the public. If possible, create a newsletter and deliver printed copies to local businesses to put on their counters – especially in those areas of town that will be affected by the policy.

Seventh **Teams of Activists.** These are the ones that get to do the grunt work. They can deliver materials like the news letter door to door. They can organize demonstrations at city hall, or at least pack the council chamber to send the message that there is strong opposition. This is best done especially on day when an important vote is to be taken on the issue. The team can also plan days to protest in front of buildings that are going to be torn down. This team provides the visual strength of the group. It can be made up of those people who want to do something but can't commit a large amount of time.

Eighth **Social Media Team.** If you've got some young people who want to get involved, this is right up their alley. Start a web page to help get your message out. Develop an on0line petition against the policy. Create a blog to share any important tidbits on the latest developments. Organize webinars to inform the town's people of your actions. How about a survey on how the people feel about the issue. If you have done your job is should be strongly in your favor and that makes it a valuable tool. You may find that the officials are watching it grow! Keep it going.

HOW TO RESEARCH

When you really want to know something, go to the organ grinder, not the monkey Researching Sustainable Development in Your Community

Sometimes it isn't easy to tell if Sustainable Development programs are being implemented in your community because its promoters deliberately use different names and terms for it. This tactic is used specifically to throw you off the trail and avoid criticism. Before your start a search for Sustainable Development in your community, read and remember the terms below:

Partnership Building, Consensus, Urban Redevelopment, Community Development, Land Use and Environment, Collaborative Approaches, Purchase of Development Rights (PRD), Maintaining a strong, diversified local economy, Preserve open space, Preserving our heritage, Heritage corridors, Heritage area, Historic preservation, Quality growth, Smart Growth, Innovative new development, Tax-free zones, Use of Eminent domain, Regional governments, Regional planning boards, Water control boards, Urban forest, non-governmental organizations (NGOs) Conservation easements, Global warming, Climate change, Sustainable farming, Comprehensive planning, Visioning process, Growth management, Resource use, Social Justice, I.C.L.E.I..

Start your search with your community web-site. Learn what information is available to you. Almost every town has a "Comprehensive Plan". Usually this plan is for a five year period. Remember the clue terms above and carefully ready the Comprehensive Plan. Check out all departments of the local government and review what the department's different missions are. You may find in Park and Recreation the exact terms of land easements. Many towns, when establishing a new program (example: land easements) will attach a program to an already established department, instead of starting a new department. So search out each department's different divisions. Research the town codes. A lot of community planning is in the town codes. Look for what grants are in force – what do they require for compliance .

Who are the players (the people leading the policy) in your community? What privately funded "stakeholder" NGO groups are there? Get to know what you can about them – other towns they have worked in – policies they have spearheaded. Where are they from? Where do their funds come from?

Is there a specific area of the community that will directly affected by a development plan? Find those to be affected by policy so you can recruit them to your cause.

Get all the details of the development plan being prepared in your community. It may already be in place, or perhaps it's being updated. You will probably find it on the town or county website.

Does the community plan call for reduction of energy use? If so, that will cost you money. Don't fall for the line that it is all voluntary – to help you save money. They haven't gone to this much trouble to be ignored. Regulations are not voluntary.

These are just a couple of examples of what to look for as you do your research.

When you have gotten all of the information you can obtain from your town's web site, its time to reach out into the Internet. Most state governments have a website that has volumes of information. Once again you must take the time to learn what information can be obtained. Use the terms listed about in general searches and see what pops up. It will bring you a treasure of information. For example, enter into the search box something like: annual report, land tax credits, and your state's name. This search will get you to the State's government website and perhaps to the State Department of Conservation and Recreation site. There you may see something like Land Preservation Tax Credit. For example, in Virginia s you find the title Land Preservation Tax Credit, click on "Click here instead." Now you will find a report from the Virginia land Conservation Foundation. In this report, on page 16 is a listing of Tax Credits given to each county.

On another page is a list of Acres of land per county that are in Conservation Easements. See if there is a list of "stakeholder" groups helping to get landowners to sign up for the easements – and if so – do they get any kind of kickbacks? Who are getting the easements? You may find that some rich land owners have found a great loophole to cut their own property taxes as the middle class makes up the short fall. This will help bring usually disinterested people to your cause.

Another page gives Land Statistics in Virginia. This information is valuable in assessing the extent of Sustainable programs and land control in the state, and especially for your county. You can also find what land trusts and NGO groups are operating inside state and local governments. That is a major goal of your efforts – whom are you dealing with?

Caution: when you find useful information, you may not remember where this information came from. To preserve information be sure to print it to save it. On the back of your printed text be sure to note the website. Another way to remember good source of information is to copy the web address and paste it to a word file. Establish a word file just for the web address you use, making it easy to keep and find your information.

Here is a valuable Research Document prepared by Pat Wood, head of Citizens for Free Speech. If you are able to fill in all of these items you will have a comprehensive file of your community, the plans and a list of the players you are dealing with.

City Survey

Getting to Know Your Community

Start a special binder to contain the following information. The more detail that you have, the better! Leave space for notes and take the binder with you to all meetings that you attend. This is critically important research that will help you understand your community.

City name

Overall demographics
>Total population
>City size in sq. miles
>Ethnic makeup
>City map

Locate and print these documents
>State constitution
>County Charter
>City Charter

Number of precincts
>Information on precinct captains (Name, phone, email)
>Precinct map

Information on Mayor and City Council members
>Name
>Party affiliation
>Age
>Male/female
>Years in office
>Previous elected positions
>Biography
>Contact information including email, phone, address
>District
>Committee memberships

Information on Key City officials & Info
>City manager

Legal counsel
City planner
City clerk
Building permits & standards

Information on County Commissioners

Name
Party affiliation
Age
Male/female
Years in office
Previous elected positions
Biography
Contact information including email, phone, address
District
Committee memberships

Information on State assemblymen and senators

Name
Party affiliation
Age
Male/female
Years in office
Previous elected positions
Biography
Contact information including email, phone, address
District
Committee memberships/chairmanships
Caucus memberships

Information on city judges

Name
Party affiliation
Age
Male/female
Years in office
Previous elected positions
Biography
Contact information including email, phone, address

Names of all local boards

Education
Water
Planning
Zoning
Energy
Fire

Where are meetings held for various events?

Calendars of Events (when and where), links to web calendars)
> City counsel
> County
> Board meetings
> County meetings

Pending legislation/ city resolutions

List of all active city projects

General Plan for City/County

City Memberships
> Regional Councils of Governments (See NARC)
> ICLEI
> Nat'l Council of Mayors
> League of Cities
> Other NGOs

County Memberships
> Nat'l League of Counties
> ICLEI
> Other NGOs

City budget (current and past)

City chamber of commerce / Visitor and Convention Bureau

Any other things that profile your city and/or affect its future

Where and how to make public records and FOIA requests

Environmental programs

List of libraries with public use meeting rooms
> Room size
> Who to contact for booking

Information on Council of Governments membership (COGS, see narc.org)
> Location and contact information
> Your representative on the council
> Other council members and their information
> Website
> Scope of operation
> General plan

NGO's working within your city/county system
> Environmental groups

Green New Deal groups
Social justice groups

How to Write an Effective Letter to the Editor:

- YOUR TOPIC: Have it clearly defined in your head before you begin.

- YOUR PERSONAL REASON FORWRITING: Angry about an issue? Want to extend public congratulations, or correct a misstatement? Would you like to introduce an idea, *influence public opinion or policymakers*, and induce others to act?

- THE RULES: Check the paper or periodical for its rules on Letters to the Editor. Often a limit of 150-300 words is set. You can say a lot with those guidelines. A small number of words often magnifies the impact.

- THE MECHANICS:

  1. Include your name, address, and contact information, as well as the recipient's (publication) name and address.

  2. State any request for anonymity.. However, unless you are writing about a provocative issue, the paper will most likely not publish your letter if you request your name withheld.

  3. If you are responding to a recent article, do so within 2-3 days of its appearance in the paper. (Or, in the next weekly cycle.)

  4. State your topic in the first sentence. Focus on one major point, and make it up front. Keep it concise, and stick to one point only. Eliminate superfluous words like "it appears obvious" or "I think". Make a statement.

  5. Provide evidence, verification to support your point.

  6. Add a personal story, if you have one. This adds veracity to your statements.

  7. Say what should be done: actions readers can take themselves, websites where they can go for more information. Instruct readers directly to call their congressman, VOTE, volunteer, etc.

  8. If requesting action from local official(s), name names! Their staffs will catch this, and bring it to their attention.

  9. Summarize and close. Keep it simple. E.g., "In support of our Constitution," and sign you name.

  10. Edit and proofread. This is not solely the job of the publisher!

In summary, KEEP IT SHORT AND SWEET. Use UNEMOTIONAL, ACCUTRATE descriptions. (For example, NOT "he acted stupidly", but rather, "his actions were obviously uninformed." AVOID JARGONJ, ACRONYMS, ABBREVIATIONS. Use commonly understood terms.

Always retain a copy of your letter. If your piece is not accepted by one publication, send it elsewhere. Don't give up. Letters to the Editor are a powerful way to reach a large audience. And OUR COUNTRY IS WORTH EVERY EFFORT!

City Council Letter: Here is a letter writtten to a city council to help explain some of the background and details of programs they were considering:

To: the Bellevue City Council:

As a recognized national expert on Smart Growth issues, I have been asked by a member of the Bellevue City Council to comment on the current debate over the proposed Complete Streets program.

Complete Streets are promoted by Non-Governmental Organizations and Planning Groups as a means to implement Smart Growth programs for the reorganization of community neighborhoods. A major goal of Smart Growth Policy is to diminish the need of automobile traffic by creating "Walkable Communities" where residents can use bicycles, public transportation and walking as their main means of transportation.

Complete Streets advocates assure residents that, under the program, streets are safe for all means of transportation and are engineered so that the entire right of way will enable safe access to all, from drivers, to transit users, pedestrians, and bicyclists. While such promises sound appealing, the reality may be a much different outcome.

First, forcing cars to share the road with every other means of transportation, including buses, trolleys and bikes, creates a dangerous and crowded situation, causing more traffic backups, leading to a greater possibility of accidents. Drivers normally have many things to watch out for as they drive, but the added hazard of additional multiple modes of transportation on already crowded city streets does not lead to the promised safety. Add to this mix the freedom of pedestrians to simply expect cars to stop as they boldly walk across the street increases the hazard for both driver and pedestrian. In Washington, D.C., where Complete Streets have been fully implemented, drivers must dodge pedestrians, bike riders, and find a way around the new trolley system that lumbers through the streets, stopping regularly, as traffic backs up behind it. The result is that driving through the Capitol City has become nearly impossible.

Leading proponents of Complete Streets are bike enthusiasts. Yet, as one travels through many communities across the nation where hundreds of thousands of dollars have been spent to establish bike lanes, one reality seems to stand out. Rarely do you see bicyclists using them. The result is that money has been invested in a program that is not widely used. How many on this Council ride their bikes to work? Worse, in several states, legislation is being considered to make it illegal for cars to pass slower bike traffic on the roads. That means massive back ups, not safer streets.

In short, as advocated by Smart Growth America, one of the proponents of Complete Streets, the real goal is to eliminate the use of automobiles. This is accomplished by making it more and more difficult to drive cars, to the point that drivers eventually give up trying. The Complete Street program has proven to be a major tool for this process. In fact, only under those conditions is the Complete Street workable. The City Council must decide – is that its goal – to eliminate cars inside the city boundaries? Such a decision will lead to a major reorganization of your local society.

Finally, let me point out that there are many special interests and planning groups advocating Smart Growth programs like Complete Streets. They do so because there are a large number of federal grants available to pay for these programs. That is good for the special interests and planners because they gain income from it. However, for the city government it may not work out so well. It is not free money. The grants come with many specifications for compliance. Those specifications may go beyond what the Council actually had in mind, forcing it to spend more money and comply with draconian regulations that will change the culture of the community way beyond simply making safer streets.

For example, several Smart Growth grants, especially from the EPA and HUD, will require the installation of Roundabouts, sidewalks in neighborhoods, curb extensions and median lanes. All will result in creating narrower travel lanes. Simply installing all of these projects will keep the city streets torn up, possibly for years. During that time, streets may be impassable, affecting local businesses, possibly even destroying some. If the city doesn't fully comply with the provisions in the grants then the city council may find itself subjected to federal law suits. Several city councils around the nation have found, as a result of such suits, that their ability to provide home rule, as they were elected by the citizens to do, will become subject to federal agencies.

These are all serious considerations that the Council must understand before considering what may now look like a good idea. Lives will be affected, taxpayer dollars will be committed, and the city will experience drastic change in how it operates. But is it for the better or for worse?

I urge all members of the City Council to independently research these programs very carefully and thoroughly. You may find the reality is much closer to my warnings than to the promises you have been given by the planners and special interests who are promoting this project.

Sincerely,

Tom DeWeese
President

TOOLS FOR MAKING PRIVATE PROPERTY THE CENTER OF YOUR EFFORTS

As previously discussed, the most effective way to combat sustainable policy is to make the center of your attacks based on protecting private property rights. Go through each program and "visioning" plan prepared for the community. For each regulation ask the question about how property rights will be protected. Carefully document each response from the officials. At first they will assure you that property rights will, of course, be protected. Some will assure you they are property owners too, and so they can be trusted to protect their own interests as well as yours. Ask them if they are willing to put that in writing! As the NGOs are flipping out behind them over that question, the officials will quickly refuse.

Here is an undeniable fact: Agenda 21/Sustainable Development cannot be enforced without usurping or diminishing private property rights. So, we need to begin to challenge the plans that affect private property rights. One major question to ask from the very beginning concerns the community's Comprehensive Development Plan. Ask your city councilmen to point out the specific wording that assures protection for private property. I assure you that such language does not exist. If it does, then it comes with several ifs, ands, and buts. Nothing will be clear and understood to be full protection of private property.

This omission gives you an opportunity to make private property protection a major issue, especially after they council members have already assured you they after in favor of protection private property. Earlier in this manual a clear definition and a means to defend it were provided. Use it.

Next, once that definition has been established it can be used as a guideline for drafting legislation and resolutions in state legislatures and city hall. Too many anti-Agenda 21 bills are being written without that definition, rendering them toothless. To use that definition to its utmost affect, I have created a new tool for you to use right in your own local county or city council meetings. It's called the

RESOLUTION TO PROTECT CITIZEN'S PROPERTY RIGHTS

The undersigned elected officials an/or community planners which are officially charged with the duty to create development planning programs for the community/county of _____ _____, do hereby agree to the following:

- That planning involves and affects the right of private property owners in their use, enjoyment, and disposal of property in which the owners are personally and financially responsible for maintaining.

- That individual property ownership constitutes an asset of unique value, as well as the foundation of individual liberty for American citizens.

Recognizing these truths, we agree that all citizen's private property rights shall be placed in the highest priority of consideration during the planning and zoning process; and in the event that any part of the planning and zoning process or recommendations resulting from the process shall potentially negatively impact any property rights, including restrictions on use, enjoyment, disposal or the value of their property, the Council and/or Planners shall:

1. Bring the affected property owner officially and directly into the discussions and deliberations of the proposed plan or policy before any action has been taken.

2. If the Council/Planners determine it is necessary to move forward with the plan, and that to do so will affect the property owner financially, such as through zoning changes, use restrictions, or takings by Eminent Domain, the Council will compensate the property owner's fair market loss, at the value of the property as it stands prior to the damaging plan/policy.

3. Finally, it is agreed that no government representatives, their assigned planning agents, or members of so-called private stakeholder groups will come on to the private property in question for any planning purposes without the prior written permission of the property owner.

Signed (Elected Officials)   Singed (Planners)

_____   _____

_____   _____

_____   _____

_____   _____

HERE'S HOW TO USE THE RESOLUTION

As you stand in front of the elected officials at their regular meeting, ask them simply, "As you bring these planners into our community and begin to implement their programs, what guarantees do I have that you will protect my private property rights?" As mentioned above, this is probably where they will rush to assure you that the certainly support private property rights. This is when you can ask them to show you any language in the plan that covers property rights protection. Finding none, you have your opening to present the Resolution to Protect Citizen's Property Rights.

At this point you haven't mentioned Agenda 21, and you haven't attacked planning. You are simply asking a non-combative question.

Now that they have assured you that they are in full support of protecting private property, but can't provide any language in the Comprehensive plan for its protection, you then say, "Well, I'm happy to hear that you support private property protection, but, I would really like to have that in writing." And you present the resolution to them.

All it basically asks for is transparency and notification of policies that will affect land owners, giving you a chance to have input on regulations that will affect you and your property.

If you can read it aloud to the meeting, so much the better. They may say they need to take it under consideration and will get back to you. Fine. Make sure you are back at the next meeting to ask about it. If they say "No, we cannot sign this resolution," you then must ask the most radical question in the English language: "Why?" and wait for their answer.

Do not attempt this alone. The key to this effort is persistence and organization. If they refuse to sign it then you need 5 or 10 people to stand up and ask again and again, WHY?

You need to escalate this at each meeting until it becomes a public issue - "Why won't your elected officials sign a simple document that says they will protect your private property rights? What are they hiding in the plans they are presenting to us?"

This can and will lead to protests, letters to the editor and other media available to you. Put the elected officials' names on signs carried by protestors who are rallying outside the next council or planning meeting.

Make THEM the issue. What you are really doing is laying the ground work for a campaign to defeat them in the next election.

Nameless, faceless bureaucrats wielding power in the backrooms, untouchable and unseen, is not freedom.

"We will map the whole nation, determine development for the whole country, and regulate it all."
Thomas Lovejoy, Science Advisor to the Department of Interior.

CANDIDATES PROMISE TO PROTECT CITIZEN'S PROPERTY RIGHTS

Do you want to shake up the next election?

Property rights are hardly ever talked about during election campaigns, even though local governments are:

- grabbing private land acres at a time

- bull dozing whole neighborhoods with eminent domain

- banning single family homes

- and threatening landlords if they simply ask prospective renters if they can afford to rent their property

The bottom line is that private property rights have no voice in our elections! Are you ready to change that? Here's how. Here is a "Candidate's Promise to Protect Citizen's Property Rights."

The Candidate's Promise is very simple. It has a very specific definition of property rights – the very one written by state Supreme Court Justice Richard B. Sanders, as defined above. Under that definition there is one question – does the candidate support property rights as defined. Right now, in the middle of the campaign, candidates want and need your support. In fact, election time is about the only time most really care about what you want or need. So, now is the time to apply pressure when you have the advantage.

Here are two ways you can use this Candidates Promise.

First, print out copies of the Candidates Promise (as provided on this page). Make a copy for each candidate you want to approach. Then when you meet your candidates in person and they are shaking your hand or appearing at a public forum – simply present them with the Candidate's Promise and ask them to sign it. If they refuse, then you know they won't support private property rights. However, if they do sign it then you have a powerful tool in your hand once they get elected.

Of course, there are lots of candidates and getting the opportunity to meet each one is a difficult task. So the second way to approach candidates is by email. Simply send a copy of the Candidates Promise directly to your local candidates. In fact, if several people in the community were to send the document to each candidate, that's even better. It will help build pressure to make property rights a major issue in the campaign. Local activists can make it a project.

Together, using this tool, you are going to finally take the forgotten issue of Private Property Rights an force it into major issue status across the nation. To achieve that, we have to start putting elected officials' feet to the fire. They must start to answer the question -- do they or do they not support your right to be secure in your home, free of the fear that private developers and greedy politicians are going to take it at their whim? The fact is, private property is being obliterated in nearly every community in the nation.

So now – stand up – use this new tool and take the property rights fight directly to those who want to represent you in government. Do they support property rights or not? Now is the time to find out.

Here are the two documents for you to use in this effort. The first is a sample email to send to your candidates. It explains the issue and the purpose of the Candidate's Promise. The second document is the actual Candidates Promise for them to sign. Just print out a copy and start applying pressure!

SPECIAL EMAIL MESSAGE TO INCLUDE WITH THE CANDIDATE'S PROMISE TO PROTECT CITIZEN'S PROPERTY RIGHTS

Dear (Candidate's name)

I have attached a "Candidate's Promise to Protect Citizen's Property Rights" which I am asking you to sign to show your support for this vital issue.

I'm sure you are aware that private property is vital to our prosperity and our freedom. Yet property rights are endangered by many government planning projects. In many communities zoning protection for single family homes is being removed. In addition, private landlords are being destroyed through rent controls. If this continues and private property is eliminated the only kind of housing that will be eventually available will be government housing. Do you want that to happen? I believe protection of private property must be a first priority as such planning projects are designed and promoted. Do you agree?

If so, I ask you to make a strong stand for the defense of property rights by signing the attached Candidates Pledge. The definition provided was written by a state Supreme Court Justice.

Please sign and return to my email address. I will then help spread the word that, if elected, you will be a reliable defender of property rights.

Sincerely,
(your name)

CANDIDATE'S PROMISE TO PROTECT CITIZEN'S PROPERTY RIGHTS

1. **I support this definition of private property rights**: "Property in a thing consists not merely in its ownership and possession, but in the unrestricted right of use, enjoyment, and disposal. Anything which destroys any of the elements of property to that extent, destroys the property itself. The substantial value of property lies in its use. If the right of use be denied, the value of the property is annihilated and ownership is rendered a barren right." Written by Washington State Supreme Court Justice Richard B. Sanders (Fifth Amendment Treatise, 1997)

I agree that individual property ownership constitutes an asset of unique value, as well ass the foundation of individual liberty for American citizens. Private property rights are under attack across the nation and its protection must be a first priority in government planning and development projects.

These are positions I pledge to promote and uphold for private property rights if I am elected to the position I seek.

Name _____

Signed _____ Date _____

Candidate for _____

HOW GOVERNMENT CAN REDUCE OR REMOVE YOUR PROPERTY RIGHTS

Eminent Domain:

The State can seize your private property without your consent to create public facilities, highways, and rail-roads, for the purpose of economic development or revenue enhancement (creating new entities on property that generates higher taxes). You are entitled to compensation, but the agency acquiring your property calculates the payments, which is often inadequate.

Federal Regulations

Government, through federal agencies, including the EPA, HUD and the Department of Transportation, impose regulations through the Clean Water Acts, Endangered Species Act, and many others, that limit of erase your property rights.

State and Regional Regulations

States create urban growth boundaries and increase the cost of services beyond those boundaries to force growth into smaller, more densely populated areas. This makes rural property less valuable and more expensive to maintain, diminishing personal wealth.

Local Planning

Local zoning ordinances can infringe upon property rights and increase the cost of ownership, rendering property less desirable and therefore less valuable when selling or borrowing money against it. Anew tactic is to remove single-family home zoning protections too allow government "affordable" housing projects to e build in the neighborhood, thereby destroying property values.

Conservation Easements

Some farmers are encouraged to sign agreements with land trusts or government agencies under the promise that their land will always be farm land. Many times they are also encouraged to sell their development rights to their property. Some farmers do this in exchange for cash or tax benefits. These are called Conservation Easements. While they appear to be a good idea at first, the landowner soon learns they have become subservient to the land trust and must obey shifting regulations and enhanced "best practices" for farming (Sustainable) mandated by the Easement holder. Often these practices become too costly, forcing the landowner to attempt to sell the land. However, with the easement in control, sale becomes difficult and often results in huge losses to the value of the property. In many cases the land trust simply gains control and ownership of the land.

Federal Grant Money

While grant money from the EPA, HUD and DOT can enticing, it frequently comes with severe strings attached that mandate how the money will be used. This can force local government to impose unplanned programs, controlling the community decisions and how property may be used.

Regionalization

Regionalization rolls up a community into a larger regional planning area that shrinks local influence over what regulations are passed, which grants are applied for, and reduces the authority of local public officials to act on behalf of local citizens. Under such a system property rights cannot be protected.

Does this mean all planning and zoning regulations is bad?

No, it means many plans contain regulations that can be damaging to property rights. It's vital that local residents and property owners be much more aware and engaged in the government process.

BEWARE OF FACILITATED PUBLIC MEETINGS

We are constantly told that these planning programs have been discussed, debated and approved by the folks in the community. That's not entirely true. Most public meetings are now run by trained and highly paid facilitators whose job is to control the meeting and bring is to a preplanned conclusion. It's all done by a psychological tactic called the Delphi Technique. If the facilitator is really good at his job, he can actually make the audience think the "consensus" the meeting has reached on an issue or proposal is their idea.

That is how Sustainable Development is being implemented across the nation, especially in meetings or planning boards that are advertised as open to the public. They really don't want you there to give real input, but they want the impression that the community came to these decision. Of course, if you do try to add your thoughts, or openly oppose their plans, you will be cut off by an expert.

But if you are prepared properly, you are the one who can through a real monkey wrench into the process and expose the fraud they are perpetrating.

Below are two presentations by experts on the subject that should start you on the path to countering and disrupting their "consensus process."

THE CONSENSUS PROCESS (DELPHI TECHNIQUE)

by Henry Lamb

In communities across America, "stakeholder" councils are being formed, or have already been formed, to advance Agenda 21 to transform cities and towns into "sustainable communities." The "consensus process" is used to gain the appearance of public support for the principles of sustainability, applied to a particular community. The process is designed to take the public policy- making function away from elected officials and place it in the hands of non-elected officials, while giving the appearance of broad public input into the decision-making process.

Stakeholder councils are called by many names and are created for a variety of specific purposes. Whatever they are called, and whatever the stated purpose for which they are created, they all have several common characteristics, and all have a common objective: the implementation of some component of Agenda 21. While each community may experience a variety of different approaches, it is necessary to recognize the common principles that guide all such councils.

Objectives

The general objective of all stakeholder councils is to promote three primary values: environmental protection, equity, and sustainable economic development. To promote these values, a comprehensive "community" plan must be developed which links, or "integrates," all three values. In some communities, stakeholder councils are formed to work on a single component of a comprehensive plan that is to be combined with the work of other councils that may be working on different components in different geographical areas of the same community. The various councils may or may not know about the work of other councils that is underway simultaneously.

Currently, the most common stakeholder councils are related to the "visioning" process to create "Sustainable Communities;" Ecosystem Management Plans, Heritage Area or Corridor Plans, River Protection Plans, Biosphere Reserves, and Economic Renewal Plans. Almost always, the plan will encompass more than one political jurisdiction. In some instances, several counties and states may be included, as in the case of the East Texas Ecosystem Plan, which embraced 73 Texas counties and a small portion of Louisiana. In other instances, the plan may be confined to a single county or city. When a plan focuses on a single town or county, someone, somewhere, is planning to incorporate that plan into a multi-jurisdictional plan.

The stated purpose of the stakeholder council may be related to environmental protection only, which is usually referred to as natural resource management. It could be related to any one of several other single subjects such as economic renewal, education, emergency response, or transportation. Or, the stated purpose could be to develop a comprehensive plan that addresses all the issues. Whatever the stated purpose, it will attempt to integrate environmental protection, equity, and sustainable economic development.

The Process

Stakeholder councils do not simply appear. Nor are they formed as the result of citizen response to a common problem. Someone creates them — with great care. They could be formed by a government agency, or by several government agencies working together; they could be formed by NGOs (non-governmental organizations) or by a combination of government agencies and NGOs — which is often the case. The Environmental Protection Agency and several other federal agencies offer grants to NGOs and local government agencies as incentives to create these councils and develop plans to achieve sustainable communities. Whoever instigates the process will carefully select individuals from the community to participate in a meeting, which will evolve into a series of meetings. The individuals selected will be chosen because they are known to share philosophical objectives, and to represent broad segments of the community. The poor, disabled, indigenous populations are specifically targeted. Representatives from government agencies are also targeted. Typically, at least one elected official from each of the political jurisdictions in the plan area are invited. Someone from industry, and a landowner or two are also among those invited.

Formation of the original group is extremely important. People who support the objectives of the originators must dominate the group. There also has to be an appearance of broad community representation. The original group may be quite small, or it could be quite large, depending upon the objectives and the size of the community and the plan area. The initial meeting is rarely advertised. Participants are invited personally, and frequently hold several meetings before the press or the community is ever informed. By the time the public becomes aware of the existence of the stakeholders council, it is pretty well organized and its work is well underway.

The Techniques

The Consensus Process — often called "collaborative decision-making" — is a process that begins with a predetermined outcome. The agencies or NGOs that assemble an Ecosystem Management visioning council, intend to establish an ecosystem management plan. The originators know what they want included in the plan before the first meeting is ever scheduled. Those who assemble Sustainable Community visioning councils intend to establish a plan to achieve their vision of a sustainable community. The literature will say that broad community input is sought. In reality, the outcome has been decided before the first meeting begins; the real purpose for the process is to "educate" the participants.

A trained facilitator will conduct the meetings. A consensus-building meeting is vastly different from a meeting conducted by Robert's Rules of Order. In a consensus-building meeting — there are no votes. There is no debate. The idea is to avoid conflict and confrontation between and among differing views. The facilitator leads the discussion with questions that are skillfully crafted to elicit no response. Questions are framed to force respondents to disagree with a statement with which most reasonable people would agree. For example, a facilitator might ask: "Is there anyone who would disagree that we have a responsibility to leave future generations sufficient resources to meet their need?" Obviously, no reasonable person can disagree with such a statement. Silence — no response — implies that a consensus has been reached on the need to protect resources for future generations. The example is an oversimplification, but it illustrates the technique used by the facilitator.

Despite the careful selection of the participants, the facilitator may encounter an individual who does disagree with the questions. The facilitator is trained to marginalize such an individual by making him or her look silly by asking another, even more extreme question, such as: "Surely you are not telling this group that you feel no responsibility to your grandchildren, are you?" With such tactics, one who objects or disagrees very often is quickly labeled as a troublemaker and is either ignored or excluded from the group.

Eventually, a professional will write a report. It will be "The Plan," or the document produced by the group. Regardless of what the group's stated purpose may be, the final document will include language that says the plan is designed to integrate ecology, equity, and the economy; environmental protection, equity, and sustainable development.

The Players

The players will include federal, state, and/or local government appointed officials. Working hand-in-hand, there will also be one or more representatives from NGOs that may or may not be recognizable. The Nature Conservancy and the Sierra Club are two of the more active NGOs instigating these stakeholder councils. Frequently, however, a new NGO will be created expressly for the purpose of instigating a stakeholder council in a given community. One or more of the larger NGOs, or an organization such as the Tides Foundation, will supply the start-up money and send a couple of professionals into a community to create an NGO such as "Friends of Hollow Rock, Inc." or something similar. Sometimes an existing local NGO will be used, with substantial financial and leadership help from a larger NGO, or with help from the federal government through one of the many grants that are available for the purpose.

Whenever it is possible, a well-known local figure — a politician, businessman, or landowner will be created to be the spokesperson. In Racine, Wisconsin, no less a figure than Samuel C. Johnson, CEO of Johnson Wax Company was chosen to convince his neighbors that sustainability was the only way to go. Such individuals give credibility to the process and can have enormous persuasive power over local residents.

With such a cast of players, using techniques that are skillful to the point of deception, in a process designed to produce a predetermined outcome, it is little wonder that the objectives of Agenda 21 are being implemented in cities, towns and across the countryside of America. Those who recognize the inherent dangers in allowing non-elected bureaucrats to develop public policy, and those who can see the socialistic underpinnings of a managed society in the objectives of Agenda 21, need to rise to the occasion to stop the underpinning of the United States Constitution.

DISRUPTING DELPHI TECHNIQUE MEETINGS

How not to be taken for a ride at your next meeting, and stop government groups from achieving consensus on issues THEY want when there is no consensus.

Have you attended a meeting of the local government and left there feeling that what you said was ignored, or the goals of the meeting were to inexplicably support everything the government group decided was what 'THEY' wanted? You may have been a victim of The Delphi Technique, a very effective tool which, when used by the wrong people, can make every meeting look as if there was participation and/or consensus when there is none.

USING THE DELPHI TECHNIQUE TO ACHIEVE CONSENSUS

How it is leading us away from representative government to an illusion of citizen participation

by Lynn Stuter

The Delphi Technique and consensus building are both founded in the same principle - the Hegelian dialectic of thesis, antithesis, and synthesis, with synthesis becoming the new thesis. The goal is a continual evolution to "oneness of mind" (consensus means solidarity of belief) -the collective mind, the wholistic society, the wholistic earth, etc. In thesis and antithesis, opinions or views are presented on a subject to establish views and opposing views. In synthesis, opposites are brought together to form the new thesis. All participants in the process are then to accept ownership of the new thesis and support it, changing their views to align with the new thesis. Through a continual process of evolution, "oneness of mind" will supposedly occur.

In group settings, the Delphi Technique is an unethical method of achieving consensus on controversial topics. It requires well-trained professionals, known as "facilitators" or "change agents," who deliberately escalate tension among group members, pitting one faction against another to make a preordained viewpoint appear "sensible," while making opposing views appear ridiculous.

In her book Educating for the New World Order, author and educator Beverly Eakman makes numerous references to the need of those in power to preserve the illusion that there is "community participation in decision-making processes, while in fact lay citizens are being squeezed out."

The setting or type of group is immaterial for the success of the technique. The point is that, when people are in groups that tend to share a particular knowledge base, they display certain identifiable characteristics, known as group dynamics, which allows the facilitator to apply the basic strategy.

The facilitators or change agents encourage each person in a group to express concerns about the programs, projects, or policies in question. They listen attentively, elicit input from group members, form "task forces," urge participants to make lists, and in going through these motions, learn about each member of a group. They are trained to identify the "leaders," the "loud mouths," the "weak or non-committal members," and those who are apt to change sides frequently during an argument.

Suddenly, the amiable facilitators become professional agitators and "devil's advocates." Using the "divide and conquer" principle, they manipulate one opinion against another, making those who are out of step appear "ridiculous, unknowledgeable, inarticulate, or dogmatic." They attempt to anger certain participants, thereby accelerating tensions. The facilitators are well trained in psychological manipulation. They are able to predict the reactions of each member in a group. Individuals in opposition to the desired policy or program will be shut out.

The Delphi Technique works. It is very effective with parents, teachers, school children, and community groups. The "targets" rarely, if ever, realize that they are being manipulated. If they do suspect what is happening, they do not know how to end the process. The facilitator seeks to polarize the group in order to become an accepted member of the group and of the process. The desired idea is then placed on the table and individual opinions are sought during discussion. Soon, associates from the divided group begin to adopt the idea as if it were their own, and they pressure the entire group to accept their proposition.

How the Delphi Technique Works

Consistent use of this technique to control public participation in our political system is causing alarm among people who cherish the form of government established by our Founding Fathers. Efforts in education and other areas have brought the emerging picture into focus.

In the not-too-distant past, the city of Spokane, in Washington state, hired a consultant to the tune of $47,000 to facilitate the direction of city government. This development brought a hue and cry from the local population. The ensuing course of action holds an eerie similarity to what is happening in education reform. A newspaper editorial described how groups of disenfranchised citizens were brought together to "discuss" what they felt needed to be changed at the local government level. A compilation of the outcomes of those "discussions" influenced the writing of the city/county charter.

That sounds innocuous. But what actually happened in Spokane is happening in communities and school districts all across the country. Let's review the process that occurs in these meetings.

First, a facilitator is hired. While his job is supposedly neutral and non-judgmental, the opposite is actually true. The facilitator is there to direct the meeting to a preset conclusion.

The facilitator begins by working the crowd to establish a good-guy-bad-guy scenario. Anyone disagreeing with the facilitator must be made to appear as the bad guy, with the facilitator appearing as the good guy. To accomplish this, the facilitator seeks out those who disagree and makes them look foolish, inept, or aggressive, which sends a clear message to the rest of the audience that, if they don't want the same treatment, they must keep quiet. When the opposition has been identified and alienated, the facilitator becomes the good guy - a friend - and the agenda and direction of the meeting are established without the audience ever realizing what has happened.

Next, the attendees are broken up into smaller groups of seven or eight people. Each group has its own facilitator. The group facilitators steer participants to discuss preset issues, employing the same tactics as the lead facilitator.

Participants are encouraged to put their ideas and disagreements on paper, with the results to be compiled later. Who does the compiling? If you ask participants, you typically hear: "Those running the meeting compiled the results." Oh-h! The next question is: "How do you know that what you wrote on your sheet of paper was incorporated into the final outcome?" The typical answer is: "Well, I've wondered about that, because what I wrote doesn't seem to be reflected. I guess my views were in the minority."

That is the crux of the situation. If 50 people write down their ideas individually, to be compiled later into a final outcome, no one knows what anyone else has written. That the final outcome of such a meeting reflects anyone's input at all is highly questionable, and the same holds true when the facilitator records the group's comments on paper. But participants in these types of meetings usually don't question the process.

Why hold such meetings at all if the outcomes are already established? The answer is because it is imperative for the acceptance of the School-to-Work agenda, or the environmental agenda, or whatever the agenda, that ordinary people assume ownership of the preset outcomes. If people believe an idea is theirs, they'll support it. If they believe an idea is being forced on them, they'll resist.

The Delphi Technique is being used very effectively to change our government from a representative form in which elected individuals represent the people, to a "participatory democracy" in which citizens selected at large are facilitated into ownership of preset outcomes. These citizens believe that their input is important to the result, whereas the reality is that the outcome was already established by people not apparent to the participants.

How to Diffuse the Delphi Technique

Three steps can diffuse the Delphi Technique as facilitators attempt to steer a meeting in a specific direction.

Always be charming, courteous, and pleasant. Smile. Moderate your voice so as not to come across as belligerent or aggressive.

Stay focused. If possible, jot down your thoughts or questions. When facilitators are asked questions they don't want to answer, they often digress from the issue that was raised and try instead to put the questioner on the defensive. Do not fall for this tactic. Courteously bring the facilitator back to your original question. If he rephrases it so that it becomes an accusatory statement (a popular tactic), simply say, "That is not what I asked. What I asked was . . ." and repeat your question.

Be persistent. If putting you on the defensive doesn't work, facilitators often resort to long monologues that drag on for several minutes. During that time, the group usually forgets the question that was asked, which is the intent. Let the facilitator finish. Then with polite persistence state: "But you didn't answer my question. My question was . . ." and repeat your question.
Never become angry under any circumstances. Anger directed at the facilitator will immediately make the facilitator the victim. This defeats the purpose. The goal of facilitators is to make the majority of the group members like them, and to alienate anyone who might pose a threat to the realization of their agenda. People with firm, fixed beliefs, who are not afraid to stand up for what they believe in, are obvious threats. If a participant becomes a victim, the facilitator loses face and favor with the crowd. This is why crowds are broken up into groups of seven or eight, and why objections are written on paper rather than voiced aloud where they can be open to public discussion and debate. It's called crowd control.

At a meeting, have two or three people who know the Delphi Technique dispersed through the crowd so that, when the facilitator digresses from a question, they can stand up and politely say: "But you didn't answer that lady/gentleman's question." Even if the facilitator suspects certain group members are working together, he will not want to alienate the crowd by making accusations. Occasionally, it takes only one incident of this type for the crowd to figure out what's going on.

Establish a plan of action before a meeting. Everyone on your team should know his part. Later, analyze what went right, what went wrong and why, and what needs to happen the next time. Never strategize during a meeting.

A popular tactic of facilitators, if a session is meeting with resistance, is to call a recess. During the recess, the facilitator and his spotters (people who observe the crowd during the course of a meeting) watch the crowd to see who congregates where, especially those who have offered resistance. If the resistors congregate in one place, a spotter will gravitate to that group and join in the conversation, reporting what was said to the facilitator. When the meeting resumes, the facilitator will steer clear of the resistors. Do not congregate. Instead gravitate to where the facilitators or spotters are. Stay away from your team members.

This strategy also works in a face-to-face, one-on-one meeting with anyone trained to use the Delphi Technique.

STATE LEGISLATIVE ACTION

State legislators have much more power than they may realize. They can block federal edicts and refuse to obey them. The Constitution, in its clearly written enumeration of powers, specifically states what the federal government may do. All other decisions are up to the states. It's called the Tenth Amendment. One of the main reasons our nation is suffering from an out-of-control national government is because the states have forgotten, ignored, or surrendered their powers and have allowed the federal government to dictate to them. To stop Sustainable Development the states must take back their rightful responsibilities.

Even if anti-Sustainable, pro-limited government legislators are in a minority they can effectively impact the legislative process.

THE FIVE BILL PACKAGE TO LAUNCH A REVOLUTION

We are always in the minority, always lacking the fire power to make real change. Well, there are ways to fight back when surrounded by superior forces and low on ammunition. In the immortal words of John Singleton Mosby, the Gray Ghost of the Confederacy – CHARGE!

Ok, so you are a state legislator who believes in limiting government. You fully understand the Sustainable Development/Green New Deal agenda and you want to stop it. But you're outnumbered. Only three or four other legislators agree with you. You've tired to introduce bills, but they go no where. What's the use? Then try this tactic.

First, talk to your fellow like-minded legislators and form a team – the Liberty Coalition. Make sure you are all in agreement by taking this Freedom Agenda pledge:
"I solemnly pledge to my constituents that I will consistently vote to defund, or vote against appropriating money for any state participation in the implementation or enforcement of an federal regulatory program or activity not specifically authorized by an enumerated power in the United States Constitution because when such program or activity is not specifically authorized by an enumerated power it is not allowed under the United

States Constitution. For any State participation I do vote to fund, I will provide the specific enumerated power constitutionally permitting it."

Second, look around at neighboring states to find similar legislators in the minority in their legislature. Begin to network with them. Open a dialogue. Third, do the same thing in more states. Make it your goal to network with such legislators in ten states and build your Freedom Coalition. Ask them to take the Freedom Agenda Pledge as well. One final action will be required in each state – reach out to the most effective activists in each state and tell them your plan.

Now, pick a day for action. On that day, in all ten states, at exactly the same time, you will all drop the exact same bills into the legislative hopper of each state. These will be a package of five bills, each designed to reduce the **S**ize, **C**ost, **R**each, **A**nd **P**ower of Government = SCRAP! After having taken that action, next, at exactly the same time, each team of the Freedom Coalition, in each state hold a news conference to announce what you have done and describe what each bill will do. This will get you a powerful start with national, and probably international news coverage. Be bold. Be determined. Stand Strong.

Now it's time for the activists that you have brought into you Freedom Coalition to step forward and begin supporting your legislative package. They need to hit the halls of the legislature, feed the news media, and hold rally and demonstrations on the state capital steps. Finally, if multiple states pass such specific legislation (even one or two of the bills) to roll back government it will catch fire and become a movement in more states, eventually becoming a vital agenda. And that's why it is important to present a package of bills, each designed to do one thing – not just one bill trying to do it all. This way each bill gets a hearing, providing more opportunity to discussion, debate and media exposure, and if only one or two are passed, you can claim victory and try again on those that didn't pass.

This is how you turn a hopeless minority into a national movement to restore freedom. Freedom Pods in the state legislatures. In fact, these exact tactics can also be used in city councils and county commissions. The power comes from people – not government – learn it– practice it - win CHARGE!

HERE ARE THE FIVE BILLS FOR YOUR SCRAP PACKAGE

Below is an outline of the bills, the entire bills can be found in the back of this book and on our website: www.americanpolicy.org/tools password apc1225

Bill #1 Prohibits International Law Over Property Rights

This bill prohibits the use of international law to infringe on property rights. This includes the 1972 Earth Summit, the 1973 Convention on International Trade in Endangered Species, the 1973 UN Environmental Program (UNEP), the 1976 Conference on Human Settlements (Habitat I), and numerous other terrible international laws, including the 1992 UN Commission on Sustainable Development.

Bill #2 Stop Eminent Domain for Private Economic Development

This bill states that private property may be taken only for public use and the taking of private property by any public entity for economic development does not constitute a public use. No public entity may take property for the purpose of economic development.

Bill #3   If Government Takes it, Government Pays For It

This bill requires government authorities to provide just compensation to property owners whenever land use ordinances, regulations, or policies adopted require the property owner to alter their property in any of numerous ways from placing signage, making an expenditure for the protection of riparian areas, or grant easements for public access on the property.

Bill #4   No Developer Entry without Property Owners Permission

This bill makes it illegal to make entry onto private property to collect resource data without legal authorization.

Bill #5   Clear Standards and Guidelines for Drone Use Over Private Property

Because technological advances have provided new, unique equipment that may be utilized for surveillance purposes (i.e. drones, etc.), and because these advances often outpace statutory protections, the legislature finds that regardless of application or size, the use of unmanned aerial vehicles, without public debate or clear legal authority, this creates uncertainty for both citizens and agencies. The lack of clear statutory authority for their use may increase liability to state and local jurisdictions. Therefore, clear standards need to be provided.

THE SILVER BULLET FOR VICTORY
THE NEED TO TAKE COMMAND OF LOCAL PRECINCTS

By Tom DeWeese

Is tyranny our fate?

The question now becomes, what do we do? Obviously, we have one of two choices. We accept our fate, or we fight. Are we finished? Do we quit? Do we surrender?
It would be easy to do any of those things. No one would blame us. We gave it the good fight. We could hide behind the idea that ancient conspiracies set our fate long before we were born. Members of secret societies somehow trumped every ideal we hold – and overpowered every move we made.

We could pat ourselves on the back and say, well, they were just too strong. What could we do? Tyranny is our destiny. Is that what you want to tell your grandchildren when they ask you what you did to preserve the ideal of America?

In another era, we could have loaded up boats and sailed to a new world to live by the ideals we hold. But that was already done. People ran from tyranny. They came here – to America. Now tyranny has caught us. And there's nowhere else to run. We either accept our pre-ordained "fate" or make a stand. This is it, my friends. This is the moment when we decide the future of our ideals.

You know the ideals I'm talking about. That you are born with liberty. That it is your natural right to speak your mind, start a business, own and control property, build your dream home – and expect it to be there for as long as you like, practice your religion exactly as you believe, and, above all, expect that the government will protect those rights at all costs.

We know by witnessing history that totalitarianism does not work. Government control of the actions of the people only leads to poverty and misery. We know that people pinned under the heavy hand of government do not produce for their masters. We know that that there are no such things as faceless, nameless masses in some undefined "common good." We know that the United States was the first nation ever created that recognized the natural rights of individuals – and America's history has proven that such a system is the only one that produces prosperity and happiness.

Do we fight for those ideals of liberty? Or will we allow them to be lost forever under some global village? Do nothing, and they have made the decision for us. What can be easier than that?

Fighting Back

But if we decide to fight, then we truly must know what we are doing. Half - hearted attempts at rallies and letter writing, like we've done in the past, didn't get the job done then and certainly won't get it done now. No short cuts. No silly rhetoric.

I've got to tell you that I get some pretty strange stuff in my office. Letters, e-mails, phone calls. People write to me with ideas they think will put us on the road to victory. Everybody's looking for that one quick fix. The right slogan. The silver bullet – that will defeat our enemies and restore freedom to America. Almost daily, I receive someone's solution – the great plan that no one else has thought of.

A good friend of mine, for example, wrote a huge book that carried all of the facts and figures to prove his position against a certain government program. He called me to say all we had to do to turn things around was to get a copy of the book into the hands of every single Member of Congress.

I tried to explain that Congressmen can't read. In fact, they now have the votes in Congress operating exactly like a fast food restaurant. Truly, about the only question they ask now is, "Do you want to super-size that?"

I've received buttons, bumper stickers and tee shirts – all created to provide "the message" that will turn everything around. I've receive phone calls resulting in long discussions about how to come up with just the right sound bite that will capture the nation's imagination and send the scoundrels to the tall grass. And my personal favorite – "we'll use words that will be so innocent sounding that the other side won't know what we are really up to".

The Silver Bullet

So, what is the silver bullet to save our liberty? I'm going to give it to you.
My friends, I often hear it lamented that the Republic is dead and that we are now controlled by Washington. You know what – I have found that isn't true. The Republic is still there buried under the weight of un-elected planning commissions, visioning statements, and review boards.

Squeezed in, under all of that, is the Republic of our Founding Fathers, rusting from lack of use. But it's still there and still armed with the silver bullet the founders provided to guarantee that no one could take it away. You see, our founders created this Republic to be self-protected by making government at the local level the most powerful force.

The Silver Bullet is the "precinct captain". You scoff? You were hoping for something much more exciting! Well, that's probably the very reason we've ignored it.

We would much rather turn our attention to Washington, Congress, or the President. Why then, are these government entities so powerful today? Because we've let them become powerful by placing all of our attention on them – while ignoring involvement in local government.

But the power still lies in the precinct captain. Our opponents know it. They have left no lowly office untouched. Check it out. Go to your local government and check out the policies being implemented by the game warden and the dog catcher – Sustainable Development and animal rights, most likely. City treasurer. City clerk. The people who collect the taxes and issue permits. What are their policies? How about the planning/development department and its policy for building permits? Sustainable Development? Now move on up to City Council and Mayor.

In 2005, the United Nations held a major conference in San Francisco on Sustainable Development. The main targets for the conference were the mayors. Those who attended were asked to sign two documents – the Green Cities Declaration and the Urban Environmental Accords in which the Mayors pledged to undertake 21 action items over the next few years to implement Sustainable Development.

These action items included water policy, energy policy, transportation, and health. The mayors were provided sample legislation and pledged to enact it. The policies called for the implementation of the Kyoto Global Warming Treaty and Agenda 21.

One week later, in Chicago, the U.S. Conference of Mayors called for the very same policies, making Sustainable Development and Kyoto the two priorities of the nation's mayors.
In short, our enemies know that the power to impose this tyranny on us is now at the local level. It will do little good to spend time trying to stop it through Congress or the White House. What does the UN understand that you and I don't? That it doesn't matter what Washington's policy is. They will just get the local cities and towns to do it anyway – because the towns and cities have the power to decide for themselves.

Think Globally – Act Locally

Think globally – act locally is not just a slogan. It's an agenda. Now, to save our Republic and way of life, we need to make it *our* agenda. The Founding Fathers did.
Make a chart of every single position available in your county. Break it down to the precinct level and then the ward level. List every office. Every board position. Now you will begin to see how large a task it is. But take it one step at a time. Start to fill those spots.

Work quietly. Please don't hold a press conference to announce to the community that you plan to take it over. Work through what ever party you want – even the Democrats. The goal here is to get our people, who understand the Sustainablist agenda, into places of decision making. It would be a dream come true to have candidates from every party running on the same issue. It's a goal to shoot for. The other side seems to have achieved it.

But make sure those candidates are people who understand the entire picture of Sustainable Development and Agenda 21. It will do you no good to help elect candidates who are, perhaps, good on one issue, like gun control or abortion, but fail to see the whole picture. Those are the very people who will fail you later.

Take over a precinct. Just one. You will control the election of every candidate at every level – at least in your little part of the city. Then take two.

You will need precinct workers to make sure our people get to the polls. You will need poll workers to make sure our votes are counted. Make sure they are people you can trust.

Run a candidate for the lowest office in town. Control it. No position is without power. Then do it again. Go up the ladder. Get more precincts. Grow, neighborhood by neighborhood.

Step by step. Control enough precincts and even presidential candidates will seek you out for help in getting elected. You will control the candidates. You can stop the bad ones from even being able to run. Again, only help elect local officials who oppose Sustainable Development. Refuse to support the lesser of two evils.

Pay attention to the non-elected review boards, policy committees, and planning commissions. Can you get one of your people on it? Who is doing the appointing?
Can you imagine the damage we could do to Sustainablist goals by getting one person on the local architectural review board?

You need to have the ability to create controversy against policies by current office holders. This will help you find like-minded folks to join you. And it will help create issues so your candidates can win. Remember, most people would oppose them if they knew the truth. Tell them. Spread out.

A New Chamber of Commerce?

Consider this idea. If your local farm bureau or Chamber of Commerce isn't representing you – start a new one. Understand this – you don't have to just take their double dealing. Go around them. Show up at council meetings, or at the meetings of any agency or board that purports to make policy that affects you.

=As a new group representing business interests, homeowners, or farmers, demand your say. Back up your demands by issuing news releases and doing interviews on local radio and television – representing your new group. Start saying over and over again that the governing body isn't representing the interests of your constituents.
If you make enough noise as the group which is truly standing up for farmers or businesses or homeowners, those individuals will follow you. You will pull the power structure right out from under the established organizations that have been taken over by our enemies.

Sure, we are way behind. Sure, we have a massive job ahead of us and we would be fools to delude ourselves otherwise. But, after all of our hard work over the years, after being a lone voice in the wilderness, something has started here.

Now is not the time to circle the wagons or give up. Now is the time to move out, get involved, and turn the tables. Stop being polite to your oppressors. Tell them their time is through. Tell those who pretend to speak for you in Washington to either get on board with our agenda – or get out of the way. We are no longer going to go quietly into the night.

Get mad. But get busy. And do what it takes to win. Organize at the local level – use the power the Founding Fathers gave us to preserve the Republic – and throw off the yoke of tyranny.

Write this down and keep it in front of you at all times: "*The right of the individual to own and control private property is the foundation of liberty.*" And now write this: "*Precinct Captain is the root to victory.*" That's the silver bullet that leads to sustained liberty. Put the two together and restore and preserve this Republic.

Now that's something to tell your grandchildren when they ask what you did in the great war to preserve American liberty. Salute, and tell them "I was a Precinct Captain."

CAN WE TAKE BACK OUR ELECTION PROCESS AND
MAKE THE PARTIES LISTEN TO US
WHAT IF WE JUST SAID NONE OF THE ABOVE!

The clamor is growing louder every day. "They don't listen." "We have no real choice of candidates." "The system is rigged for the elite." "There's no difference between the two parties."

You hear it every election. Endless talk about the need to create jobs, build the economy, make the nation a "better place to live for our families," and, my favorite – "restore trust!" Who's not for those wonderful things! The slogans work for Democrat and Republican alike. These so-called issues are interchangeable. They are, in fact, nothing more than empty rhetoric.

Meanwhile, do we hear a discussion about our money becoming more worthless every day from government spending and rampant inflation? What about the destruction of our education system as it is used for behavior modification while true academics are eliminated for the curriculum? Does any candidate dare mention the hopelessness taking over our inner cities as federal welfare policies are enslaving whole generations to the ever-expanding government plantation? And of course there is the fear campaign in every city in the nation about the need to control development and population, leading to the utter destruction of private property.

None of these issues are ever mentioned in local, state or federal campaigns. Any candidate who tries is immediately labeled an extremist!

So our political parties choose for us candidates that are "acceptable," middle of the road, not rocking the boat, and not too extreme. In short, we are forced to choose the lesser of two evils. Election after election the drone goes on. And what are we to do? These are the candidates those in charge have chosen for us for city council, county commission, state legislature, Congress and President. Yes, we have primaries to choose, but I think we all know those are pretty much rigged to assure the powers in charge get whom they want – just ask Bernie Sanders.

Is it any wonder that there are millions of Americans who don't vote or participate in our nation's debate because they think it doesn't matter anyway? The "average voter" increasingly feels that the decisions have been made for them.

Those who hold conservative points of view that our nation should live within the Constitution now believe socialism is inevitable, so why bother going to the polls.

The poor think they are simply pawns in a vice grip between big money and special interests which control the elections. Why bother? Helplessness now rules the world's greatest representative democracy. As people stay home or trudge to the polls to unenthusiastically vote for the next lesser of two evils, 93% of incumbents are routinely returned to office – year after year after year.

The instant a candidate is elected and joins the ranks of the incumbents he/she begins the dance. Get the money for the next campaign. How? Special interests groups, corporations and foreign interests flood into their offices to make deals, promote their personal agendas and show the way to fame, fortune and perpetual office – if only the incumbents go along. They have the whole process well in hand. Campaigns become little more than big PR projects, promoted in positive platitudes, specifically designed to assure nothing negative sticks. Just get through it and keep the gravy train running.

Above all, do not talk about controversial subjects like dollar values, global trade or immigration; just stick to issues like health care, and the environment – coincidentally, two issues bought and paid for by the special interests. See how it works?

So year after year, we officially hold elections and politicians pontificate about how our going to the polls is a revered right, a valued tradition, the underpinning of a free society. And they wonder why there is such division in the nation. How did we end up in such a mess? We voted for these guys. But did we enjoy it? Are we satisfied with the results? Would we like to demand a do-over?

So is it hopeless? Is there any way to change it? Do you want the people to, again, have control of the election process and of the choice of candidates offered? Do you want to force the power elites to listen to you? I've got a solution.

Don't despair. Don't give up. There is a logical, effective way out of this. But it won't happen by depending on political parties to lead the way. We have to take things into our own hands. We need an effective, binding form of protest to say "NO" to bad candidates. There is such a way.

Imagine going into the voting booth and looking down the list of candidates offered. None really appeal. None seem to offer satisfaction as an answer to the issues that concern you. If only there was something else you could do. A write in won't help. It would take such a difficult, expensive effort. It rarely works.

Then you look further down the ballot. Something new. It says "NONE OF THE ABOVE." It's a final choice after each of the candidates in every category, from president, to congress to city council. What does it mean?

It means you have the power to decide who will hold office – not the power brokers. When the votes are tallied, if "NONE OF THE ABOVE" gets a majority of votes over any of the candidates listed, then "NONE OF THE ABOVE" wins. And that means none of those candidates will win the office. The office will remain vacant until a new election is held. To set up another election and fill the spot would work exactly like the process provided in the Constitution when an incumbent dies or resigns, and a special election is held. Now new candidates will have to try to win the public's support.

Fixing the election process could be that simple. You, the voter, would be completely in the driver's seat with the power to reject candidates, forcing a new election with new choices. The political parties would be forced to provide candidates the people want -- or face being rejected. They would have to talk about real issues – or face being rejected. Incumbents would have to answer for their actions in office – or face being rejected. "NONE OF THE ABOVE." Period. The power of labor unions and international corporations would be broken.

Think of the consequences. No longer would voters have to settle for the lesser of two evils. If all the candidates are bad – none would be able to force their way into office. It would mean that powerful special interests could no longer rely on their money to buy elections. They could buy all the ads they wanted, spend millions on "volunteers" going door to door and sling their dirt, but if the voters aren't buying, none of it will save their candidate from being rejected by "NONE OF THE ABOVE."

Moreover, the power of entrenched incumbents who have been unbeatable because of their massive war chests and party ties would be broken. Picture John McCain or Nancy Pelosi unable to run for office because they were rejected by "NONE OF THE ABOVE."

However, in order to work, "NONE OF THE ABOVE" would have to be binding. It would have to have the power of law behind it. It cannot be just a "protest" vote that has no other meaning.

"NONE OF THE ABOVE" is completely non-partisan. There is no way to control its outcome. There is no need for a massive campaign chest to support "NONE OF THE ABOVE," although it could certainly be done. But the option, once permanently placed on the ballot, would always be there. America's representative system would be restored.

To get the job done, activists in every state would have to begin a campaign to demand that "NONE OF THE ABOVE" be given a permanent spot on the ballot. It would not require a Constitutional Amendment. It would have to be done state by state. Some states have ballot referendums and initiatives using petition drives to get an issue on the ballot so the people can decide. It's difficult and expensive to do, but popular ideas have a chance.

In other states, "NONE OF THE ABOVE" advocates would have to find a friendly state representative or senator to introduce the idea before the state legislature and then get enough votes to pass it in both houses and then have it signed by the governor. The main drawback to that effort is that, if the effort is successful, then every one of those legislators is an incumbent who will have to face "NONE OF THE ABOVE" on the ballot for their re-election. They probably won't be too excited about the idea.
So why would they support the idea? It would be only because supporters succeed in creating a strong movement of voters which demand it. No one is saying this will be an easy process. But such movements have succeeded before. For example, local activists could begin by demanding that candidates support the measure much like they now sign "no tax" pledges. In short, they would support it because there is strong popular support and they simply have no choice.

Of course, one of their main objections to the "NONE OF THE ABOVE" idea would be the requirement for holding a new election, should it win. Too expensive, our responsible public servants would say as they dismissed the idea. However, if it means getting better candidates, isn't it worth it to hold a new election, especially considering how much a very bad candidate would cost us if he actually got into office? The fact is, such a need for a new election would probably not arise often once political power brokers began to understand that they must offer candidates acceptable to the people rather than to the special interests. That's all they really have to do. It's all we want. It only takes a couple of "None of the Above" victories to see that the electorate is back in charge.

The idea of "NONE OF THE ABOVE" has been around for a long time. Over the years, most states have had some kind of legislation introduced supporting the concept. Nevada actually has it on the ballot – but it is not binding. It doesn't force a new election. It is just a measure of protest. That's not good enough to make it effective.

One of the reasons it has not been successful is because there has never been a serious national drive to promote the idea. However, with the growing dissatisfaction voters are feeling with the lack of quality candidates seeming to get worse every election, perhaps there has never been a better time to start a national discussion on the issue.

The best part is that "NONE OF THE ABOVE" isn't a conservative or liberal idea. It's not a Republican of Democrat proposal. In fact, Republican leadership might see it as a good way to break the back of big labor's influence over elections. Equally, Democrats could see it as a way to stop the power and influence of the Republican's big business money. However the parties want to look at it, the bottom line is that the voters win.

This will be a long-term process and is primarily aimed at local, state and congressional candidates. While it should certainly be used in presidential elections as well, the real power comes from rejecting the lower level candidates.

But all of that depends on the voters. Do you want to take back control, or are you satisfied to have your choices made for you behind closed doors? Because that's what we have now. How's that working for you?

WHY DON'T ELECTED REPRESENTATIVES AND THEIR AGENTS RESPOND TO CITIZENS? LEGAL ACTION: SECTION 1983 MAKE THEM PERSONALLY RESPONSIBLE FOR THEIR OWN ACTIONs

The Civil Rights Act of 1991, Section 1983

Many people complain that their government simply pays no attention to them as it imposes damaging policies. For that reason, many citizens give up the fight, feeling there is no hope in making a difference. There is a very specific reason why you are ignored. Those officials suffer no consequences for their actions. Even if you were to successfully sue the city over such a policy, the government officials feel no pain. They don't pay the fines, taxpayers do. Nor do they face jail time or firing. Meanwhile, they are surrounded by Planners and NGO representatives who are plying them with more programs, money, and potential political power. Why should they bother to listen to you? There is nothing to gain, nothing to lose. That can be changed. Little known to most activists is a legal means to make these government representatives personally responsible for their actions and if it is successfully employed, it can change the entire game of government as the guilty ones pay their own fines, reparations, and can actually face jail time, depending on the situation. It's called Section 1983 of the Civil Rights Act of 1991. Here are the details.

All persons born or naturalized in the United States, and subject to the jurisdiction thereof, are citizens of the United States and of the state wherein they reside. No state shall make or enforce any law which shall abridge the privileges or immunities of citizens of the United States; nor shall any state deprive any person of life, liberty, or property, without due process of law; nor deny to any person within its jurisdiction the equal protection of the laws.

American Policy Center has put together the details to help attorneys and laypeople use Section 1983 to the law to take back their rights. In today's bureaucracies our rights are being trampled on and denied with virtual impunity. Whether it is a city or county using zoning to deny you the use of your property, illegal search and seizure often done under 'civil forfeiture', the 'taking' of your property by forbidding you to use it as you see fit, warrantless wiretapping, denying Freedom of Information Act by reclassification and increased secrecy; and red flag gun confiscation, you have the right to sue. And we are looking at Real ID, forced vaccinations, 5G, shutting down churches. A perfect example: Pamela Geller sued NYC Mayor Bill De Blasio, May 2020. "The lawsuit challenges Mayor de Blasio's recent announcement that, pursuant to his executive orders, the First Amendment no longer applies in the City of New York as he has made it unlawful to peaceably assemble and protest."

After the Civil War, the 13th, 14th, and 15th, Amendments abolished slavery, make the former slaves citizens, and gave **all men** the right to vote. These were all civil rights laws. And they were pretty much ignored. It wasn't until the late 1950's that people pushed for strong laws to protect Blacks, and, in 1963 President Kennedy took up the crusade for civil rights. President Johnson sign the 1964 Civil Rights Act that has been updated a couple of times, but is the basis for what we are using today.

Our civil rights, according to FindLaw "are an expansive and significant set of rights that are designed to protect individuals from unfair treatment; they are the rights of individuals to receive equal treatment (and to be free from unfair treatment or discrimination) in a number of settings – including education, employment, housing, public accommodations, and more -- and based on certain legally-protected characteristics."

There must be an act by a municipal policymaker to establish municipal liability. The Supreme Court had earlier defined a policy as a deliberate choice to follow a course of action from among various alternatives.

If your rights have been infringed upon, American Policy Center has videos, teleconferencing, and an online toolbox full of documents to help you or your attorney take on the fight.

Walking through a Civil Rights Act, Section 1983 lawsuit section 1,: All persons born or naturalized in the United States, and subject to the jurisdiction thereof, are citizens of the United States and of the state wherein they reside. No state shall make or enforce any law which shall abridge the privileges or immunities of citizens of the United States; nor shall any state deprive any person of life, liberty, or property, without due process of law; nor deny to any person within its jurisdiction the equal protection of the laws.

When you believe your civil rights have been denied you by bureaucrats, you have to right to redress through the Civil Rights Act. It is not difficult, but it requires that you follow all the steps. There are a couple of caveats that you need to know: 1. Our courts have been taking on, and agreeing with, thousands of these cases – from the Left, and 2. The person or persons you wish to sue must have sworn their oath to uphold the Constitution.

Get all your facts lined up. Tell the story. Tell it thoroughly. The whos, whats, whens, and hows.

- **What** is the specific right you are claiming that is being violated?

- **Who** is violating it?

- **How** are they violating it?

- **What** damages are you suffering or will be because of the violation?

- **What** result are you looking for? This is the theme for the lawsuit.

Write it out. Make sure you have all the necessary points covered. In other words show that the person/persons were acting as representatives of their office. **And** it must show which of your Constitution rights (or federal statutes) were violated.

The six steps you will need to cover are:
Jurisdictional
Background
Allegations of fact
Relief
Conclusions of Law
The 1983 action

2. Using the New Attorney's Guide to the Steps in a Lawsuit, https://www.lexisnexis.com/legalnewsroom/lex-is-hub/b/how-to-build-your-professional-skills/posts/new-attorney_2700_s-guide-to-the-steps-in-a-lawsuit you start by filing a complaint which lays out exactly what you put together in the story. Draft it right so it is not subject to dismissal. (This is where being OCD is not a handicap.)

3. **When you serve your complaint**, it is going to get the attention of the person served. Let's say you are going after a city councilperson who introduced a law or regulation that will change the zoning code on your place of business and, while your business might be grandfathered in, you intended to retire by selling your business. But now that won't be possible.

You now might want to serve notice on his/her fellow council members. That will get their attention and, hopefully, get them to encourage a settlement. When you do this, each is now separated; they cannot all use the same attorney.

If others in the community file suit also it will have an even greater impact. On the other hand, filing a class-action suit gives them the opportunity to use the bureau's attorney or a single attorney to represent all of them.

At the same time, you need to be spreading the word of your suit far and wide – local press, radio talk shows, speak at civic organizations. The public is the focus of your message; get them riled up so they are concerned about their rights and will begin calling their council representative.

All of this is to bring pressure upon your target. You would like to have them settle before going to court. $$$$$

4. But, if they don't cave: When/if you get to discovery, make sure you ask for everything the opponent has that can help you. You will need as much info as possible for interrogatories – depositions. You need to have been working on this from day one. Watch videos of meetings, get copies of emails, whatever *might* be relevant.

NOTE To successfully prevail in an action under Section 1983, the courts have held that plaintiffs must allege and prove two essential elements. First, *plaintiffs must show that the alleged conduct occurred under color of state law*. Second, *plaintiffs must show that the conduct deprived plaintiffs of rights, privileges, or immunities secured by the United States <u>Constitution</u> or a federal statute*.

An intent to violate the constitution is not required for liability under § 1983,[7] but procedural due process liability attaches only for intentional and not for negligent deprivations.[8]

To sue under a federal statute:

The Supreme Court case _Cort v. Ash_ provided the following four-part test for determining whether a claimant has the right to sue under a federal statute:

The claimant has membership in the class for whose benefit the statute was enacted;
There is evidence of congressional intent to confer a private remedy;
There is consistency between the right to sue and Congress' statutory intent; and
The claim involves a cause of action not traditionally relegated to the states.
The test effectively requires both a private right and a private remedy.
https://criminal.findlaw.com/criminal-rights/42-u-s-code-section-1983.html

"Under Color of" State Law
For Section 1983 to come into play, the person to be sued (the defendant) must have acted "under color of any statute, ordinance, regulation, custom, or usage, of any State or Territory or the District of Columbia … ." (42 U.S.C.A. § 1983 (2017).)

Courts have determined that the "under color of" clause requires that the wrongdoer qualify, at least in some sense, as a representative of the state when depriving the victim of civil rights. In a nutshell, the clause refers to people who misuse some kind of authority that they get from state law. Police officers who use <u>excessive force</u> generally fit this bill.
Judges can consider a number of factors to decide whether, when violating someone's federal rights, an officer was acting under the color of state law. Among them are whether the officer:
was on duty was wearing a police uniform used police equipment (like a squad car or handcuffs) lashed a badge or otherwise claimed to be an officer, or carried out an <u>arrest</u>.

When a Section 1983 suit has to do with an arrest—a central police function—a court will normally consider the officer to have acted under color of state law.
https://www.nolo.com/legal-encyclopedia/what-is-a-section-1983-lawsuit-against-the-police.html

LINKS

States have their own civil rights laws which you can look up:

https://statelaws.findlaw.com/

For those fighting 5G, Smart Meters, Towers,etc. I recommend looking at Raymond Broomhall's site for information. While Australia does not have our Bill of Rights or Civil Rights Act, they have a similar laws.

https://www.wesaynoto5ginaustralia.com/raymond-broomhall-action

https://www.radiationresearch.org/articles/raymond-broomhall-action-wesaynoto5g/

https://ecsfr.com.au/barrister-raymond-broomhall/

http://www.emraustralia.com.au/announcements/class-action-talk-by-raymond-broomhall

For those fighting Wind and solar power

See doc Wind Net in APC toolbox

For those fighting a police action:

"Under Color of" State Law
For Section 1983 to come into play, the person to be sued (the defendant) must have acted "under color of any statute, ordinance, regulation, custom, or usage, of any State or Territory or the District of Columbia … ." (42 U.S.C.A. § 1983 (2017).)
Courts have determined that the "under color of" clause requires that the wrongdoer qualify, at least in some sense, as a representative of the state when depriving the victim of civil rights. In a nutshell, the clause refers to people who misuse some kind of authority that they get from state law. Police officers who use <u>excessive force</u> generally fit this bill.
Judges can consider a number of factors to decide whether, when violating someone's federal rights, an officer was acting under the color of state law. Among them are whether the officer:
was on duty was wearing a police uniform used police equipment (like a squad car or handcuffs) flashed a badge or otherwise claimed to be an officer, or carried out an <u>arrest</u>.

When a Section 1983 suit has to do with an arrest—a central police function—a court will normally consider the officer to have acted under color of state law.

This is an overview of Section 1983 and how it can work. In the Activist Training Tool Kit on americanpolicy. org/tools (password apc1225) there are extensive documents to help you fully understand how to word, file, and research, depending on your area of interest including: property rights, civil asset forfeiture, wind and solar, 5G, personal privacy and medical invasion.

<u>Instructions for Civil Rights Claims Under Section 1983</u>

This is the handbook for everything needed in filing a 1983 claim

<u>Liability Under Section 1983</u>

This explains how to successfully prevail in a 1983 case, whom/what you may sue, who has immunity, the damages you may claim, the awards of damages, and others issues that may come up in your claim.

<u>42 U.S. Code § 1988. Proceedings in vindication of civil rights</u>

This article explores the history and purpose of the Fifth Amendment's privilege against self-incrimination, examines subsequent judicial interpretations, and recommends that the Eighth Circuit follow a broad approach, liberally defining when a case commences. It also calls for allowing section 1983 claims to proceed when compelled statements are used in the early stages of criminal proceedings.

<u>1983 Needs No Intent</u>

<u>Land Use Actions Under Section 1983 of the Federal Civil Rights Act</u>

Gives the basic scope of the Statute regarding property rights

<u>New Attorney's Guide to the Steps in a Lawsuit</u>

This is a Lexus/Nexus guide for submitting a basic Section 1983 complaint

<u>14th Amendment</u>

This explains the equal protection under the law under the 14th Amendment, with expanded definitions of rights and with examples of suits brought under Section 1983 pertaining to the 14th Amendment.

Typical Section 1983 Claims

- Amended Claim Against San Joaquin County

- Bodin Order

- George Jercich Vs. County Of Merced

- Judge Dismisses Prime Vs Harris Lawsuit

- Motion to Return Property

For those who are suing under Section 1983 against wind/solar power, 5G, an similar issues.

Wind Net Economics Summary

Notice Of Default And Imminent Liability Concerning Trespassing Technology

EXAMPLES OF BATTLES FOUGHT
LOCAL BATTLES TEACH US WHY WE LOSE AND HOW TO WIN

Many people want to engage in their communities and take effective action to assure government overreach is contained and rights are secured. Some do it right and win decisive victories. Others don't fully commit for the long haul and wonder why they lose.

Many times I've spoken with activists who have attempted to take up the fight. Often they are alone, unable to get friends and neighbors to join them. Acting alone is a sure way to be ignored by government officials. We must understand that they are surrounded by an effective, well-organized, well financed gang of private Non-governmental organizations (NGOs) who have a specific agenda to impose, a well-worn path to get there, and the ability to bring in reinforcements when challenged. They usually have close ties with federal and state agencies and the grant money that comes with them. Most importantly, they are there in every meeting. Their faces are known to the officials because they have established a relationship.

This is why, when local activists, concerned citizens, just plain folk, attend a public meeting and attempt to speak out on their own they are basically dismissed. Many times I have talked with local activists who tell me they tried to fight back but nothing was accomplished. Recently I was told, "We had over 100 people show up at the city council meeting to oppose a project. It didn't do any good because they just ignored us and went ahead with it." I then asked, well, what did you do the next day after that meeting, and the next, and the next? The answer, "nothing, it didn't do any good."

That is why we lose. The secret to winning is being a consistent thorn in their side, meeting after meeting. To win you must network, research, plan, and organize with others dedicated to the fight.

Here are five examples of major local fights. Each one shows a different approach and a different outcome. Some won, some lost. A learning lesson in each.

MARTHA BONETA

Martha bought a beautiful Virginia farm. Unfortunately she bought it from a land trust called the Piedmont Environmental Council (PEC). This group practically controls local city councils and county commissions in several counties of the state. They are powerful and determined to impose a radical, anti-development agenda. What Martha didn't know was that the PEC had slipped in a conservation easement in to the purchase agreement.

Martha took over the farm that had been left in great disrepair by the PEC. There was a tree growing in the barn. The fields were near barren. There was an historic burial ground on the property that the PEC has left exposed to grazing animals. Martha spent thousands of dollars to repair the damage and make the farm a showcase. She even converted the barn into a useful and profitable farm store to sell her homegrown products.

The PEC became determined to reclaim the now-improved property. They began to use the conservation easement as a weapon, subjecting Martha to surprise inspections, looking for violations in an attempt to force her to sell the property. They used their powerful connections with the county government which now created violations out of thin air. To that end her farm store was closed down, fines were imposed for supposed violations, and she was even subjected to an IRS audit. It's interesting to note that a member of the PEC board of directors included a former IRS executive. The PEC actually attempted to buy her mortgage from her lending bank.

Martha refused to give in. She mobilized concerned citizens in the country, building an effective property rights coalition. She stormed the news media, even taking her story to Fox News. Incredibly, she managed to get support in the Virginia legislature to introduce and pass the Boneta Bill to force local governments to back off such suffocating regulations on farmers and she was finally able to get her farm store reopened. She also filed a law suit against the PEC and won

But Martha had one more card to play. She held a rally on the Virginia state house grounds, and then she and many of her supporters stormed a hearing of the Virginia Outdoors Foundation to air grievances against the PEC. . It was one of the first times ever that a land trust actually begged to get out of a conservation easement!

Note what she did. Martha contacted property rights leaders from across the state to make her case a major part of their programs. So doing, she built an effective property rights movement that is still active today. Then she took her case to the media and drummed up major support for her cause. With each new surprise inspection of her property by the PEC she video taped those actions and got it to the media. Then she sent straight to the county government, where the PEC held such a stronghold. She didn't shy away. She made anyone in the government who played ball with the PEC feel pain! And then she took the fight directly to the state legislature and to the courts.

That's how we fight and win.

JENNIE GRANATO

Jennie Granato is a citizen of Montgomery County, Ohio. She and her family own a 165-year-old historic house just outside of Dayton. They've lived there for over 40 years. On July 31, 2013 her front years was demolished thanks to county planning commission bureaucrats. The Miami Valley Regional Planning Commission (MVRPC) had seized Jennie's and other private property for its "essential project," a $5 million bike path extension. On Jennie's property the path was placed within 5 feet of her front door. To prepare for it, bull dozers destroyed all of her front yard, including her hedge along the highway and her mother's beloved Magnolia Tree.

Jennie and her family tried for over a year to negotiate with the unelected planning commission. Unfortunately her lawyers advised her to not say anything publicly about the4 pending land grab. Most lawyers have little understanding of the systematic land grabbing policies of Sustainable Development. Instead, lawyers use old-school tactics from a bygone era. That's why many people lose their cases. In Jennie's case, the lawyers didn't want to make waves, just be "reasonable." In the end the tactic worked to the planning commission's advantage. So, when the bull dozers arrive, the news media treated it like a non-story.

Jennie never got a meeting with the planning commissions and were never warned when the bull dozers would arrive. They just suddenly hear a commotion outside. When Jennie's mother ran out to see what was going on, she reached the yard just in time to see her beloved Magnolia tree collapse. So over come with shock at the site, Jennie's mom grabbed her chest with a heart attack and died on the spot. The planning commission defended its actions, saying it was just promoting the "public welfare" of the private "stakeholders" and pressure groups it works with.

Jennie went to the county commission to complain. But was told it was the unelected MVRPC that was responsible. So she went to the MVRPC and was told they had only applied for the grants for the project. No one was responsible. This is how the new Sustainable Development policies have successfully eliminated representative government across the nation.

In the end, she was offered as pittance of compensation for the land grab. Meanwhile, the value of her property was reduced to next to nothing as a bike path wide enough to drive a car through made stepping out of her front door nearly impossible for fear of bicycles whizzing by at 10 to 20 miles an hour. The front yard is gone and a local developer was allow to run a drainage ditch onto her land.

Jennie had no legal force, no organized group of activists on her side, and no political or media support. A few dedicated property rights activists did stage some sign-wavings, and some did attend county government meetings to speak on her behalf. But it just wasn't enough to cause a stir. Jennie's story is the all-too common result of a lack of organized, trained support for property rights.

That's how we lose.

CADDO LAKE, LOUISIANA

National Heritage Areas (NHA) are one of the most despicable stealth land grabs in the nation. That's because this program plays on Americans' love of history and the preservation of significant places that played an important role in the making of our unique nation. National Heritage Areas, then, serve as a powerful tool to capture the support of more conservative- minded Americans who would otherwise oppose government control and planning policies. Unfortunately, study shows that, far from preserving the ideals of freedom,. National Heritage Areas are just another well-hidden excuse to use tax dollars through the National Park Service to fill the coffers of powerful NGO's who use the funds to stealthfully pressure for more land grabs, top-down government control, and bogus environmentalist strategies. Such proof can be found in the 49 National Heritage Areas already in existence across the country.

One of the latest efforts to impose a National Heritage Area took place around Caddo Lake, near Shreveport Louisiana. When the legislation was introduced in Congress to establish the Caddo Lake National Heritage Area, proponents put forth a feasibility study to explain the true purpose was to *"Identify and evaluate alternatives for managing, preserving, and interpreting nationally important cultural and historic landscapes, sites, and structures existing under and around Caddo Lake."* Of course for every one of those items to be identified and evaluated there is an NGO that makes it their mission to impose it, and a federal grant to enforce it.

Property owners around the Caddo Lake have proven themselves to be good stewards, protecting the lake and the property around it. That's why the area around the lake is beautiful, well- kept and teaming with wildlife,. As a result, there is a thriving tourist industry and lots of environmental protections around the lake. Unfortunately for the locals, that's also why the area became noticed and coveted for control by the forces behind the NHA.

Local businessman Danny McCormick and others immediately understood the threat the Caddo Lake NHA represented to property rights and local control of their government. They studied other National Heritage Areas and were alarmed by how the designated areas became immersed in more layers of government bureaucracy and massive amounts of grant money. History of other NHAs showed that property owners on the shore line would likely lose their private boat docks as their use of the land would be pushed back from the edge of the lake. Worst of all, decisions over natural habitat would take precedent over their own, even though they had lived in harmony with the environment for two hundred years.

So the local residents sprang into action. They attended meetings, asked questions, researched, handed out reasonable arguments, and they never allowed proponents to simply dismiss their opposition. Again and again, they attended, they turned out, and they flooded the news media with and endless stream of facts and details. They fully understood that they were engaged in a battle to preserve their private property rights and their ability for self-governance –true history preservation. Above all, they understood that the only way to make sure government doesn't abuse power is to not grant it in the first place. In this very rural area, hundreds of local residents got involved, stood their ground and made their battle cry "Not one inch of this land will be put into a National Heritage Area."

Finally, so strong was their resistance and their resolve to see the battle won that the very surprised sponsoring congressmen withdrew their bill. But here is the important lesson of the Caddo battle – the locals fully understood that this battle was won, but the war was far from over. They knew the forces of control would return with a new battle plan and the residents began immediately to prepare for what ever that new attack would be. They didn't have to wait long.

The next step came from the city of Shreveport as its city council began to expand the boundaries of its Unified Development Code. The boundaries of control were extended clear out of the city and to the shores of Caddo Lake, completely outside the jurisdiction of the city of Shreveport. And what were the rules of the Unified Development Code that would now be enforced on the lake properties? Of course, they were basically identical to the controls called for in the NHA. The second battle of Caddo Lake broke out.

Again led by Danny McCormick, who had now been elected to the Louisiana state legislature, he created the

Caddo Alliance for Freedom. Now, the rural residents stormed city hall, packing council chambers, they held rallies and training meetings, opened a face book page and rocked the media. The fight goes on, but to date, Shreveport City Council has been rocked by overstepping its bounds and are on alert to not mess with Caddo Lake. That's how we organize to win.

BAYOU LA BAITRE, ALABAMA

In the Bayou of Alabama there is a beautiful, small, quaint village called Bayou La Baitre. Boat building is the major industry of the community, especially shrimp boats. There are at least ten such ship building yards and a vibrant seafood-processing industry that supply jobs and fill the tax base for the 2,500 residents. For over two hundred years the folks of Bayou La Baitre have lived quiet, happy, productive lives.

But we live in a time of massive upheaval. The NGOs and their agenda of control over our lives never sleep. Their raised its ugly head in Bayou La Baitre in the form of a 200 page zoning proposal which was developed by the city's planning commission with assistance from the Southeast Alabama Regional Planning Commission (SARPC), plus input from some environmental groups. The proposal was two years in the making and enjoyed the support of some powerful forces including the National Oceanographic and Atmospheric Administration (NOAA). In fact, NOAA was to provide federal grant money to the SARPC to help implement the plan. Immersed in all of this national attention and promises of big bucks, the plan was also strongly supported by Mayor Terry Downey.

What was this grand plan? Eco-tourism! It means land locked away from development. It means every fly, snail darter, and mosquito has more rights than the people who own and live on their property. The planners prepared an entire "visioning" plan, outlining the town's future, which would lead to lots of rules and regulations that were never there before. In other words, Bayou La Baitre was about to be locked into a time warp, restricting growth, destruction of property rights, and denial of freedom of choice for the residents. All would be surrendered to the vision of those who had a different agenda than those who actually lived and worked there.

However, as news of the plan leaked out, its zoning proposals were widely seen as hostile to the generations-old seafood and shipbuilding industries which opponents feared would be displaced by eco-tourism businesses such as kayak and come rentals and outing to view migratory birds. Local business owners were also upset over language to the proposed ordinance that, they said, would affect where their businesses could operate if they had to be rebuilt or changed hands.

To keep the residents calm, the new plan called for "grandfathering in" the existing ship building companies and fish processing plants. No muss, no fuss, nothing to worry about. All is well. We re just going to bring lots of new revenue to the community with the new plan, plus we will keep it growth-free for the good of the environment. However, the small print in the plan told the truth. If a ship builder's property, for example, happened to be severely damaged or destroyed by a hurricane, fire, or flood, they were forbidden to rebuild. Instead, the property would be taken over and used for the Eco-tourism plan, perhaps becoming a bistro for the tourists.

What the planners didn't count on were some residents who were well-versed on Agenda 21 and its true purpose. They went into social media and began spreading the word. Anger spread across the community. As the opposition built, Mayor Downey became exasperated and when he went to the media to defend the ordinance, he actually called Bayou La Baitre "nothing but a mudhole." Angry residents then stormed city council and demanded that the mayor resign. He didn't, but opposition continued to build. One city

councilman, Henry Barnes, was shown by the activists that the language in the ordinance was nearly identical to language in Agenda 21. In an interesting twist, it so happens that Alabama is the only state in the Union to have a law against Agenda 21. Councilman Barnes was able to show that identical language to other members of the City Council and told them that the ordinance was illegal. The council then voted unanimously (7-0) to scrap the ordinance completely and threw it out.

When we understand the agenda that's being played we win.

The lessons learned in all of these examples is that to win you must not fight alone, research, network, organize, be determined, stop being polite in the face of government overreach, and above all, in the words of Winston Churchill, "Never Give In, Never, Never, Never." A victory is a victory – no matter how small – build on it.

STATEMENT OF PRINCIPLES
FOR A WORLDWIDE PRIVATE PROPERTY RIGHTS MOVEMENT

Private property ownership and control is one of the fundamental requirements in establishing and maintaining a free society. Private property ownership is a means to building individual wealth and eradicating poverty. Private property ownership includes lands, homes, businesses, possessions, papers, fruits of ones labor and ideas. Without private property ownership freedom is not sustainable.

PRIVATE PROPERTY RIGHTS MEANS

• The owner's exclusive authority to determine how private property is used;

• The owner's peaceful possession, control, and enjoyment of his/her lawfully purchased, real private property;

• The owner's ability to make contracts to sell, rent, or give away all or part of the lawfully purchased/real private property;

• That local, city, county, state, and federal governments are prohibited from exercising eminent domain for the sole purpose of acquiring lawfully purchased/real private property so as to resell to a private interest or generate revenues;

• That no local, city, county, state, or federal government has the authority to impose directives, ordinances, fees, or fines regarding aesthetic landscaping, color selections, tree and plant preservation, or open spaces on lawfully purchased/real private property;

• That no local, city, county, state or federal government shall implement a land use plan that requires any part of lawfully purchased/real private property be set aside for public use or for a Natural Resource Protection Area directing that no construction or disturbance may occur;

• That no local, city, county, state, or federal government shall implement a law or ordinance restricting the number of outbuildings that may be placed on lawfully purchased/real private property;

• That no local, city, county, state, or federal government shall alter or impose zoning restrictions or regulations that will devalue or limit the ability to sell lawfully purchased/real private property;

• That no local, city, county, state, or federal government shall limit profitable or productive agriculture activities by mandating and controlling what crops and livestock are grown on lawfully purchased/real private property;

• That no local, city, county, state, or federal government representatives or their assigned agents may trespass on private property without the consent of the property owner or is in possession of a lawful warrant from a legitimate court of law. This includes invasion of property rights and privacy by government use of unmanned drone flights, with the exceptions of exigent circumstances such as protection of life, limb or the private property itself.

PRIVATE PROPERTY RIGHTS DEFINED

Throughout history, experts have left a clear understanding of what property means:

Land Patents are a contract or document of title issued by a government or state for the conveyance of some portion of land from the public domain to private individuals. According to Blacks Law, a Land Patent Contract means the complete and absolute ownership of land. A paramount and individual right of property in land.

"Property in a thing consists not merely in its ownership and possession, but in the unrestricted right of use, enjoyment, and disposal. Anything which destroys any of the elements of property, to that extent, destroys the property itself. The substantial value of property lies in its use. If the right of use be denied, the value of the property is annihilated and ownership is rendered a barren right."
-   From "Fifth Amendment" treatise by State Supreme Court Justice Richard B. Sanders (12/10/97)

"LIFE, LIBERTY, and PROPERTY... are so related that the deprivation of any one of these rights may lessen or

extinguish the value of the other two." Smith Vs State of Texas, 233 US 636 (1914)

"As a man is said to have a right to his property, he may be equally said to have a property in his rights." James Madison (Meaning that even if a person owned nothing else, he still owned his rights, which are the mot valuable property of all.)

"The moment the idea is admitted into society that property is not as sacred as the law of God, and that there is not a force of law and public justice to protect it, anarchy and tyranny commence." - President, John Adams

"Ultimately, property rights and personal rights are the same thing."
  - President Calvin Coolidge

"If you don't have the right to own and control property then you are property."
  - Wayne Hage, rancher

PRIVATE PROPERTY OWNERSHIP AND THE ERADICATION OF POVERTY

International economist Hernando deSoto estimates that nearly 5 billion people around the world are legally and economically disenfranchised by their own governments because they are denied a comprehensive, legal property system. That means their property cannot serve as an asset.

While it is a common practice in the United States to buy property, hold it for a few years and sell it at a substantial profit or move up to a better home, thereby creating individual wealth, such a system is basically unheard of in most nations of the world.

This incredible ability to build wealth is possible because private property rights are recognized and every bit of land ownership is recognized through complete recognition by government records of the undisputed property ownership.

Because of that system, average Americans can use their property as a tool to obtain loans. At least 60% of American companies have been started through equity loans on private property. And those privately held companies now employ about 60% of the American workforce.

That is how private property ownership made the United States the richest nation in the world, almost over night.

Lack of such a system is the reason most of the rest of the world is falling into extreme poverty. The people have no way out of poverty and are forced to rely on government handouts. Yet, the laws and practices of most countries in the world make it nearly impossible for average citizens to own property or to prove ownership of property. That is the root of devastating and growing poverty in most parts of the world.

The Worldwide Private Property Rights Movement calls for all governments to protect the private property owner's unrestricted right of use, enjoyment and disposal of their legally purchased/deeded private property. In doing so, this allows individuals, all over the world, the opportunity to stand on their own, to achieve their own hopes and dreams without interference.

Private property ownership and its unrestricted use are the foundation for a worldwide revolution of Freedom. Let that revolution begin with a worldwide demand for the universal recognition and protection of the private property rights for each individual on Earth.

PART 2
DOCUMENTS, HANDOUTS, DETAILS, PROGRAMS, QUOTES, AND THE PLAYERS
ALL THE DETAILS YOU NEED TO UNDERSTAND THE AGENDA THAT IS TRANSFORMING OUR LIVES

There are five paths being used to transform America from a free, sovereign, independent nation to a piece of the global village. They are:

- "Wildlands Project" to control the rural areas

- "Smart Growth" to control the large cities/metro areas

- "Public/Private Partnerships" (P3s) to control businesses

- "Regionalism" to transform your local governments

- "No Child Left Behind" to brainwash and control children in schools

It's in every community in the nation. We hear it talked about in county commission meetings and state legislatures. It's even used in advertising as a positive practice for food processing and auto sales. It's used as the model for building materials, power sources and transportation policy. It's sold as the bold visionary plan for the future. The nation is being transformed under the banner of "Sustainable Development"; and that is Agenda 21 or the Green New Deal – same evil, different clothing.

A. What is Agenda 21/Green New Deal?

In the rural areas, the Greens' selected tactic is to control the land, water, energy, and population of the Earth. To achieve these ends requires, among other things, the destruction of private property rights and elimination of every individual's ability to make personal life-style choices, including personal diet. That's why the American Beef Industry is such a necessary target.

First they had to create a false crisis so everyone would feel the need to take immediate action. Their tactic was to declare that beef was not sustainable – not as a product to grow — and not as a healthy food for people to consume. This put the cattlemen in the middle of a pincer move between the radical environmental movement seeking control of land use, and the Animal Rights movement which demanded the end of the consumption of animals.

Their most effective tactic is the never-ending threat of Global Warming. Say the Greens, global warming is driven by energy consumption and cows are energy guzzlers. That's because you need trucks to ship the cattle to market. In their vision of a perfect sustainable community, nothing would be shipped in to consume. Everything needed would be produce right in the city. The Soviet Union called those gulags. And they starved.

So, these are some of the reasons why it's charged that beef is unsustainable and must be ruled, regulated and frankly, eliminated. These are charges brought by anti-beef vegans who want all beef consumption stopped. In cahoots, are environmentalists who seek to stop the private ownership and use of land under the excuse of environmental protection.

We are assured by elected officials that Sustainable Development is simply a tool or a guideline to help direct the carefully-planned growth of our cities and rural areas while protecting our natural resources for future generations. "We must guard against a chaotic, unregulated growth in our cities," say its earnest proponents as they sell the concept through familiar, non-threatening words and beautiful pictures.

Citizens are assured by their community leaders that all such plans are just local, local, local, created with the participation of the whole community. Sustainable Development policy, they say, is just an environmental land conservation policy, a sensible development policy. Sustainable…what's wrong with that?

As usual, the answers are hidden in the details. Are we hearing the truth? What are the consequences of the policy that has taken over every level of government? Are there hidden dangers most just can't see? Or, as its proponents claim, is opposition to Sustainable Development really just a silly, overblown conspiracy theory found in a twenty-year-old meaningless document called Agenda 21?

The UN's Brundtland Commission on Global Governance described Sustainable Development as *"Development that meets the needs of the present without compromising the needs of the future."* It's just common sense to assure we don't overuse our resources, say proponents. If everyone will do their part, we can achieve total sustainability.

A couple of years later, in 1992, at the UN's Earth Summit, 50,000 delegates approved a plan describing in great detail how to meet those future needs. They issued a document called Agenda 21, which the UN labeled as a "comprehensive blueprint for the reorganization of human society." The UN sold Agenda 21 as a "soft law" policy, meaning it was an idea that nations would need to take up and impose through their own mechanisms.

To that end, in 1993, newly elected President Bill Clinton created the President's Council on Sustainable Development. Serving on the Council were the representative of nearly every federal agency, along with representatives of Nongovernmental Organizations (NGOs) who had helped to write Agenda 21 on the international level. Also on the Council were representatives of major global corporations. Their task was to create the policies to turn the Agenda 21 goals into official government policy and provide the means to fund it.

The President's Council released a report describing its Sustainable Development goals, saying, *"Sustainable communities encourage people to work together to create healthy communities where natural resources and historic resources are preserved, jobs are available, sprawl is contained, neighborhoods are secure, education is lifelong, transportation and health care is accessible, and all citizens have opportunities to improve the quality of their lives."*
It all sounds pretty neat. Nothing to fear here! It sounds like Utopia is truly ours for the taking. Again, what are the details? How do we put such ideas into action? What are the consequences? Is the environment better off? Are we better off? Well, let's take each of these glowing ideas one at a time and just see where it all leads!

- **Sustainable communities encourage people to work together**   There certainly are members of our society who take the whole Sustainablist agenda to heart and love to get involved improving their community. They clean out riverbanks, collect trash along roadways, recycle, watch their thermostats, and ride their bikes whenever possible. Good for them. That's their decision and they are free to make it.

But there are others who may have a different vision on how they want to live. Perhaps they don't agree with the dire predictions that we must comply or face environmental Armageddon. How do they fit in the Agenda for the 21st Century? They are dealt with.

Children in the public schools are pummeled with the political correctness of being proper environmental stewards, as detailed in Agenda 21. Guilt plays a huge part in that indoctrination. It's necessary that everyone think alike without questioning policy so future generations will be prepared to "work" together in their communities. In addition, in many schools now, the children are required to fulfill a certain number of hours of community service in order to qualify for their diploma. In a Sustainable world, proper attitude is more important than academic scholarship. Today's curriculum to ensure proper citizenship is called Common Core. It is the curriculum of Agenda 21 and is intended to be "life-long, " and the key focus is Sustainability.

Cooperation from adult citizens is just as structured. In the recent past, public meetings to discuss new policy were based on the guidelines called "Roberts Rules of Order" through which everyone got a fair chance to have their say and then a vote was taken. Today, in the Sustainable world, we have "facilitators" trained in psychology to assure they lead a gathering in exactly the direction needed for the predetermined and desired outcome of the community planners. If the facilitator is really good at his job, everyone in the meeting will believe the outcome was their idea. And those in charge hail the meeting as a huge success in which all in the community "worked together" to put these plans in place.

- **to create healthy communities**   This can mean many things. Healthy? We see the growing power of the food police today who have declared many things in our diet unhealthy. We see the Mayor of New York declaring large sodas unhealthy and banning their sale. We see fast food establishments picketed for selling fries made with grease or hamburgers that are cruel to animal rights. There are mandatory vaccinations, without which children can't be enrolled in schools and parents are charged with child abuse. New policies are beginning to arise that lean toward mandatory exercise and controls on diets. These are called Blue Zones.

Local governments enforce grand comprehensive plans designed to pack and stack people on top of each other in massive highrise buildings. Is that what they mean by healthy? History would show that forcing people into massive containers reduces quality of life, spreads disease and promotes violence. These aren't healthy communities. The Russians called them Gulags.

- **Natural resources are preserved**   The message is that over-consumption will bring shortages of natural resources, and so the sustainable plan is to erect endless forests of windmills. That is the natural way, we are told. Man will live on the surface of the Earth doing no harm. Of course, they never seem to mention that the huge wind turbines will take more energy to build than they will ever generate in their lifetime. In addition, to bring the power online so it can be used by society requires a massive infrastructure of wires, cement and roads. While one nuclear power plant located on ten acres can supply enough energy for a megacity, wind power would require thousands of acres of clearcut, cement wastelands. Then the power proves to be unstable and unreliable, causing the power grid to falter, forcing controls on home thermostats that fail to heat or cool the homes when needed. How is that healthy for our communities? Moreover, there is the not insignificant side effect of millions of birds that are chopped up in the turbines, including "endangered" raptors like eagles. And they call that environmentally sound?

And one more question comes to mind as we lock away resources for future generations. At what point would these locked away resources ever be allowed to be used by a society so afraid of itself? Won't there always be a future generation that might need them? Meanwhile, science keeps discovering that the dire predictions of resource depletion are outrageously overblown. It has recently been discovered that the United States has the largest oil and gas supplies in the world. Hydraulic fracturing is a benign American technology that is ecologically sound and economically advantageous. But it has been deemed "unsustainable" by those enforcing Sustainable policy as they quickly oppose any source of cheap energy. Yet, fracking stretches our energy reserves several hundred years into the future. That would certainly give science ample time to come up with new workable technology.

- **Historic resources are preserved**   Frankly I have no idea what a historic "resource" is. But I do know that Sustainablists prey on America's love of history as an excuse to lock away any land where once a historic person may have taken a walk. And they use it to generate massive federal grants so planners can stop development, even in towns where nothing of historic significance ever occurred. It's a growth industry in the world of sustainable lock-aways.

- **Jobs are available**   What will magically happen in a Sustainable Community to suddenly create jobs that aren't there now? Government doesn't create jobs. Creative, driven, free people create jobs to fill needs they have discovered. No government-controlled economy would ever have created a factory that makes designer clothes, dandruff shampoo, or little pieces of plastic that go on the ends of your shoe laces. Bureaucrats don't think that way. They only think in terms of need, urgency – bare minimum. Luxury is never part of the government plan. The fact is, Sustainable Development is one of the biggest killers of jobs. Its rules and regulation make it near impossible for many companies to survive. The EPA, enforcing Sustainable policies, is killing power plants, mines, and farms. They're destroying economies of whole states. So where will these glorious Sustainable jobs come from? Government jobs! Perhaps the high-rise apartments in the mega cities will need lots of NSA type eavesdroppers for mandatory surveillance to assure people are following the rules for compulsory health policy!

- **Sprawl is contained**   Evil sprawl (suburbia to normal folk) — those areas of community growth where people run to escape the mega cities. In nearly every case, those new homes in their shiny developments are a place where families first opened the front door with smiles on their faces because this was *their* home. They have backyards where the kids can play. They have a real sense of community. And those terrible strip malls that spring up around the new developments that supple goods and services for the new residents also create jobs and enhance the economy. Stack and pack cities are not livable if you actually believe in fresh air and a place for the kids to play. Cities are full of government regulations, high taxes, drugs, and disease. Do the Sustainablists focus on stopping murders by drug cartels and beatings by gangs of illegal aliens? You never seem to hear anything about that in their plans. All of these facts were actually exposed in a report by the American Planning Association on the effects of Smart Growth. The report revealed that it doesn't work. But that hasn't changed the APA's policies because Smart Growth is full of government grants. And that's the real game – Sustainable income for Non-governmental organizations (NGOs).

- **Neighborhoods are secure**   How is this done? Massive police control? Cameras on every corner? Gun control? TSA in the subways and bus stations? NSA listening in on every conversation, and computer keystroke? Security over privacy and individual choice? Certainly, there is no Sustainable "freedom" in such a scheme.

- **Transportation is accessible**   This one is easy. Public transportation. Trains for long distance, bikes for the quick run to the store. No cars. You will rarely leave your neighborhood. Imagine the hassle involved in taking the family on a trip to the beach using inconvenient train schedules? Of course, humans flocking to the beach are an unsustainable danger to the environment. Ban that too. Stay in the city.

- **Healthcare accessible**   Well, we used to have accessible healthcare, then government got into the game. Perhaps you think it's unfair to mention Obamacare in an article about Sustainable Development. Simply Google "Sustainable Medicine" and find more than 5,850,000 references on the subject, and you will find almost all the provisions of Obamacare.

- **All citizens have the opportunity to improve the quality of their lives**   Really? What part above leads to improvement of the quality of life? We used to call it tyranny – now we call it quality of life. As George Orwell said in his landmark book, 1984, it's all called doublespeak. Look around you now as Sustainable policy is being forced on us. America's economy is in shambles and not improving. Costs of everything, especially healthcare, food and energy are skyrocketing. These industries are the very first to be impacted by Sustainable Development. How will it improve under a policy of planned shortages and locked away resources? What or who are they counting on to pull us out? Answer: individuals who will continue to produce no matter how many shackles they lock them in. Eventually, even the most determined give up.

The Sustainablists use such innocent, attractive sounding descriptions of their plans for us. Then they deny they are even doing it, and anyone who calls them on it is labeled a fringe nut. But there is another way to say it, a much older description of Sustainable Development that explains the motivation behind the policy in a much more direct manner: "*From each according to his ability. To each according to his need.*" If you recognize that quote, then you fully understand the true nature of Sustainable Development.

Here are two more quotes that will drive reality into daylight of the true purpose of Sustainable Development.

First, does this sound like something your local planners may have said? "*The chaotic growth of cities will be replaced by a dynamic system of urban settlement…The region is formed by the economic interdependence of its development, from the industrial complex to the industrial region. The region has a single system of transportation, a centralized administration, and a united system of education and research.*" This was written in 1968 by Alexei Gutnov. He was a Soviet Russian architect writing in a book titled *The Ideal Communist City*.

And finally there is this very recent quote from New York City Mayor William DeBlasio from an interview in New York magazine. "*What's been hardest is the way our legal system is structured to favor private property. I think people all over this city, of every background, would like to have the city government be able to determine which building goes where, how high it will be, who gets to lie in it, what the rent shall be.*"

These quotes represent the true origin and process of Sustainable Development and its goal to reorganize human society. In such a process, there is no room for the independence of free enterprise, private property ownership or individual choice. This is why we fight to stop it.

How sustainable forces intend to use pandemic fear tactics to impose GND at local and state levels.

In their own words:

"I hope that the shock of this pandemic will jolt people out of their desire to ignore global issues like climate change. I hope our growing sense of urgency, of solidarity, of stubborn optimism and empowerment to take action, can be one thing that rises out of this terrible situation. Because while we will, eventually, return to normal after this pandemic, the climate that we know as normal is never coming back." **Christiana Figueres, Time Magazine**

"All this looks like good news for the planet — at least in the short term. "Suppose you were a policymaker, and you were thinking about what you would do to lower emissions — you just got a pretty good instruction." **Amy Jaffe, director of the Council on Foreign Relations' Energy Security and Climate Change program**

"To curb the spread of the virus, there have been lockdowns across the world, with less industrial activity, far fewer car journeys and vast numbers of flights cancelled -- this presents a roadmap for the future. We need only look to the improved air quality in some of the world's major cities and the return of wildlife to our communities and waterways. When the current crisis is over, I hope the world would reflect on how it might help shape a more environmentally friendly future." **Prince Charles at Earth Day event 2020**

"A burgeoning chorus of climate campaigners and experts is urging political leaders to learn from how governments handle the coronavirus outbreak and, as the pandemic subsides, to seize the opportunity to both revive the world's economy and battle the climate emergency by implementing a global Green New Deal." **Jessica Corbett, Common Dreams**

"With the coronavirus there are no interest groups which benefit directly from promoting inaction and delay like the fossil fuel industry does with climate change. Supposedly innate characteristics of human perception are certainly not the whole story – politics and vested interests matter too. Perhaps the pandemic will produce changes which make societies more willing to act on the climate crisis in the long run." **Andrew Norton, Climate Home News**

When people hear Non-Governmental Organization and Civil Society, they think do-good, non-profit organizations that care for people, animals, the earth, and even stuffed bears. Nothing could be further from the truth. These organizations have been either established by the globalists who are beind the Global Agenda, are far-out environmental and animal rights organizations that are bein used as extreme outliers to do the dirty work for the globalist, or are newly established by those same globalist to fill a need for a new program that needs to be pushed. When you see them listed in any material you get encouraging you to get on a bandwagon, look them up

https://www.un.org/development/desa/disabilities/conference-of-states-parties-to-the-convention-on-the-rights-of-persons-with-disabilities-2/list-of-non-governmental-organization-accredited-to-the-conference-of-states-parties.html

or https://esango.un.org/civilsociety/login.do

THE FORCES BEHIND A21/GND

A. NGOs (Non-governmental Organizations)

The UN wrapped up yet another international meeting attended by thousands of delegates and world leaders. This time they introduced and unanimously approved the 2030 Agenda for "Sustainable Development". This is the 17-Goal reboot of Agenda 21 with plans to fully enforce it by 2030. To make it even more certain that they achieve their goal of a one-world government, a new propaganda campaign has been added to clinch the deal. That is the "Green New Deal" – which is not green, not new, and certainly no deal for the American people. But, basically it is Agenda21/2030/Sustainable Development for Dummies – an easy, dumbed-down way of teaching people by their political propaganda which they present to the world as looking like it is helpful to our world when the opposite is true.

Many ask, "Who writes these Agendas and who attends these meetings?" They especially want to know how they wield so much power and influence over our government. It's a vast matrix composed of both private Non-governmental Organizations (NGO) groups and representatives of the UN, and representatives of a large number of US federal agencies – all working together behind the scenes, quietly making policy for the rest of us.

The global elite scoff at our efforts to expose and fight Agenda 21, calling it a "conspiracy theory." Through their condescending chuckles, they boldly claim that Agenda 21 policy has no power of enforcement and that "*there are no blue-helmeted troops at City Hall.*" The truth is that the UN doesn't need troops at City Hall because they have a private army doing the job for them – the NGOs working behind the scenes applying the pressure on elected officials.

One rarely hears of it. Few elected officials raise an eyebrow. The media makes no mention of it. But power is slowly slipping away from our elected representatives. In much the same way Mao Tse Tung had his Red Guards, so the UN has its NGOs. They may well be your masters of tomorrow, yet you don't even know they exist.

There are, in fact, two parallel, complimentary forces at work in the world, working together to advance the global Agenda21/Sustainable Development plan, ultimately leading toward UN global governance. Those two forces are the UN itself and its faithful soldiers, the non-governmental organizations (NGOs.)

Beginning with the United Nations, the infrastructure pushing the "Sustainable Development" agenda is a vast, international matrix. At the top of the heap is the United Nations Environmental Program (UNEP). Created in 1973 by the UN General Assembly, UNEP is the catalyst through which the global environmental agenda is implemented. **Virtually all of the international environmental programs and policy changes that have occurred globally in the past three decades are the result of UNEP policies and propaganda**.

But the UNEP doesn't operate on its own. Influencing it and helping to write policy are thousands of non-governmental organizations (NGOs). These are private groups, which seek to implement a specific political agenda. Through the UN infrastructure, particularly through the UNEP, they have great power.

The phrase "non-governmental organization" came into use with the establishment of the United Nations Organization in 1945 with provisions in Article 71 of Chapter 10 of the United Nations' "Charter." The term describes a consultative role for organizations that are neither government nor member states of the UN.

NGOs are not just any private group hoping to influence policy. True NGOs are officially sanctioned by the United Nations. Such status was created by UN Resolution 1296 in 1948, giving NGOs official "Consultative" status to the UN. That means, they can not only sit in on international meetings, but can actively participate in creating policy, with these global government representatives.

There are numerous classifications of NGOs. The two most common are "Operational" and "Advocacy." "Operational" NGOs are involved with designing and implementing specific projects such as feeding the hungry or organizing relief projects. These groups can be religious or secular. They can be community-based, national or international. The International Red Cross falls under the category of an operational NGO.

"Advocacy" NGOs are promoting a specific political agenda. They lobby government bodies, use the news media and organize activist-oriented events, all designed to raise awareness and apply pressure to promote their causes which include environmental issues, human rights, poverty, education, children, drinking water, and population control – to name a few. Amnesty International is the largest human rights advocacy NGO in the world. Organized globally, it has more than 1.8 million members, supporters, and subscribers in over 150 countries.

Today these NGOs have power nearly equal to the member nations when it comes to writing U.N. policy. Just as civil service bureaucrats provide the infrastructure for government operation, so to do NGOs provide such infrastructure for the U.N. In fact, most U.N. policy is first debated and then written by the NGOs and presented to national government officials at international meetings for approval and ratification. It is through this process that the individual political agendas of the NGO groups enter the international political arena.

Agenda 21 has grown from a collection of ideas and wish lists of a wide variety of private organizations to become the most widely implemented tool in the U.N.'s quest for global governance.

The three most powerful organizations influencing UNEP policy are three international NGOs. They are the World Wide Fund for Nature (WWF), the World Resources Institute (WRI), and the International Union for Conservation and Nature (IUCN). **These three groups provide the philosophy, objectives, and methodology for the international environmental agenda** through a series of official reports and studies such as: *World Conservation Strategy*, published in 1980 by all three groups; *Global Biodiversity Strategy*, published in 1992; and *Global Biodiversity Assessment*, published in 1996.

These groups not only influence UNEP's agenda, they also influence a staggering array of international and national NGOs around the world. Jay Hair, former head of the National Wildlife Federation, one of the U.S.'s largest environmental organizations, was also the president of the IUCN. Hair later turned up as co-chairman of the "Presidents Council on Sustainable Development".

The WWF maintains a network of national chapters around the world, which influence, if not dominate, NGO activities at the national level. It is at the national level where NGOs agitate and lobby national governments to implement the policies that the IUCN, WWF and WRI get written into the documents that are advanced by the UNEP. In this manner, the world grows ever closer to global governance.

Other than treaties, how does UNEP policy become U.S. policy? Specifically, the IUCN has an incredible mix of U.S. government agencies along with major U.S. NGOs as members. Federal agencies include the Department of State, Department of Interior, Department of Agriculture, Environmental Protection Agency (EPA), the National Park Service (NPS), the U.S. Forest Service (USFS), and the Fish and Wildlife Service. These agencies send representatives to all meetings of the UNEP.

Also attending those meetings as active members are NGO representatives. These include activist groups such as the Environmental Defense Fund, National Audubon Society, The Nature Conservancy, National Wildlife Federation, Zero Population Growth, Planned Parenthood, the Sierra Club, the National Education Association, and hundreds more. These groups all have specific political agendas that they desire to become law. Through their official contact with government agencies working side-by-side with the UNEP, their political wish-lists become official government regulations.

How can private organizations control policy and share equal power with elected officials? Here's how it works.

When the dust settled over the UN's 1992 Rio Earth Summit, five major documents were forced into international policy that forever changed how national policy is made. More importantly, the Rio Summit produced the United Nations Conference on Environment and Development (UNCED). UNCED outlined a new procedure for shaping policy. The procedure has no name, nor is it dictatorial. It is perhaps best described as "controlled consensus" or "affirmative acquiescence."

Putting it in simple street language, the procedure really amounts to a collection of NGOs, bureaucrats, and government officials, all working together toward a *predetermined* outcome. They have met together in meetings, written policy statements based on international agreements, which they helped to create and now they are about to impose laws and regulations that will have dire effects on people's lives and national economies. Yet, with barely a twinge of conscience they move forward with the policy, saying nothing. No one objects. It's understood. Everyone goes along. For this is a barbaric procedure that insures their desired outcome -- without the ugliness of bloodshed, or even debate. It is the procedure used to advance the radical, global environmental agenda.

The UNCED procedure utilizes four elements of power: international government (UN); national governments; non-governmental organizations, and philanthropic institutions.

The NGOs are the key to the process. They create policy ideas from their own private agendas. The policy idea is then adopted by one or more U.N. organizations for consideration at a regional conference. Each conference is preceded by an NGO forum designed specifically to bring NGO activists into the debate. At those conferences, they are fully briefed on the policy and then trained to write papers and lobby and influence the official delegates of the conference. In this way, the NGOs control the debate and assure the policy is adopted.

The ultimate goal of the conference is to produce a "Convention," which is a legally- drawn, policy statement on specific issues. Once the "Convention" is adopted by the delegates, it is sent to the national governments for official ratification. Once that is done, the new policy becomes international law.

Then the real work begins. Compliance must be assured. The NGOs come into the picture again and they are responsible for pressuring Congress to write national laws in order to comply with the treaty. One trick used to assure compliance is to write into the laws a concept of third-party lawsuits.

NGOs now, regularly, sue the government and private citizens to force policy. They have their legal fees and even damage awards paid to them out of the government treasury. Through a coordinated process, hundreds of NGOs are at work in Congress, in every state government, and in every local community, advancing some component of the global environmental agenda.

However, the United States Constitution's Tenth Amendment bars the Federal Government from writing laws that dictate local policy. **To by pass this roadblock, NGOs encourage Congress to include special grants to help states and communities fund the new policy, should they want to "voluntarily" comply.**

If a community or state refuses to participate "voluntarily," then local chapters of the NGOs are trained to go into action. They begin by pressuring city councils or county commissioners to accept the grants and implement the policy. If they meet any resistance, they begin to issue news releases telling the community their elected officials are losing millions of dollars for the community. The pressure continues until the grant is finally taken and the policy becomes local law. This practice has resulted in the NGOs gaining incredible power at the local levels. Today, a great number of communities are actually run by NGO members as city and county governments are staffed by NGO members. They are routinely appointed to serve on local unelected boards and regional councils that the NGOs helped to create. In that way, local representative government is slowly relinquishing its power to the NGOs and, ultimately, to the global agenda of the United Nations.

Americans must begin to understand that the debate over environmental issues has very little to do with clean water and air or community planning, and much more to do with the establishment of power. NGOs are gaining it as locally-elected representatives are losing their rightful position to influence and guide policy on behalf of the citizens of their community who elected them. Through the creation of the non-elected boards, councils, and regional governments, fueled by the federal grants, the structure of American government is being systematically changed to a top-down, non-elected dictatorship controlled by the NGOs, sanctioned from the UN.

Some of the NGOs working with the United Nations

There are thousands of NGOs and they cover *every* aspect of life on earth. Here are just a few:

AARP
Council of Churches
Greenpeace International
Humane Society of the United States
American Bar Association
Lions Clubs
Planned Parenthood
United Cities and Local Governments
American Heart Association
Advocates for Human Rights
American Diabetes Association
Chamber of Commerce
American Cancer Society
American Civil Liberties Union
American Conservative Union
Climate Institute
American Human Rights Council
United Way
Climate Action Network
American Planning Association
YWCA
 Association for Integrated Sustainable Development Initiatives Association for Promotion Sustainable Development
Association for Sustainable Community Development
Association for Sustainable Human Development
Center for Development of Civil Society
Chamber of Commerce
United Cities and Local Governments
Salvation Army
American Heart Association Center for Sustainable Development, Earth Institute at Columbia University
ICLEI - Local Governments For Sustainability
International Society of Doctors for the Environment
The Nature Conservancy
World Wildlife Fund for Nature
World Wide Fund for Nature

There is also another level of influence on elected officials from a large group of associations that many interpret to be government entities, but, in fact, they are 501c3 non-profit foundations that only wield influence if your elected officials grant it to them. Among them are:

National Conference of Mayors

- made the UN's Kyoto Global Warming Treaty a centerpiece of its agenda, calling on cities to cut their carbon footprint based on the Treaty demands.

- support the Kelo decision that took away protection of property rights.

- promotes Smart Growth and Sustainable Development polices

- established the **Center for Sustainable Communities**

National League of Cities

- opposes any restrictions on state governments taking private l   and.

- support the Kelo decision that took away protection of property rights.

- promotes **Smart Growth** and **Sustainable Development** policies.

National Governors Association

- advocate **Smart Growth**

- support more government benefits for illegal aliens

- worked to block 'workfare' requirements for welfare benefits.

Council of State Governments

- promotes world-wide Sustainable zoning.

- provides model uniform and regulatory status for legislatures.

National Conference of State Legislatures

- works to ensure that federal programs are embedded in state policy in a seamless and harmonized manner, creating the appearance that such policies are local rather than federal mandates.

National Association of Counties

- established the **Center for Sustainable Communities**

- provided the framework for Clinton's **President's Council on Sustainable Development.**

American Farmland Trust (AFT), which started out as a group of farmers and preservationists to preserve farm and ranchland in the U.S. Over the years, their methods of "protecting" the lands switched to acquisition and control of development rights. In 2007, they signed on to the President's Climate Action Plan. Through Purchase of Agricultural Easements (see Rural) and Transfer of Development Rights (see questions to ask below)

American Planning Association (APA) (see Planners and non-elected Regional Councils). While the APA in earlier forms has always been in the control of the globalists, it has become one of the leading proponents of Smart Growth and Sustainable Development. The APA was paid by HUD and other federal agencies to create the *Growing Smart Legislative Guidebook,* a 1,500 page that, according to John Anthony, is "a compendium of boilerplate legislation and planning practices that operationalizes the principles of UN Agenda 21 as implemented through the now disbanded President's Council on Sustainable Development". The APA's work has been embedded in every university, state, and county.

Metropolitan Association of Planning Organizations (MAPO) was formed, as its names indicates, to provide to all metropolitan planning organizations across the country with federal transportation policy, air quality planning, and subject to all EPA regulations and guidelines. And they are dedicated to Smart Growth and the elimination of automobiles as a transportation mode.

National Association of Regional Councils (NARC) (see non-elected Regional councils)

B. The Sustainablists

For the past several years, those people who have been pushing the Agenda 21 policy have denied it's United Nations origins, ignoring the many documents that clearly prove that the very term "sustainable development" can easily be traced back to the 1987 UN report titled, "Our Common Future." That radical report has been used by the UN as a virtual springboard for a "wrenching transformation" (Al Gore's words) of human society. The words "sustainable development" are used in nearly every federal, state, and local development plan; on nearly every federal, state, and local government web site; and in nearly every public statement on new development policies. We even had a President's Council on Sustainable Development, created by an Executive Order of Bill Clinton, with the stated purpose to impose the policies of Agenda 21 into United States law. Many serving on the Council helped write Agenda 21, including John Sawhill of the Nature Conservancy, Jay Hair of the National Wildlife Federation and Michele Perrault, international Vice President of the Sierra Club.

The exact words of "Sustainable Development" came from UN documents and its exact policies are imposed at the local level – yet, we are told by its proponents, none of these development plans have anything to do with UN policy. It's an amazing tap dance. As local residents question their county commissioners, city councilmen, mayors, state legislators, and governors about the origins of their policies, it has become routine for these "representatives of the people" to get a puzzled look on their faces and a wrinkle in their brows, as they say, "I've never heard of Agenda 21." "That's just a conspiracy theory."

Yes, we've heard it for years now. But as more and more citizens begin to learn the truth and opposition builds, what is the response of the Sustainablists? Do they now stand up and proudly defend their policies?" Do they attempt to open debate and allow other voices to be heard in a legitimate discussion about our "Common Future?" Do they try to find reasonable solutions for citizens who have become victims of such policies? None of the above.

First they have ignored those protests with the usual excuse of, "I don't know what they are talking about." Then they have tried to ridicule those of us who have led the charge against the policy, calling it a conspiracy theory. As our anti-Agenda 21 (and now Green New Deal) movement has picked up steam, they have enlisted the big guns to attack our credibility, including front page articles in the *New York Times*, and in the pages of the *Washington Post*. Each of those articles took the position that protestors at public meetings are simply wasting the valuable time of legitimate professional planners who are just trying to do their jobs. How dare we question their motives or the origins of their schemes? There's serious business going on here. Will the peasants please get out of the way of progress?

But such arrogant, strong-armed tactics which used to confuse and disperse opposition has ceased to work. Too much information is out there and too many citizens have become victims of the policies of SD/GND. Opposition has become fierce and organized in the face of this wrenching transformation of our lives.

So, since they can't beat us with strong arms, the Sustainablists are rushing to change the entire playing field, changing tactics, re-educating their storm troopers to employ non-confrontational new-speak, and rewriting the dictionary to "avoid polarizing jargon." In an attempt to neutralize their opposition they seek to lull us all into believing the policies they continue to enforce aren't "Sustainable Development". There is no hidden agenda, they now promise. It's just local planning by local officials, so they claim with a straight face.

HIDING THEIR AGENDA IN "NEWSPEAK"

The worst of the worst of the Sustainablists is the American Planning Association (APA). This American Trojan Horse is so panicked over growing opposition to its policies that APA has organized a "Boot Camp" to teach its operatives how to counter our opposition. Recently APA released a memo entitled "Glossary for the Public." It is quite telling on how an organization that is supposed to be one of the most respected planning groups in the nation, operating in nearly every city, will teach its people to lie at all costs in order to maintain their power and influence over our communities.

A recent memo introduction given to your local planners from the APA says, "*Given the heightened scrutiny of planners by some members of the public, what is said – or not said – is especially important in building support for planning.*" Here is a list of words the APA warns planners **not** to use – because they cause "*critics to see red,*" as they have become "*highly politicized and generate suspicion among some citizens:*"

Affordable; Agenda 21; Collaboration; Consensus; Delphi technique; Density; Livable; Localized planning; Long-term; region-wide planning; Organize and facilitate; Public visioning; Public-Private Partnerships; Regional, regionalism, regional planning; Smart growth; Stakeholders; Sustainability; Walkable.

The very policy they are implementing, the policy they have invoked time and again – Sustainability – is no longer to be used. So, what instead? The APA memo continues by saying, "*Some may find the words 'district' or 'central' to be an indication of a 'top down' or 'Big Brother' process. Using the common word 'downtown' or 'business area' may be more neutral and preferable.*"

More words not to use: "*Code enforcement, design review, design review standards.*" Why? Explains the APA memo, "*Avoid talking about or linking plans and planning with regulatory matters.*" It is apparently necessary to point out to these stealth controllers of our lives that their planning process has everything to do with regulatory matters and *that* is precisely *why* we are objecting to and fighting their policies in the first place! It's the "regulatory matters" that are taking our private property rights and creating victims.

And here are more words to be eliminated: Councils of government; metropolitan planning organizations; regional planning; Density; clusters; Eminent domain; police powers; Green infrastructure; Mixed-use development; Urban growth boundary; Zoning; and many more. The entire language of Agenda21/Sustainable Development is to be eliminated. And yet, says the memo to the planners – "stay on message."

What will the message now be? Some examples of the NewSpeak now provided by the APA: "*We have a responsibility to think through the long term consequences of our decisions. Planning enables us to do that.*" "*We need to understand together how to make sure our local community and our local economy are strong enough for our children to grow up and have a good life here. Planning helps us do that.*" "*We need to make decisions that are careful, cost effective, efficient, and fair to everybody. That is the purpose of this meeting. There is no hidden agenda.*"

In every one of those canned descriptions of the "planning process" you will find the tenets of Agenda 21. The use of the word "we" is the standard "Delphi technique" of the consensus process they are trying to hide. The reference to the future for the children is right out of the UN Agenda 21 definition: "*Development that meets the needs of the present without compromising the ability of future generations to meet their own needs.*" Of course, as we have learned, that to accomplish such an innocent-sounding goal, means locked away lands and resources. Agenda 21.

The APA intends to dazzle citizens with meaningless statements designed to appeal to their personal interests, appeal to their local patriotism, and crush them with the results when they aren't watching.

As the late Henry Lamb of "Freedom 21" described the true American tradition of planning, "*The process is truly similar to a sausage-making machine. At open meetings, ordinary citizens are free to suggest new ideas about community needs, for consideration by the governing authority. Other citizens are free to oppose those ideas. Ultimately the elected officials discuss and debate the suggestions then vote.*" Now is that so hard? But none of those easy and established practices of honest and open government are used by the APA and their ilk. In fact, they are adamantly opposed and crushed every step of the way.

The American Planning Association and their allies have chosen to counter the anti-Agenda 21 movement with lies, double-speak and stealth. Why? Aren't they proud of their policies? Seattle planner J.Gary Lawrence said it best, when he admitted several years ago, that "*participating in a U.N. advocated planning process would very likely bring out many...who would actively work to defeat any elected official...undertaking Local Agenda 21. So we will call our process something else, such as comprehensive planning, growth management or smart growth.*" Now, even those words have caught up with their secret agenda. Soon they will have to start inventing their own words.

For almost 30 years, Agenda 21 has made a steady, unchecked advance across America, eradicating property rights in the name of "Sustainable Development", while cloaked in environmentally friendly terms like open space, smart growth, and climate change. It is changing our style of government, our way of life, and our hope for a happy, peaceful future.

The latest tactics by the American Planning Association reveals the dark intent of the Sustainablists and the lengths they will go to hide their goals. Honest intent doesn't have to hide in lies and double speak. Those are the tactics of tyranny.

THE PROGRAMS OF AGENDA21/GREEN NEW DEAL

In the Urban Areas

When researching your community's Comprehensive Plan to find evidence of Agenda 21/Sustainable programs, here are some to watch for:

FORM--BASED CODES

A form-based code is a land development regulation that fosters predictable built results and a high-quality public realm by using physical form (rather than separation of uses) as the organizing principle for the code. A form-based code is a regulation, not a mere guideline, adopted into city, town, or county law. A form-based code offers a powerful alternative to conventional zoning regulation.

Read that definition above of Form-based Code again. Note: "**a regulation, not a mere guideline for every city, town, or county**". And "**a powerful alternative to conventional zoning regulation**". You bet it is! Once accepted by your city council, community planning commission staffs will simply follow in lock-step the dictates of
Form-Based Codes. Local planning will not exist. There will be **no** exceptions.

Form-Based Codes:

• Regulate land development to achieve a specific urban form.

• Regulate the form, scale, and character of buildings, including floor ratios, swelling units per acre (Smart Growth), and parking ratios.

• Enforced in International Building Codes (IBC). (see below)

• All communities to look exactly alike.

• A scheme to enforce energy and land use controls under Sustainable guidelines.

AFFIRMATIVELY FURTHERING FAIR HOUSING (AFFH)

The <u>Federal Register says</u> that AFFH "does not impose any land use or zoning laws on any government." And that is true. AFFH grants, **like all other federal programs that work to further Sustainable Development, come with strings**. That is how the government captures neighborhoods, with the monies HUD offers to applicants for CDBG and other grants. **Once the grant money is accepted**, there is no going back; but going forward is community hell.

In 2013, in a speech before the NAACP, HUD Secretary Shaun Donovan clearly revealed HUD's determination to take control of American cities and neighborhoods in the name of fair housing when he said, "There are no stones we won't turn. There are no places we won't go. And there are no complaints we won't explore in order to eliminate housing discrimination."

In 2015, HUD issued a new 377-page ruling called Affirmatively Furthering Fair Housing (AFFH). The purpose is further enforcement of Smart Growth through social justice standards instead of the rule of law. Affordable Housing has become the new battle cry to oppose free enterprise, property rights, and individual wants and needs in favor of the collective. Property ownership is now called "racism" and "white privilege" as "community property" replaces private property through Sustainable Development.

AFFH is the tool of choice for that fight. To achieve its goals, AFFH requires local government agencies that apply for HUD grants to provide a massive profile of the community, including detailed income levels of residents, the breakdown of various religions affiliations and populations, color and national origin of the population, all broken down by neighborhood. Then, using the Livability Principles, HUD determines any "imbalances" in the makeup of the neighborhoods. If necessary, HUD then forces a major shift of the "proper" people into certain neighborhoods to assure the desired "balance." Every five years communities must supply HUD with updates on the progress to achieve balance to assure progress. This is top-down dictatorship by the national government and is nothing less than social engineering!

The next step for communities that fail to comply to AFFH rules is to bring lawsuits. And HUD has begun to file a bunch of them. There is one major problem in dealing with AFFH lawsuits -- there is no set definition as to what AFFH compliance is. Instead it's whatever HUD claims it is. All they need to start legal action is a complaint against the community.

To assure there are plenty of complaints, HUD expects each city to invite participation in their planning programs by civil rights groups, affordable housing developers, community development organizations and any interested members of the public to assist in identifying potential areas of discrimination. Does anyone notice a problem with this situation? The very groups that benefit from these programs, NGOs, agitators, and multiple special interests assure that problems will be found and lawsuits will be filed

For example, in Baltimore, Maryland, the NAACP discovered that the community put Section 8 Public Housing in the same areas of the city. This situation, they claimed, caused ghettos as low-income people, combined with drug dealers, MS13 gangs and others, all seemed to congregate together, creating a high crime area. So the NAACP filed a lawsuit. And they won. The result of the suit -- Baltimore must now spend $30 million of local taxpayer money to begin to build 1,000 low-income housing units inside upscale neighborhoods over the next ten years. That, says the NAACP, will make it all fair. Never mind how the property owners in those neighborhoods will be affected. Never mind that pure logic says this will destroy their property values. It's racism and white privilege to express such ideas!

For those who live in ethnic neighborhoods of their own choosing, being close to family and friends that share traditions and outlooks, it means being forced into neighborhoods where they are not wanted and where they do not want to be. It means a loss of freedom of choice and loss of the right to be secure in their home.

In this day of constant accusations of racism for nearly every act, does no one see the irony of the built-in racism in a regulation that assumes those of certain ethnic origins or economic levels are oppressed and unhappy simply because they live in a different kind of environment than that of the enforcers? What could make them feel more lost and hopeless than to be forced into living in government controlled housing in a neighborhood where they are shunned and resented?

Under AFFH rules, Americans will simply have no choice in the kind of neighborhood in which they wish to live. Using the excuse of equality, HUD- dictated quotas are being enforced. As a result, property values will plummet. Equity in home values will be lost as resale prices fall. Poverty will grow – not diminish -- by these tyrannical rules to reorganize our society.

However, the danger of AFFH goes beyond the destruction of American neighborhoods. It is, in fact, a direct threat to locally elected home rule in communities across the nation. The danger lies in the taking of federal grants. If a community has taken such grants to fund local development, create low income housing programs, and more, then that community has essentially sacrificed its independence to HUD. The fact is, nearly every community has already taken such grants in the name of Smart Growth, Sustainable Development and the creation of Comprehensive Development Plans.

Now, HUD is coming back to collect its due and communities are about to find out there is no such thing as free money. No matter what the city fathers desire for local policy, after taking such grants, HUD will now dictate the use of that money under AFFH rules. President Trump has taken action to remove AFFH Policy. Joe Biden intends to Strengthen it!

URBAN GROWTH BOUNDARIES/SMART GROWTH

According to the Greenbelt Alliance Urban Growth Boundaries accomplish two goals:

- Safeguarding greenbelts from sprawl development.

- Encouraging climate-smart growth, which creates more mixed-use, walkable, affordable, and thriving neighborhoods within urban limits.

Compact cities and towns, rather than sprawling development, tend to be less dependent on cars, which is good for the environment as well as the community's health. It's easier for residents to walk, bike, or take public transportation, which reduces the city's carbon footprint while also encouraging exercise and decreasing harmful air pollution. Additionally, a higher-density city uses less water.

In truth, none of that is true but the sales pitch is for a perfect lifestyle in what they call healthy, happy communities -- where neighbors interact, parents play with their children, and there is no stress from long commutes because all the conveniences of living are just a walk down the street. It all sounds so warm and wonderful, creating images of a near Eighteenth-century atmosphere of peace and tranquility, yet with all the conveniences and technology of our modern age, all leading toward a "sensible growth plan" for future development.

Smart growth planners promote their schemes by insisting that Americans live the wrong way. And they use their comprehensive land-use regulations to impose on others what they insist is the right way to live.

In Omaha, Nebraska, government and NGO forces have been working hard to sell the community on a grand plan for the future called Heartland 2050. Of course, as usual, it's not just for Omaha – but for eight full counties in the surrounding area, all combined into the same regional plan run by an unelected regional council. And the plan openly says it is for the implementation of Sustainable Development.

Listen to the sales pitch. According to the promoters, the goal of Heartland 2050 is to create a strategic "vision" for the region's development over the next 30 years to assure "proper growth." "The Metro area is always changing," say proponents, "but is it moving in the right direction?"

Stop right there! You must ask – moving in the right direction, according to whom? This massive plan will lay the ground rules for transportation, housing, jobs, property/land-use, education, and even health care.

Here's how Smart Growth works. First the planners draw an imaginary line around the community and declare little or no growth will take place outside that line. According to the creed of the planners, growth must be tightly controlled otherwise urban sprawl takes place. It must be stopped.

Why? What is urban sprawl? It is growth outside the pre-determined metro area. It's the building of housing developments that require infrastructure like roads and utilities. Then, of course, such growth causes the creation of shopping malls to serve the needs of the new developments. That, of course, leads to "traffic!" All of those actions are deemed unsustainable by those who appointed themselves our protectors.

The Sustainablists argue that urban sprawl is an added expense to local government, requiring tax dollars to be spent on infrastructure and roads. The answer, they say, is to keep everyone inside the pre-determined line where development, transportation and energy use can be tightly control – all for the common good.

Of course, all of those arguments come with massive holes in them. The new housing developments are built for several reasons. First there is population growth. New families want to start their own homes with all of the advantages, including a place for the kids to play, the personal wealth such an investment provides, and the peace and security a private home of their own brings. Many of these families are escaping the cities because of crime, high taxes and over-crowding. If one could place a video camera at the front door of these new houses to record the home-owning families as they enter for the first time, you would see joy, smiles, and excitement. That's what these new homes mean to the new owners. It used to be called the American Dream. Now such ideas are derided as "sprawl!"

Second, those developments are not a burden on the taxpayers to pay for the infrastructure. Each of those new homes provide increased income for the community through new property taxes. Also, the builders provide the basic streets in the new neighborhoods, In recent years some builders have started to help widen main roads leading to the new developments, in fact that is usually now one of the stipulations for the permit. So the higher taxes argument simply has little basis in fact.

Third, the new shopping malls which spring up around such developments not only provide goods and services for them, they also provide jobs for the new residents. That also adds to the tax rolls. In short, this is how economies are built.

The main enemy of the dedicated Sustainablists is the automobile. To them urban sprawl is the breeder of cars. The sustainable planners have to devise ways to get people out of their cars. That's the first role of Smart Growth.

INTERNATIONAL BUILDING CODES (IBC)

One of the planning tools the APA uses to enforce Sustainability is the International Code Council (ICC), an international set of standards based on a one size fits all set of regulations. The ICC also develops the International Energy Conservation Code, a model for energy efficiency codes used in planning. And it develops a standard for Accessible and Usable Building Facilities. In addition, most communities are now adding enforcement of International Building Codes (IBC) to development plans. Each of these codes is aimed at cutting back energy use, controlling private property use, and -- in short -- enforcing Sustainable Development.

Remember where the concept of Sustainable Development was first introduced and perfected as an agenda for development? Oh yes, in Agenda 21. As international codes are enforced on local communities using the consensus process, there is no room for discussion, reason, or consideration for exceptional local situations. The APA brings these codes and others into the community planning as a pre-packaged deal inflicting the community with (yes) foreign regulations. And, yes, dedicated Americans are protesting that this is not local government or planning, but the enforcement of an international (UN) agenda.

COMPLETE STREETS

The main enemy of the dedicated Sustainablists in the automobile. To them urban sprawl is the breeder of cars. The sustainable planners have to devise ways to get people out of their cars. That's the first role of Smart Growth.

That means the focus for future housing will be the establishment of high-density neighborhoods with residents living in high-rise condos. Walkable communities, as the Sustainablists call them, means the use of private cars will be discouraged in favor of public transportation, bicycles or walking.

How is that done? Several ways. Higher taxes on cars and on gasoline – and there are now plans being developed in various states to tax every mile you drive. Your mileage is kept in the computers of today's cars, like the black boxes in airplanes. Mandatory auto inspections by the state will provide the opportunity to read that information, determine the number of miles driven and a bill will be sent to the car owner each year. Oregon is the first state to announce its intention to collect such taxes, now California has jumped on board.

Heartland 2050 includes the program called the "Complete Street." That is an edict that cars must share the road with bicycles. It calls for "Traffic Calming," which means large speed bumps placed in the center of residential streets that make driving a very unpleasant experience. In addition there are traffic circles that are a menaces to emergency equipment as well as the normal driver. Across the nation, through smart growth plans, communities are now building residential apartment buildings without parking. It's all designed to discourage interest in driving so that residents use bikes for short trips or public transportation, including light rail trains.

In many cities, such as San Francisco, as they eliminate parking from residential areas, they have closed some major streets to vehicle traffic, and have reduced some four-lane streets to two lanes to provide a whole lane for bicycles.

New York City implemented what is called "progressive street projects." They built more than 400 miles of new bike lanes, and they created a massive pedestrian plaza in Times Square by closing five blocks of Broadway to cars.

The announced purpose was to "change the culture." The pedestrian plazas are placed in the center of what were once busy streets, blocking off traffic, and, again, making it difficult to drive in the city. But here, promises the planners, people can congregate, sit at tables in an out of doors atmosphere, and enjoy each other, rather than rushing around by themselves in cars.

One of the leaders of this project said, "*What we're trying to do is see equity of public space. When you build your streets for cars, you're actually building in the expectation that people are going to have cars.*" So, if you stop having streets, obviously people will stop wanting cars.

She went on to explain, "*It costs $10,000 per year for a household to own and maintain a car. We're talking about building an affordable option for people to get around.*" This edict for the drivers of New York City is nothing short of social justice/ social engineering. It's all designed to reduce your ability to drive so that you are forced to use bikes for short trips and public transportation including light rail trains for trips outside the neighborhood. If you want to take a vacation, or visit grandma on Thanksgiving, take the bus, on their timetable and space availability. Of course, forget about taking the kids to see the many Heritage Areas along the way, these buses are not tour buses.

WHAT WORKS CITIES

What Works Cities are located in every region of the United States and in 37 states. This NGO operation supplies communities with workshops, training, data, and all the information and evidence needed to guide your city into the "right" programs that work. It is viewed as a useful tool by local governments to assure they are doing it right. By adopting the WWC Standard, the community becomes part of a national network of local governments. In short, they will be fully invaded by armies of NGOs to help them "do it right!" Of course, all What Works Cities policy is based on Sustainable Development programs.

According to Bloomberg Philanthropies, their What Works Cities program is run in collaboration with the Bill & Melinda Gates Foundation and Ballmer Group; Results for America; the Behavioral Insights Team; Harvard Kennedy School's Government Performance Lab; Johns Hopkins University's Center for Government Excellence; and the Sunlight Foundation.

"In 2017, the program created What Works Cities Certification, a standard that **measures the extent to which cities have the right people, policies, and practices in place to use data for decision-making**, and inspires many more cities to improve their practices."

- What Works Cities, supply communities with workshops, training, data, and all information needed to guide our cities into the "right" programs.
- Eliminate the need for elected officials (see non-elected Regional councils
- Under WWC standards, the city becomes part of a national network of local governments.
- Sustainable policies are enforced by an army of NGOs in WWCs.

TRANSITION

Ten years ago Transition Towns were 'happening'. First begun in the U.K., the goal was to disengage from an oil-based society: *Another important aspect of Transition that differentiates it from other efforts is in it's ultimate goal of creating an Energy Decent Action Plan (EDAP). An EDAP sets out a vision of a powered-down, resilient, relocalized future, and then backcasts, in a series of practical steps, creating a map to get there from here. Every community's EDAP will be different, both in content and style.* In simple words, no oil, green energy only, and then try to figure out, any way you can, how you can exist in that world.

Being trendy, the Transition Towns went the way of the bell-bottom trousers. Today, rather than "towns", the body politic of Sustainable Development has taken the word, added the adjective "just", and voila 'Just Transition', and sold it to the unions as their piece of the carbon tax pie.

JUST TRANSITION

Obviously, 'just' is not used as an adjective, 'righteous, impartial, fair', but as an adverb, 'simply, narrowly, merely'; because the transition from carbon-based energy to so-called green energy is not at all impartial or fair. It is 'just' another tool in the box of civilization-deconstruction brought to us by those working for a world government.

So, in the words of the UN and its NGOs, here is Just Transition. From the Organization for Economic Cooperation and Development (OECD), another branch of the UN, Just Transition is: *essential if the global economy is to make the shift to a low-carbon and resilient economy at the scale and pace required to avoid catastrophic climate damage in a fair way. Governments, international institutions, businesses, trade unions, civil society, communities and, increasingly, investors are placing growing emphasis on the workplace and wider social dimension of the transition.*

"Ambitious action on climate that keeps the warming of the planet as far below 2 degrees as possible is an imperative if we are to ensure a future for humanity. There can be no doubt that a zero-carbon world is possible, but we have choices about how we manage the transition. A just transition ensures environmental sustainability as well as decent work, social inclusion and poverty eradication. Indeed, this is what the Paris Agreement requires: National plans on climate
change that include just transition measures with a centrality of decent work and quality jobs.

"The sectoral and economic transformation we face is on a scale and within a time frame faster than any in human history. There is a real potential for stranded workers and stranded communities. Transparent planning that includes just transition measures will prevent fear, opposition and inter-community and generational conflict. People need to see a future that
allows them to understand that, notwithstanding the threats, there is both security and opportunity.

"Nonetheless, the just transition will not happen by itself. It requires plans and policies. Workers and communities dependent on fossil fuels will not find an alternative sources of income and revenue overnight. This is why transformation is not only about phasing out polluting sectors, it is also about new jobs, new industries, new skills, new investment and the opportunity to create a more equal and resilient economy."

"In 2015, the UN agreed Sustainable Development Goals that collectively represent the agenda of just transition, particularly the goals of decent work for all (Goal 8), clean energy for all (Goal 7), climate protection (Goal 13) and poverty eradication (Goal 1). Again, unions had campaigned for these goals, in particular Goal 8. Thereafter in 2015, the **UN's International Labor Organization** produced a definitive model for just transition: Guidelines for a just transition towards environmentally sustainable economies and societies for all. The Guidelines are the result of a tripartite multilateral negotiation between **unions**, employers' organizations and governments. In the negotiations leading up to the Paris Agreement, the global climate deal negotiated in 2015, unions and their allies worked hard to get strong text on just transition in the Agreement. In the end the Parties agreed to include the text in the Agreement's preamble: "Taking into account the imperatives of a just transition of the workforce and the creation of decent work and quality jobs in accordance with nationally defined development priorities ..." Paris Agreement (2015).

"The ILO's vision of just transition is broad and primarily positive. It is a bridge from where we are today to a future where all jobs are green and decent, poverty is eradicated, and communities are thriving and resilient. More precisely, it is a systemic and whole of economy approach to sustainability. It includes both measures to reduce the impact of job losses and industry phase-out on workers and communities, and measures to produce new, green and decent jobs, sectors and healthy communities. It aims to address environmental, social and economic issues together.

"The process, its participants and its goals are key. Workers, employers and government are active and collaborative partners in developing plans for transition and transformation that simultaneously consider environment, social justice and poverty alleviation."

But the governments of the world do not have enough money to support this boondoggle of fake science, so the Just Transition Center, an NGO, is working to encourage businesses and investors to make "responsible investments for "a just-transition and sustainable development to tackle the growing threat of climate change need to incorporate the full range of environmental, social and governance (ESG) dimensions of responsible investment."

"Climate action + social inclusion = the just transition
The transition to a resilient, low-carbon economy is underway and investors are increasingly taking action to drive this shift. However, the pace of change is still too slow and too limited to achieve the goals of the 2015 Paris Agreement on climate change or to realize the economic and social benefits that climate action can bring. Investors can do much more to bring about the needed change. The just transition builds on and deepens the core investment case for action on climate change. It focuses on the management of the social aspects of climate change in the workplace and wider community so that rapid decarbonisation is achieved in ways that contribute to inclusive and resilient growth.

"In the words of economist Nicholas Stern, Chair of the Grantham Research Institute on Climate Change and the Environment: '*We should see the just transition as part of the new story of inclusive, sustainable growth. This is a highly attractive economic model, with strong innovation and growth and able to overcome poverty in an effective and lasting way. But it requires us to manage the process of change in much better ways within modern market economies. We need to be organizing for transitions in the plural including technologies, economic structures, cities and the international division of labor. And we must accelerate the pace of decision-making if we are to respond to the urgency of climate change.*"

In the RURAL Areas look for any way that can be used to capture your property, in part or in whole. Conserveation Easements can sould like a godsend, but they steal your property without having to pay for it. The Endangered Species Act lets you keep your property, but you might not get to live one it. National Historic Trust turns wonderful towns into the cheapest of destination tourism. There are so many ways to have your property taken that you need to be awake and aware.

THE WILDLANDS PROJECT

The legal framework for the plan is found in Article 8a-e of the *Convention on Biological Diversity.* (This is the treaty that President Clinton had already signed and that the U.S. Senate was very nearly duped into ratifying in September 1995. Section 10.4.2.2.3 of the *United National Global Biodiversity Assessment (GBA)* defines the enabling and enforcement protocols for the Biodiversity Treaty.

According to the GBA, reserves would include wilderness areas and national parks while inner buffer zones would permit no agriculture, no more than 0.5 miles of road per square mile of land, primitive camping, and only light selection harvesting of forests. The June 25, 1993 issue of Science magazine reported that the plan calls for 23.4% of the land to be put into wilderness (no human use) and 26.2% into corridors and human buffer zones (very limited use by humans). The Wildlands Project is a massive program for restructuring society around nature as the organizing principle. The concept is Earth First founder, Dave Foreman's, but the plan was developed by Dr. Reed Noss, under grants from The Nature Conservancy and the National Audubon Society. It was first published in *Wild Earth,* a publication of the Cenozoic Society, of which Foreman is also chairman.

The Wildlands Project was set up as a corporation with offices in Arizona and Oregon; Foreman is Chairman of the Board; Reed Noss is a Director. Working in tandem with the Wildlands Project is the Biosphere Reserve Program, a creation of the United Nations Educational, Scientific, Cultural Organization (UNESCO). The objective of the program, *conceived in 1971*, has been to designate sites worldwide for preservation and to protect the biodiversity of chosen sites on a global level. Toward that end, the Sierra Club has redrawn the map of North America into 21 "bioregions." In turn, each of the 21 bioregions has been divided into three zones: 1) Wilderness area, designated as habitat of plants and animals. Human habitation, use, or intrusion is forbidden. (2) Buffer zones surrounding the wilderness areas. Limited, and strictly controlled, human access is permitted within this zone. (3) Cooperation zones, the only zones where humans will be permitted to live.

According to the late Dr. Michael Coffman of Environmental Perspectives, Inc., a strategy to implement reserves and corridors (in the northern Rockies, for example, would be to: 1) Start with a seemingly innocent-sounding program like the "World Heritage Areas in Danger." Bring all human activity under regulation in a 14-18 million acre buffer zone around Yellowstone National Park. 2) Next, declare all federal land (except Indian reservations) as buffers, along with private land within federal administration boundaries. 3) Next, extend the U.S. Heritage corridor buffer zone concept along major river systems. Begin to convert critical federal lands and ecosystems to reserves. 4) Finally, convert all U.S. Forest Service, grasslands, and wildlife refuges to reserves. Add missing reserves and corridors so that 50 percent of landscape is preserved.

Investigative reporter Karen Lee Bixman, in her article, "The Taking of America," states that "each of the 21 bioregions will be governed by bioregional councils. Although in its infancy stage, the setting up of such a council is taking place [now] in the south in conjunction with the *Smokey Mountain National Park in Tennessee*. When these councils come into play, local, state and national government will not be able to interfere with their enforcement. It will be under the strong arm of the UN Environmental organizations such as the Sierra Club, Nature Conservancy, and other green organizations will be given the green light [to be] the enforcement arm of these councils at the local level." Karen Lee Bixman, "The Taking of America," *The Investigative Reporter*

It cannot be too strongly emphasized that this is a radical agenda designed to control not just the land, but all human activity, as well. Under the Wildlands Project, at least 50 percent of the land area of America would be returned to "core wilderness areas" where human activity is barred. Those areas would be connected by corridors, a few miles wide. The core areas and corridors would be surrounded by "buffer zones" in which "managed" human activity would be allowed, provided that biodiversity protection is the first priority. Reed Noss's words put it very, very plainly: "the collective needs of non-human species must take precedence over the needs and desires of humans." ["Rewilding America," *eco-logic Magazine* (Publ. By Environmental Conservation Organization,

CONSERVATION EASEMENTS

In a typical conservation easement, a private land trust organization purchases some or all of the "bundle" of a property owner's rights. The bundle includes an agreement to give up development rights for the property; the ability to overrule the owner's choice of how to use the property, including adding more buildings or renovating or rebuilding existing buildings; in the case of farmers, it may include decisions on which fields can be used for planting or even which crops can be grown and the technique to be used. All of these things come under the command of the easement. And all of it may become the decision of the land trust, because, once the conservation easement agreement is signed, the owner's rights are legally subservient to his new partner, the trust.

True, in exchange, the property owner receives charitable deductions on federal taxes based on the difference between the values of the land before and after granting the easement. The property owner also receives relief from federal estate or inheritance taxes. Many states provide income tax credits and property tax relief. And the owner receives a payment for his development rights.

In the beginning it all sounds good. Money in the pocket; the farm safe from development and the ability to practice the beloved tradition of farming. Well, maybe.

The fact is, under the easement, the owner has sold away his property rights and therefore no longer has controlling interest in his property. Through the restrictions outlined in the easement, property usage is now strictly controlled, including everyday decisions on running the farm. In many cases, the Land Trust that controls the easement demands strict adherence to "sustainable" farming practices. That means strict controls on how much energy or water can be used in the farming process, access to streams for the livestock, use of fertilizer, etc, are all under the direction of the Land Trust. And there's more. Certain details weren't revealed to the landowner as he signed on the dotted line. For example:

- Trusts often re-sell the easement to other conservation groups. They sell and resell them like commodities. Eventually the farmer may not know who actually holds the control over his land. For these groups, the easements become a significant profit center as they rake in fees for each new easement they sign up.

- Worse, the land trust may work directly with government agencies, helping to establish new regulations which alter best management practices, driving up compliance costs. Eventually these cost increases can force owners into a desperate situation and they are more than ready to sell the land.

- In certain targeted areas where the land trusts are especially interested in locking away the land, owners who refuse to sign an easement may find themselves under massive pressure to do so. The Nature Conservancy is a master at this trick, creating millions of dollars of income for the group. Its favorite practice is to tell the landowner that the government intends to take the land, but, if they sell to the Conservancy, it will guarantee that the land will stay in private hands, but of course, since the government intends to take the land it is now worth much less. So they get the landowner to sell at a reduced rate. Then the Conservancy calls the government agency to tell them the good news that they have the land. And the agency pays the Conservancy full market value. They call that, "Capitalism with a heart!!"

- Because ownership rights are muddled between taxes, restrictions, and best practices requirements, it can be difficult to find a buyer willing to pay a fair market price for the land. In a sense, once the easement is signed, the owner has just rendered his land worthless on the open market.

- Conservation easement deeds use broad language that expands the trust's control but very specific language that limits the landowner's rights.

- When productive land is taken off the local tax rolls, a revenue shortage is created that has to be made up by other taxpayers, causing rate hikes in property taxes and other tricks the government can come up with to keep the same amount of money coming in even though thousands of acres are being taken off the tax rolls.

At a January, 2013, meeting of the Fauquier County, Virginia planning commission, it was revealed that 96,600 acres of county land is in conservation easements (or 23% of the total land mass of the county). A little research revealed an interesting detail. It seems that, as the conservation easements are sold to the public as a way to save the small family farm, in reality, of the 23% of the land in easements, only 2% of it is actually small family farms. The rest is basically the vast estates of the landed gentry who have found a way to not only keep the land open for their fox hunts – but to also reduce their property taxes.

10 QUESTIONS TO ASK BEFORE SIGNING A CONSERVATION EASEMENT

Are You Asking the Right Questions about Conservation Easements (CE) or Purchased Development Rights (PDR)?

Special thanks to Ric Frost – Economic Policy Analyst

Many landowners have placed portions, or all, of their private land holdings into a split estate situation without fully understanding the impacts to themselves, or their community. This is largely due to not asking enough questions, or the right questions.

1. Why would someone want to pay to control my land, and where is the money coming from?

2. I have signed away my rights, but can the Land Trust transfer their rights? What will my kids have left if I do this?

3. Do Conservation Easements protect agriculturalists from the real pressures of ownership, as is claimed by land trusts?

- These pressures would include:

- Government restrictions and regulations that affect farming;

- Tax Exempt, Non-Government Environmental Organization Lawsuits against property owners;

- Weather Fluctuations;

- Market Fluctuations;

- Protection for farmers market pricing structures (or the ability to pass on increased business costs, such as fuel expenses);

- Protection from Subsidized Foreign Market Dumping.

- Protection from Estate Taxes and compliance costs.

    These are the real reasons farmers can't stay in business and are forced to sell their land – not pressure from developers.

    Here's the answer to that question -- Conservation Easements **DO NOT** protect farmers from these pressures.

5. If land trusts are concerned with protecting agriculture, then what have they done to alleviate these real pressures?

Splitting the title of private land through Conservation Easements has other consequences as well. Some comments on CE and PDR impacts by financial officers:

> "Owners give up management and control of the land": Jimmy Hall, PCA, NM

> "Severely diminished loan value of land": John Johnson, First Western Bank, SD

> "CEs eliminate property loan value": Dee Gidney, Texas Bank Ag Loans, TX

> "Fragmentation of land title to deny future generations a full range of productive land-use options": David Guernsey, Alliance for America

> Loan Value for operational and other loans is reduced up to 90 percent with an Easement

6. What are the real facts vs the misguided sales pitches?

- "Perpetual means 99 years." False: **PERPETUAL is FOREVER**.

- "I retain full title to the land." False: title becomes split with easement holder.

- "A CE (PDR) is the only way the land is managed to my intent." **False**: the easement holder and future easement holder (LAND TRUSTS) can change management practices at any time, including development! Easement management loopholes also allow easement holders and third party non-easement holder interests to sue the landowner (not the easement holder trust) and impose habitat restrictions.

- "A CE (PDR) allows me to use the property as I always have had." **False**: you give up management control of all easement property forever!

- "Property with a CE (PDR) will sell easy." **False**: a CE (PDR) may reduce the property value, and affect the willingness of financial institutions to loan money on a split title.

7. Questions landowners and local governments should ask before accepting   or promoting Conservation Easements:

- What could be unexpected economic impacts that may be encountered as the result of Conservation Easements and Property Development Rights? Some of the impacts already experienced by landowners and communities have been:

- Reduced management options on taxed lands of landowner and heirs,

- Restrictions on farm and ranch management practices, Restrictions on chemicals used, Restrictions on seed and plant types, Restrictions on farm and ranch management practices,

- Reduction of income due to restrictions,

- Reduction in management options with land and business value decline, forcing owner into a "willing seller" status (actually a compromised seller),

- Imposition of Environmental Assessment (EA) and Environmental Impact Study (EIS) expenses on landowner for management changes, especially if a Federal Nexus exists,

- Legal expenses incurred by the Land Trust for enforcement and penalty expenses for CE and PDR violations (It's built into the fine print),

- Vulnerability from non-trust third party interest lawsuits – Litigation Exposure is in the Easement Act,

- Decreased or eliminated production translating into negative economic impacts to agriculture and related industries within community, county, and state.

- **Recent reports indicate a majority of lands with CEs (PDRs) have not remained in agriculture, and are rendered to untaxed "open space" in the hands of the government, or owned by wealthy non-agriculturalists comfortable with "open space" restricted lands without production,**

- Reduced Management Options on taxed lands of landowner and heirs,

- Reduction of income due to restrictions of direct, induced, and indirect economic benefits to all related industries within community, county and state,

- Reduction of county tax base forcing tax increases and reduction of county services on other property owners to make up the loss (a disproportionate burden).

8. Questions that landowners, who are approached for CEs or Purchase Development Rights (PDRs), should ask are:

- What are CE (PDR) impacts to private landowners and communities?

- Do the "benefits" offset the impacts? (Lost tax revenue and future earnings opportunities)

- What are the other impacts and implications from imposing a CE (PDR) on private land? (Federal Nexus and Section 7)

- What is the long-range outcome from imposing a CE (PDR) on private landowners?

- According to whom? (A tax-exempt organization?)

- Would a limited liability company or incorporation better serve the landowner's tax needs, instead of a CE (PDR) that brings in tax-exempt third party litigation and potential federal agency management?

9. Would it not be better to protect agriculture by:

- Supporting reduced environmental restrictions on agricultural producers?

- Stopping the dumping of foreign commodities on our markets by foreign subsidized products, at prices lower than producers' cost of operation?

- Making agriculture attractive as a viable business career and encouraging our youth to remain in agriculture as a productive and fulfilling life?

10. Questions that State and County officials should be considering for CE and PDR regulations are:

- License and regulate land trust agents as real estate agents.

- Regulation of tax-exempt land trusts by state real estate commission (they are acting as land brokers).

- Bonding requirement on each CE and PDR transaction equivalent to value of encumbered property before transaction.

- Renegotiation language built into CE contract that allows grantee to renegotiate every 5 Years (North Dakota has 10 year limits – no perpetuity allowed!).

- If renegotiations cannot be accomplished to satisfaction of landowner, the CE contract becomes null and void.

- Land Trust pays back-taxes on land if this occurs, not landowner (don't forget that if a CE or PDR is ended, under current IRS law the landowner pays the IRS the back-taxes back to the time of the origin of the CE or PDR, not the tax-exempt land trust).

- Land trust pays taxable value of severed development right to county to prevent erosion of tax base as community infrastructure demands increase (check with county appraiser for development right tax values).

- No CE shall be valid and enforceable unless the limitations or obligations created by the easement are clearly presented in writing on the face of any document creating the CE or PDR Including Information From the UCEA 1981 (Uniform Conservation Easement Act).

- Water, grazing, farming and mineral rights shall not be encumbered by conditions or restrictions imposed or agreed to in the CE or PDR Contract. Grantee (landowner) retains rights of transfer on all rights not expressly identified in CE or PDR.

- Local and state legislation expressly prohibiting transfer of CE or PDR to other parties without formal written consent of landowner (a common practice of land trusts is to trade CEs and PDRs without knowledge or consent of landowner).

- Elimination of third-party enforcement clause language from CE contracts – must be state law! (Colorado has this law, and it has been upheld in at least one case).

Remember, restricting land through Conservation Easements or Purchased Development Rights in the name of "protecting agriculture" simply put, does not protect agriculture!

Perhaps the simplest way to end the tyranny of conservation easements over the landowners is for state government to allow a five year opt out of the conservation easement for the landowner. This would allow enough time for them to decide if the easement is working for them. And what about the tax credits they have already received? Simple. They received them while under the easement. They stop receiving the tax credits when they opt out. No muss. No fuss.

Better yet, stop the massive taxes and regulations and let the landowners use they property as they wish. Of course that would be contrary to the agenda for reorganization of human society.

Conservation easements are not a tool for property owners to preserve their land. All the tax breaks and rhetoric about helping farmers is just that – rhetoric for the specific purpose of pressuring the owner to give up control of the land. In truth, the creation of the conservation easement ruse is a brilliant tactic by the Sustainable Development forces to get landowners to give up their property rights voluntarily.

ENDANGERED SPECIES ACT

In 1973, the Endangered Species Act (ESA) was signed into law by President Richard Nixon. Its announced purpose was to protect and help recover species that were disappearing from the earth. Whales, polar bears, wolves, grizzly bears, and bald eagles, were some of the most highly publicized species in need of rescue.

As a tool for "recovering" endangered species the ESA has been a monumental failure. In its thirty-year history, of the 1304 species that have been listed to save, only 12 have been officially recovered. That's a success rate of only 1%. Why? What went wrong?

Answer – the ESA was created as a tool to take and control private land, not recover species. In fact, once a species has been listed no recovery plan is ever required. If that seems strange concerning an act that is so highly touted as a major plan to protect wildlife, then one must remember the true purpose of Sustainable Development. Again, it is not an environmental plan, but a diabolical policy to reorganize and control human civilization.

Here's how the ESA really works. With pressure from NGO groups, the federal government declares that a certain species is endangered so the species is placed on the ESA list. Now, if that endangered species is discovered on a farm or a ranch – or in the middle of a proposed building project, all *human* action on the affected property is stopped. No ranching, no farming, no drilling, no timber or mining activity, and no building may take place. Essentially the land is rendered worthless and locked away. Understand that 90% of all species (endangered or otherwise) claim habitation on private land, so the ESA becomes the perfect tool if your goal is to lock away land and stop industry. Not much good, however, for the animals.

Punishment of the landowner is the direct effect of the ESA. It's interesting to consider that if an endangered species is found on a property, perhaps it's because the landowner has actually been doing something right to encourage and provide the proper habitat. Such thoughts are never considered by government agents and their Green stormtroopers. The result has been that any landowner who discovers the existence of an endangered specie on his land quickly understands that, in order to keep it, he needs to adopt the SSS policy -- shoot, shovel and shut up! Get rid of the foul creature and say nothing of its existence – or lose your land and go to jail. Not a very effective atmosphere for trying to save wildlife, but sometimes the only way to save a person's property.

Yet every attempt to fix the deadly punitive affects of the ESA has been refused by the environmentalists. They will not hear of changing a single comma in the ESA. Again, saving species is not the purpose. Land control is the goal. Facts about whether listed species are really endangered simply get in the way.

THE SPOTTED OWL

Two decades ago, the nation was warned that spotted owls were disappearing because big bad timber companies were cutting down "old growth" forests. Old growth is an invented term to define forests that have not yet been harvested by the timber industry.

So the Sustainablists rushed to the forests, hugged the trees, and issued news releases to decry the evils of the logging industry. Save the owl! Save the trees! Kill the timber industry! Of course, that was the point. As a result of the hysteria to save the "endangered" owls, U.S. timber sales were reduced by 80-90%, forcing sawmills to close, loggers to go broke, and whole towns, which depended on the industry, to die. The federal crackdown on the industry caused a shift from U.S. domestic lumber purchases to those from foreign soils. In short, American industry suffered in the name of protecting the spotted owl. Turns out it wasn't endangered.

First, the spotted owl is a sub-species of the Mexican spotted owl. There are lots of them! Second, it wasn't the timber industry driving down the spotted owl populations – it was the completely natural consequence of competition with another species of owl – the barred owl. Third, the spotted owl didn't have to have "old growth forests" to live. They were found living (and procreating) in McDonald signs, under bridges, and many other places. Another Green lie that accomplished the desired and pre-determined outcome – death to the timber industry – all in the name of environmental protection.

POLAR BEARS

The next frantic endangered species crisis was the dying population of polar bears – all because of man's encroachment on their northern habitat as well as the evil drillers of oil in the arctic. To this day, the World Wildlife Fund continues to run dramatic, heart rendering ads on television, showing drowning polar bears clinging to life as they cling to a melting hunk of ice.

Oh the tragedy. Immediately, Congress rushed to the rescue as Representative Ed Markey, Chairman of the House Select Committee on Energy Independence and Global Warming, issued legislation to stop drilling rights in the Chukchi Sea. He said this area of drilling "may be" needed as critical habitat for the polar bears' survival. Of course, Global Warming was to blame for the melting ice. Another man-made assault on nature.

Again, it was all a lie. According to the National Oceanic and Atmospheric Administration (NOAA) average Alaskan temperatures were NOT climbing. The ice was not melting. Today, it is at an all time high thickness.

Most importantly, polar bear populations are not declining. They are growing. The total population in the area was about 22,000 bears. Now, according to the Canadian government, local hunts are necessary to keep the populations under control.

WOLF REINTRODUCTION

For several hundred years our ancestors worked diligently to remove predators from the land so they could live in peace, without fear for their children and livestock. Over the past several decades, the forces of Sustainable Development have demanded that government enforce policy to bring back the wolves and grizzly bears that ranchers and farmers had fought so hard to keep at a viable but controlled number.

When the people protested, saying the wolves and grizzles would destroy their lives and livelihood, the Greens insisted man could live in harmony with these predators because there had never been a case of wolves killing humans. Moreover, they argued that the wolves would be good for the elk populations and that the wolves only kill what they need to eat. The government, of course, acceding to the Greens' demands and brought the wolves and bears back as protected species.

So, wolves were dropped on the plains of Montana, Idaho, and other western states. Then reality set in. With no predators of their own, the packs of wolves grew rapidly, reproducing at a rapid rate. Over 2,000 wolves caused 45% of known deaths of radio-collared female elk on the northern ridge of Montana. Elk populations decreased from 16,791 in 1995 to 8,335 in 2004, doubling the rate of kills predicted by the ESA. In addition, contrary to the noble narrative of wolves killing only what they needed to eat, it was discovered that they actually will eat their prey while it's still alive, sometimes eating only a portion and leaving the prey to suffer as they die slowly. Wolves, it was discovered, were actually treacherous and not to be trusted.

Humans soon became the prey. Hunters reported being surrounded by packs of wolves, cleverly hunting them like a scene from Jurassic Park. One resident in Idaho reported a pack of wolves sitting in her yard as she walked down her driveway. As she tried to call a neighbor for help, they surrounded her, closing in, almost upon her before help finally arrived. In New Mexico, two school children were followed home from the bus stop by three wolves. In Idaho a wolf kill was found 70 yards from a school bus stop. Yet the wolves are the ones our own government chooses to protect, not our children.

Meanwhile, wolves routinely attack and kill pets and livestock, just as predicted by the ranchers and farmers. The Sustainable movement is based on anti-human policy, perpetrated by deceit and promoted by myth as it drives its plan to destroy human society. Yet it's hard for most humans to comprehend that other humans want to rid most of us from the earth.

HIDING THE SLAUGHTER CAUSED BY THE WINDMILLS

If you are caught simply carrying the feather of an endangered eagle it could lead to huge fines and even imprisonment. They are sacred and not to be messed with – according to accepted environmental lore.

Of course, it's also accepted lore that wind power is natural and therefore sacred. Wind energy advocates insist that those gigantic turbines, which now cover vast acres of the nation, "only" kill an "acceptable" number of birds, perhaps 440,000 annually.

That is hundreds of times more than were killed in the Exxon Valdez or BP Gulf of Mexico oil spills. It's also 1,900 times more dead birds than the 2011 case which prompted the U.S. Justice Department and Fish and Wildlife Service to prosecute oil companies operating in North Dakota in 2011.

The "acceptable" kill rate by wind turbines is also pure fabrication of numbers, aided and abetted by the same government officials and Sustainablists who never miss an the opportunity to pillory and prosecute oil producers. The actual death toll from wind turbine blades is an intolerable and unsustainable 13,000,000 to 39,000,000 birds and bats annually, year after year, in the United States alone. And the number grows with the increase of new turbines. But don't worry, those kills are acceptable because wind power is environmentally and politically correct!

NATIONAL HERITAGE AREAS (NHA)

Preserving history! How much more American can you get? The major opponents of the Sustainable power grab are the folks who love our nation, revere our Constitution and will do almost anything to preserve the ideals that created our beloved nation.   Visiting historic areas, walking the hallowed ground of our battlefields, learning the details of the Founders' every thought and action, these are the things that set the passions of America's patriots on fire. These are the people who would oppose any action that would violate the Constitution or infringe on private property rights as they defend free enterprise every step of the way. They are the greatest opponents of Sustainable Development's drive for an all-powerful central government.

How do the power mongers guide such opponents into their trap? Answer! Historic Preservation! There are a lot of programs popping out of the federal government under the name of historic preservation. It's interesting to note how many have come about since the drive began to impose Sustainable Development. There are Scenic Rivers designations. We've already discussed the American Heritage Rivers Initiative. Of course there's the National Register of Historic Places and the National Historic Landmarks Program, to name just a few.

Then there are National Heritage Areas. Heritage areas are sold as a means to honor historic or cultural events that took place in a specific locale. We are told that they will preserve our culture and honor the past, that they will preserve battlefields where our forefathers fought and died for freedom, and they will preserve birthplaces, homes, buildings and hallowed grounds for posterity. Of course, we are assured that Heritage Areas will also help build tourism and boost local economies.

What is a National Heritage Area? To put it bluntly, it is a pork barrel earmark that harms property rights and local governance. Why is that true? Because Heritage Areas have boundaries. These are very defined boundaries with very definite consequences for folks who reside within them. National historic significance, obviously, is a very arbitrary term; so anyone's property can end up falling under those guidelines.

Here are the details as to how a Heritage Area operates. Specifically, funding and technical assistance for Heritages Areas are administered through the National Park Service, a federal agency with a long history of hostility toward private landowners.

The recipient of these funds, in partnership with the Park Service, become a "managing entity" for the activities and development of the Heritage Area. Who are the recipients of these funds? As usual, they are typically strictly ideological special interests groups and local government officials. The managing entity sets up non-elected boards, councils, and regional governments to oversee policy inside the Heritage Area. In other words, Heritage Areas are set up just like all Sustainable Development operations.

In the mix of special interest groups you're going to find all of the usual suspects: environmental groups, planning groups, historic preservation groups, all with their own private agendas – all working behind the scenes, creating policy, hovering over the members of the non-elected boards (even assuring that their own people make up the boards), and all collecting the Park Service funds to pressure local governments to install their agenda. In many cases, these groups actually form a compact with the Interior Department to determine the guidelines that make up the land-use management plan and the boundaries of the Heritage Area itself.

After the Heritage Area boundaries are drawn, and after the management plan has been approved by the Park Service, the management entity and its special interest groups are given the federal funds, typically a million dollars or more per year, and told to spend that money getting the management plan enacted at the local level.

Here's how they operate with those funds. They go to local boards and local elected officials and say, "Congress just created a new Heritage Area and you are within the boundaries. We have identified certain properties within these boundaries as those we deem significant. We have also identified certain businesses that we deem insignificant and harmful to these properties and a harmful to the Heritage Area. We don't have the power to make laws to regulating control over these properties and businesses, but you do. And here is some federal money. Now use whatever tools, whatever laws, whatever regulatory procedures you already have to make this management plan come into fruition."

Incredibly, proponents argue that National Heritage Areas do not influence local zoning or land-use planning. Yet by definition this is precisely what they do. Found right in the language of Heritage Area legislation, the management entity is specifically directed to restore, preserve, and manage anything and everything that is naturally, culturally, historically, and recreationally significant to the Heritage Area.

This sweeping mandate ensures that virtually every square inch of land within the boundaries is subject to the scrutiny of Park Service bureaucrats and their managing partners. That is the way it works. It's done behind the scenes – out of the way of public input.

It is also worth noting that these are permanent units of the Park Service. Proponents claim NHAs are merely seed grants and that, sooner or later, they will attain self-sufficiency and no longer need federal funding. Yet National Heritage Areas almost never meet their funding sunset triggers. Once created, they are permanent units of the National Park Service and always dependent on increased federal funds. And the Park Service has testified several times that they, indeed, could be considered permanent units of the Park Service because they always need oversight.

In addition, within the Heritage Areas, the Park Service looks for opportunities to create other Park Service programs. Former Deputy Director of the National Park Service, Donald Murphy, testified before the Senate Subcommittee on National Parks that one of the things the Park Service does when administering National Heritage Areas is survey land that would be suitable for future National Parks or National Park expansions.

Of course, as with so many other invasive planning schemes, there is always the assurance that these are local initiatives, and that Heritage Areas are something citizens want in order to bring an honorary federal designation to help drive tourism into their regions.

It simply isn't true. For the most part, Heritage Areas are first dreamed up by national organizations or small wealthy organizations within the locality, which are looking to promote their own agendas – paid for by federal tax dollars. The process then becomes federally driven by the National Park Service, which uses the legislation to hand out cash to the very organizations that are pushing them.

THE CONNECTION BETWEEN HERITAGE AREAS AND SUSTAINABLE DEVELOPMENT

The language used in Congressional legislation (H.R. 4099, a bill from 2012, to "Authorize a National Heritage Area Program) has been very revealing. Describing the "need" for Heritage Areas, it said: "Certain areas of the United States tell nationally significant stories; they illustrate significant aspects of our heritage; possess exceptional natural, cultural, scenic, and historic resources; and represent the diversity of our national character."

Ok, so, name a section of our nation that doesn't contain "significant stories." Or locate a place where people from the past didn't walk, live, or carry on their lives. That definition is simply too broad to be practical, if the real purpose is to honor significant events in our history.

But the bill goes on to explain: "*In these areas, the interaction of natural processes, geography, history, cultural traditions, and economic and social forces form distinctive landscapes that should be recognized, conserved, enhanced, and interpreted to improve the quality of life in the regions and to provide opportunities for public appreciation, education, enjoyment, and economic sustainability.*"

Where have we heard these very words before – economic and social forces; conserve; improve the quality of life?

Well, again, lets go back to this quote from the 1993 President's Council on Sustainable Development which said, "*Sustainable Communities encourage people to work together to create healthy communities where natural resources are preserved, jobs are available, sprawl is contained, neighborhoods are secure, education is lifelong, transportation and health care are accessible, and all citizens have opportunities to improve the quality of their lives.*"

We've already learned that the purpose of the President's Council on Sustainable Development was to create policy to reduce or eliminate "unsustainable" activities by controlling such things as consumerism, high meat intake, use of fossil fuels, roadways, automobiles, dams, pastures, golf courses, and much more.

So, now wait a minute. Are we talking about historic preservation where we just want to honor our past – or are we talking about a massive zoning process involving central planning? Because that's what Sustainable Development is. Even the planning groups will admit that. So, why is the same language of Sustainable Development in a bill on Heritage Areas? Could they possibly be part of the same top down agenda?

In that light, consider this additional quote from the President's Council: "*Private land-use decisions are often driven by strong economic incentives that result in several ecological and aesthetic consequences…the key to overcoming it is through public policy.*" That means new legislation and government programs. And so, what are Heritage Areas but legislation for a new government program.

Did the people of the affected areas really ask for a Heritage Area or did this idea just appear for no apparent reason? Is there an emergency? Is there a dire need? If so, can anybody name those needs? These questions must be asked before such policy is put in place.

And finally, there is this quote from the same policy making source – the President's Council: "*We need a new collaborative decision process that leads to better decisions, more rapid change and more sensible use of human, natural and financial resources in achieving our goals.*" Better decisions for whom – by whom? More sensible use of resources, according to whom? Ask these same questions about any of the policies so far detailed in this report – from Conservation Easements, to American Heritage Rivers. Where is the urgency?

This description of government leads away from elected representatives doing the people's bidding. Instead it establishes non-elected boards, councils, and regional government entities in which local citizens have little or no input. The language is the same between Sustainable Development and Heritage Areas because they are both part of the same "collaborative" process and for the same purpose – control of the land and all human activity inside it.

As proponents talk about historic preservation and heritage inside the Heritage Area, you will also find the catchwords "resource conservation" and "resource stewardship," for example. It's all about control. Control of the land. Control of resources, Control of decision-making. And how does that fit with the claim of preserving the American culture - which was built on the ideals of free enterprise and private property? The fact is, it doesn't.

In reality, National Heritage Areas are nothing more than land targeted by the NPS for future national parks, historic sites, landmarks, and land acquisition for the specific purpose of limiting human activity – adding to the Wildlands.

Proponents of NHAs also claim that they are "locally driven" projects. Nothing could be further from the truth. Landowners within the boundaries of proposed Heritage Areas are left in the dark throughout the entire process. Why? Because each and every Heritage Area bill refuses to include simple written notification to property owners. Seemingly the Park Service and their management "partners" are not too eager to share all the good news with the local citizenry.

I have personally been in meetings with congressional staffers to discuss Heritage Areas, specifically the staff of former Congressman Frank Wolfe, a major proponent of Heritage Areas. I asked them if they intended to notify affected landowners living inside the boundaries of a specific Heritage Area. They looked at me like I had two heads. They shuffled their feet and looked down at the table and then said, "there's no way to do that." "It would be too costly." "How could we reach everyone?" And then they quickly moved to change the subject.

Of course the ability is there. The mailman delivers to each and every one of the homes in the designated area every day. The fact is, they don't want to tell residents in advance, they might object. And that would disrupt the "process." No matter how noble a project may sound, alarm bells should go off when proponents want to enforce their vision in secret.

If these National Heritage Areas were truly driven by local enthusiasm there would be no reason to keep the plans secret. Instead, local enthusiasm would have attracted and generated local funding to create local Heritage Areas. But, National Heritage Areas depend on federal tax dollars because they lack local interest, and not a single Heritage Area has ever succeeded in attracting that interest throughout their entire infinite lives.

The federal money is the villain. If local residents just wanted to honor an area for its historic or cultural achievements, a simple resolution from Congress and a plaque at the county line could do that. That alone would help bring in the promised tourism, of course, it's not about that. It's about money, control, and agendas.

There are currently 49 National Heritage Areas across the country so far. Here are just a few tidbits about them and how they operate:

- The entire city of **Baltimore** is a National Heritage Area.

- The entire State of Tennessee is covered by the **Tennessee Civil War National Heritage Area.**

- In Waterloo, Iowa, which is a major part of the nation's breadbasket and home of John Deer tractors, **Silos and Smoke Stacks Heritage Area** was sold as a means to "honor" the farmers. Since its creation, not much has changed for farmers inside the Heritage Area. There has been no focus by its leaders to actually help farmers by keeping taxes down or helping them compete with oversees competitors. Instead, they are essentially putting American farmland in a museum. But Waterloo's slumlords who owned dilapidated buildings and empty store fronts in the downtown area did receive massive taxpayer funding to fix up their buildings and raise their rents. There are strict controls on use of the buildings, including how they can be repaired or upgraded. Grants flow like water to special interests in the name of historic preservation. There are educational programs paid for by taxpayers for such vital subjects as why manure is important to farm life. And in the process, downtown Waterloo has been designated as an historic area. There's only one problem -- nothing much of historic significance actually happened in downtown Waterloo. As usual, follow the money.

- Along the Mississippi River there are two Heritage Areas, **Mississippi Delta National Heritage Area and Mississippi Gulf Coast National Heritage Area**. Now here is a region rich in history. There must be all kinds of good things happening along the mother of all rivers. Well, today you won't find people participating in one of the grand historic traditions of the river – living on riverboats. There were once whole generations of river people living on such boats. Talk about American Heritage – right out of Mark Twain. But, back in the 1990s, as part of Bill Clinton's American Heritage Rivers Initiative, those living on houseboats were moved off the river. Certain other boat traffic and river activities were also curtailed. It was all in the name of environmental protection, of course. In addition, the traditional flood plain designations were moved to an extreme distance from the river, making it impossible for existing homes to get flood insurance, and stopping any further building along the river. This was land-use planning – right out of the Sustainable Development plan and the Wildlands project. So, the Heritage Areas were used to honor what? Certainly not life on the river. They are essentially putting the Mississippi River in a museum.

- In West Virginia we find the **National Coal Heritage Area**. Introduced in 1996 by Congressman Rahall, it was sold as a way to honor the coal industry. Apparently, Rahall thought that since the miners have all lost their jobs to environmentalism, perhaps he can make up for it by throwing a few extra bucks their way to give tours of their bankrupt area. Take this challenge – just try to mine a lump of coal inside the National Coal Heritage Area. Not on your life. Restricted. Taboo. In short, they have put West Virginia coal in a museum. Do you get the picture?

- **The Journey Through Hallowed Ground Heritage Area** created a 175- mile-long federal corridor, encompassing portions of Virginia, Maryland and Pennsylvania. Of course it was sold as a means to honor and protect some of the most precious historic areas of the nation, running from Jefferson's Monticello to the Gettysburg battlefield. The chief sponsor was Virginia Republican, Congressman Frank Wolfe, who promoted it saying, "The Journey Through Hallowed Ground Corridor holds more American history than any other region in the country and its recognition as a National Heritage Area will elevate its national prominence as deserved." He also claimed that it was an "effort to create economic opportunity by celebrating the unique place in American history the region holds." **There's one major problem with all of those promises. Every one of those designated sites are already preserved and are major tourist attractions.** The only difference is that now all of the homes, businesses and towns inside the borders of the Heritage Area are subjected to the control of the National Park Service. The legislation assigned the usual "management entity" consisting of the Journey Through Hallowed Ground Partnership. This was an umbrella group of preservation activists and lobbyists which helped move the legislation through Congress. They now stand to directly benefit from the power gained from the bills passage. Also strongly pushing for passage was the Department of Interior, which saw the Heritage Area as a means to oversee development and land-use in the area. An additional example of a group that pushed hard to establish the JTHG Heritage Area was the National Trust for Historic Preservation. Another was Scenic America.

These last two named are national groups that have very benign titles but very serious missions. But are they interested in just historic preservation or massive top-down controlled land-use restrictions?

Well, here is some insight into the answer to that question. You may have heard about Measure 37 in Oregon passed in 2004. This is a basic property rights initiative that isn't very hard to support no matter who you are, even if you are indifferent to property rights. All it does is reaffirm the Fifth Amendment to the Constitution. It simply says that when state or local governments pass laws that take away somebody's property rights and devalue their property, those states and local governments have to compensate that person, or if they can't compensate then they have to waive the regulation. It is that simple. It basically stops state and local governments from stealing private land.

It passed overwhelmingly despite a massive campaign by Greens to try to prevent it, and it was even upheld by the Oregon Supreme Court. And groups like the National Trust for Historic Preservation and Scenic America actually fought this ballot initiative tooth and nail. It had nothing to do with historic preservation per se, or a scenic America, but obviously these groups have a much bigger agenda they are trying to protect.

Of course proponents usually claim that Heritage Areas are just honorary designations that are designed to enhance tourism. But the bills that they actually write and support have very little to do with driving tourism to the region. Tourism is typically a result of good advertising. The bills have very little to do with advertising, but they have a lot to do with giving these groups power to influence land-use decisions.

When property owners express concern that their property could be taken in the process the proponents always have a ready-made answer. Don't worry, they say, as they quickly point to language in the Heritage Area bills that assure property rights protections. Former Congressman Wolfe actually wrote property rights language into the Heritage Area legislation saying "Nothing in this subtitle…abridges the right of any property owner… including the right to refrain from participating in any plan, project, program, or activity conducted within the National Heritage Area…"

In other words, that language is written to give assurance that that you actually have the right to opt out of the Heritage Area – so, of course, there is absolutely no threat to your property rights. However, further study has shown that this language is basically worthless.

The fact is, it is physically impossible to opt out of an official government boundary when you live inside it. It is also impossible to simply declare that you are going to opt out of any of the land-use regulations, down-zoning, or other restrictions that result from the Heritage Area designation. When your local government passes legislation that affects your property rights because of a Heritage Area, you can't go to them and say, wait a minute. I opt out. They will just laugh.

You don't believe that to be true? Then go down to the County Supervisor's meeting next week and tell them you want to opt out of any rules that say you have to have a building permit for a new porch. See how that works for you!

It must be understood that the Heritage Area affects all the land in the designated area, not just recognized historic sights. The federal designation, made from congressional legislation creating federal regulations and oversight through the National Park Service, requires a contract between state and local governmental entities and the Secretary of the Interior. That contract is to manage the land-use of the region for preservation. That means federal control and zoning, either directly, under the terms of the "management pact" or indirectly. Either way the federal government controls the land-use.

Such "indirect" control is the real danger. In spite of the specific language in the bill which states property rights will be protected, the true damage to homeowners may well come from the private groups, non-governmental organizations (NGOs) and preservation agencies which receive public funds through the Park Service to implement the polices of the Heritage Area.

The funds flowing from the Park Service provide a seductive pork-barrel system for NGO advocacy groups to enforce their vision of development of the Heritage Area. The experience with more than twenty-four such

Heritage Areas now in existence nationwide clearly shows such groups will convert this money into political activism to encourage local community and county governments to pass and enforce strict zoning laws. While the tactic makes it appear that home rule is fully in force, removing blame from the federal designation, the impact is fully the fault of the Heritage Areas designation. The result is that private property owners' rights are diminished and much of the local land-use brought to a standstill.

Zoning and land-use policies are and should be local decisions to be made by locally elected officials who are directly accountable to the citizens they represent. However, National Heritage Areas corrupt this inherently local procedure by adding federal dollars, federal oversight, and federal mandates to the mix.

Specifically, when an area is designated a National Heritage Area, the Park Service partners with environmental or historic preservation special interest groups to "restore, preserve, and manage" anything and everything that is naturally, culturally, historically, and recreationally significant to the Heritage Area. This sweeping mandate ensures that every square inch of land, whether private or public is a prime target for regulation or acquisition.

But what of the promised tourism that is supposed to help local communities? Many members of Congress admit they support the concept of Heritage Areas for that very reason: jobs created by people visiting their little part of the world to see why it's so special. Is it true?

As already stated, those boundaries have consequences – strict control over the use of the land. Certain industries may prove to be too "dirty" to satisfy environmental special interests. Eventually such existing industrial operations will find themselves regulated or taxed to a point of forcing them to leave or go out of business. Property that is locked away for preservation is no longer productive and no longer provides the community with tax dollars. Roads most assuredly will be closed (to protect the integrity of the historic area). That means land is locked away from private development, diminishing growth for the community. It also means hunting and recreational use of the land will most certainly be curtailed.

Eventually, such restrictions will take away the community's economic base. Communities with sagging economies become run-down and uninviting. Preservation zoning and lack of jobs force ordinary people to move away. Experience has shown tourism rarely materializes as promised. And it's never enough to save an area economically.

These are the reasons why the specific language in the Heritage Area legislation designed to protect private property rights is basically meaningless to the actual outcome. While the land is not specifically locked away in the name of the federal designation, its very existence creates the pressure on local government to act. The result is the same.

The fact is the Heritage Area designations are completely unnecessary. Most of the historic sites are already under the control of the National Park Service, including Thomas Jefferson's home, Manassas Battlefield (Bull Run – to you Yankees) and Gettysburg Battlefield. Several other birthplaces and significant historic sights are also well preserved.

The boundaries of Gettysburg, for example, were specifically laid out by the men who fought there. Most of the land was private and was donated to the park by the owners more than 125 years ago. While protecting private property and the farms across which the battle raged, they preserved the most significant parts into what today is today a comprehensive memorial.

This old system of voluntary contributions and non-coerced purchases of the land is far superior to a process that uses the massive power of the federal government to rip out the roots of property owners who are simply unlucky enough to live near something that should be special and precious. Given their way, many preservationist special interest groups would set out to turn the entire nation into a museum.

In contrast, it is significant to note that today, as a coercive preservation policy is imposed in Gettysburg, the community has seen the near destruction of its once vital downtown where private businesses are being forced out. Many parts of downtown now are void of significant businesses like clothing shops or hardware stores. Most businesses in the downtown area today are restaurants and tee-shirt shops designed for the tourist industry. That's not the way for a town to build a solid economic future.

Every step of land had something from the past occur on it. But let us remember, those who fought on these fields of "hallowed ground" did so to protect our liberty, including ownership of private property. One must ask how they would react to huge government restrictions over the land now, simply because they fought there. One can envision them again taking up arms to free it from government clutches.

It's interesting to note that the recent protests demanding to remove historic statues have not been opposed by a single Heritage Area management entity. So much for actually defending our American Heritage.

The forces of Sustainable Development have no intention of honoring true American heritage. The rational for preservation legislation is simply another excuse to hide the real goal – reorganizing human society for complete control. The American heritage of individual liberty, free enterprise, and private property aren't even in the equation.

The sustainablists have been after the farmers and ranchers for decades. They've done some nasty, underhanded things in the past. tTake Wayne Hage, a rancher. The Forest Service put non-native elk on his land to compete with his cattle for grass and water; they canceled his grazing permits, auctioned off more than 100 cows, and on and on. All because someone wanted his land, but didn't want to pay for it. Now they are getting sneakier, nastier, and more underhanded if that is possible.

THE ATTACK ON AMERICAN AGRICULTURE
HOW THE BEEF INDUSTRY IS CONTROLLED BY ANTI-BEEF ZEALOTS

Attacks on American agriculture are growing rapidly. The beef industry has actually come under the control of radical environmentalists such as the World Wildlife Fund, which promote an agenda to eliminate beef consumption, a major goal of the Green New Deal. Individual ranchers and beef growers are at the mercy of once-trusted representatives such as the National Cattlemen's Beef Association to represent their interests and protect them. Instead, these representatives, as well as nearly the entire industry, including the packing companies that hold the key to the marketplace, are siding with the enemies of beef.

Meanwhile, other farm communities are experiencing the same betrayal as they are being forced to accept "sustainable" regulations that raise their costs, lock away large parts of once productive areas of their farms for wild animal habitat, and force acceptance of climate change policies such as the use of wind and solar energy systems that are expensive and unworkable. **In Lyon Country, Kansas, new zoning proposals would convert all agriculture tax bases to commercial. The policy would require special permits to own any livestock,** repair wire fences, fence posts, etc. and require rural houses to be on city water and sewer (at farmers expense). Again, these farmers are being betrayed by the very agriculture representatives on whom they have always relied. Twenty-one such organizations, such as the National Farmers Union, American Farm

Bureau Federation, United Egg Producers, and many more, are all now on the radical sustainable bandwagon, systematically imposing the Green New Deal agenda that will eventually destroy their industry.

American Policy Center has been working to sound the alarm that the American beef industry is under massive assault from the radical environmental and animal rights movements that seek its ultimate destruction. In the rural areas, the Greens' selected tactic is to control the land, water, energy, and population of the Earth. To achieve these ends requires, among other things, the destruction of private property rights and elimination of every individual's ability to make personal life-style choices, including personal diet. That's why the American Beef Industry is such a necessary target.

First they had to create a false crisis so everyone would feel the need to take immediate action. Their tactic was to declare that beef was not sustainable – not as a product to grow — and not as a healthy food for people to consume. This put the cattlemen in the middle of a pincer move between the radical environmental movement seeking control of land use, and the Animal Rights movement which demanded the end of the consumption of animals.

Their most effective tactic is the never-ending threat of Global Warming. Say the Greens, global warming is driven by energy consumption and cows are energy guzzlers. That's because you need trucks to ship the cattle to market. In their vision of a perfect sustainable community, nothing would be shipped in to consume. Everything needed would be produce right in the city. The Soviet Union called those gulags. And they starved.

So, these are some of the reasons why it's charged that beef is unsustainable and must be ruled, regulated and frankly, eliminated. These are charges brought by anti-beef vegans who want all beef consumption stopped. In cahoots, are environmentalists who seek to stop the private ownership and use of land under the excuse of environmental protection.

Incredibly, to help deliver the cattle industry into line with this world view the National Cattlemen's Beef Association (NCBA) has accepted the imposition of the Global Roundtable for Sustainable Beef, which is heavily influenced, if not controlled, by the World Wildlife Fund (WWF), one of the most powerful environmental organizations in the world and a leader of the United Nations Environmental Program (UNEP), which basically sets the rules for global environmental policy.

This is the same World Wildlife Fund that has openly stated its opposition to beef production. They insist that to "*Save the Earth it is demanded that we change human consumption habits away from beef.*" Keep in mind that the WWF is working diligently with environmental groups to gain control of the Northern Great Plains which spans more than 180 million acres across five states and into Canada. It's part of the Wildlands Project. Under the false flag of wildlife restoration and conservation, the true purpose is to remove domestic livestock from the grasslands.

When you submit to powerful forces like the WWF, which has a specific political agenda for your future, you are actually giving them the keys to public lands and your private property. Put another way, what if it was the law that you had to have the approval of your competition to start a new business? That's the reality of dealing with the WWF and its Roundtable. Sustainability means a one size fits all straightjacket that destroys individual creativity and thought. It's the death of innovation, progress and the very roots of free enterprise.

So why would the NCBA, the organization so many cattlemen have trusted to represent their interests, allow itself to be used as the Judas Goat to lead the beef industry to sustainable slaughter? Well, recently, the NCBA issued an article in an attempt to explain its reasons. Said the article, titled Why Sustainability? *"…it's difficult to accept that outsiders have influence in how we're doing business. Increasingly, though, that's exactly what's happening. In the case of sustainability, consumers have decided they ought to have a better understanding and perhaps even a say in how their food is produced."*

Is the NCBA saying that its purpose is to let people who have no idea how to grow beef decide how it's to be grown? Do we now throw out reality for someone's misguided feelings? The article's author, NCBA Vice President of Government Affairs Ethan Lane, explains his reason is *that "the natural evolution of that interest was a conversation about sustainability and whether a product is viewed by consumers as sustainable."* He goes on to say that *"Groups like WWF and many others have tremendous influence over corporations in the United States and foreign countries."*

Here's a little secret. Allowing the "conversation" on sustainability is the TRAP! The reason there is confusion and conversation about sustainability is because the industries that know how to produce their products haven't taken the lead to explain their own needs and explain to the general public why they do what they do. Instead they have submitted to green bullies and remained silent, letting the bullies determine the argument.

Oh, but the NCBA has a remedy for that – just for the cattlemen, of course. Says Lane, proudly, *"NCBA participates in the Global Roundtable for Sustainable Beef and the US Roundtable for Sustainable Beef … to make certain that the voice of cattlemen and women is heard in conversations about cattle and beef production."* In other words, he's claiming that NCBA has gained a seat at the table to stand just for the beef industry!

Well, how's that working for them now that they have a seat at the table? In short, cattlemen have been forced to accept an endless list of rules and regulations to make them sustainably certified, or acceptable for market under the new rules. To continue to produce, cattlemen will be required to submit to a centralized control of regulations that will never end and will always increase in costs and needless waste of manpower.

To follow the sustainable rules and be officially certified, cattle growers must agree to have much of the use of their land reduced to provide for wildlife habitat. That's the start. Just a little bit. And little bit more. Just to help improve your product and help the environment. Then come strict controls over water use and grazing areas. This forces smaller herds, making the process more expensive and economically unviable for the industry. In addition, there is a new layer of industry and government inspectors, creating a massive bureaucratic overreach, causing yet more costs for catttlemen. On its website, the WWF calls that "consulting" with the cattle growers.

The Roundtable rules are now enforced on them through the packing companies. As a result, their ability to get cattle to market is getting harder every day – unless they comply with rules that are simply designed to put them out of business. And of course, if cattle growers do comply, they will certainly go out of business.

But the NCBA says it is protecting them because they have a seat at the table!! Oh yes, the cattle growers voice is being heard alright! Bull! Over the past several years, industry after industry has been subjugated and destroyed using this exact game plan. Submit, be silenced, be destroyed. This is why McDonalds is a major backer of the Roundtable. First they were attacked by the animal rights thugs. They submitted and started granting their demands. Walmart, same thing. Now they all cling to and promote the Roundtable out of fear. Home Depot did the same thing to help destroy the timber industry. In addition, the oil industry started donating massive funds to the green movement, while ignoring the very groups that have been fighting for their cause. It's not black mail – it's green mail!

Go along to get along. They all decided they needed a seat at the table too. Not one ever stood up and said

NO! And not one has ever seen their industry or their business improve by going along with these thugs. That's why the WWF calls the shots. FEAR.

The only reason the World Wildlife Fund and their green buddies have any influence or power is because every industry, every corporation, every business they attack gives it to them. We've allowed them to become terrorists on our markets, spreading fear and lies.

So this question must be asked of the cattlemen who are suffering under this oppression, do you understand the game that is being played on you? You are not supposed to win – you are supposed to quietly comply and then die. You cannot reason with them. You cannot compromise with them – because they have a very specific agenda. You follow their rules. They own the game. The fact is this is really a game of strip poker and the NCBA has left you all in your underwear!

There are only four main packing companies in the United States. They are all part of the Roundtable, working side by side with the World Wildlife Fund to force sustainable certification on the cattle growers. Hiding behind the Roundtable and its so-called certification, the packers that have played the game have become near monopolies able to destroy any attempts to create competition to them. Tragically, the packers themselves don't understand that they too have been played and have signed their own death warrant because when beef is banned the packers will be gone too.

Of course, one of the first tactics was to remove the country of origin labeling from packaging so that consumers have no idea where their product is coming from. As the packers force these expensive, unnecessary, and unworkable sustainable certifications on American cattlemen they are systematically bringing in cheaper product from other countries. As a result there is a noticeable rise in news reports of recalls of diseased chicken and beef in American grocery stores.

This then is the situation that is threatening the American beef industry. If one reads the documents and statements from the World Wildlife Fund, the United Nations Environment Program and others involved, it is not hard to realize that the true goal is not to make beef better, but to ban it altogether. And believe it or not, the fact that some of the inferior, foreign beef sold in stores is lower grade and even diseased, works in the Sustainablists favor too – because the ultimate goal is to stop the consumption of beef. So fear of dangerous beef is a valuable tool.

However, the beef industry cannot recover by relying only on legal and legislative fights. The cattle growers must get the American consumer behind them. If consumers are confused, as Mr. Lane claims, that's because they have never heard the truth. They have only heard the fear spread in the deliberate political agenda of the vegans, animal rights movement, and environmental propagandists. By the way, these are people who would never buy beef, no matter how sustainably certified you become. But if the industry insists that cattlemen submit to them, then the industry will most certainly lose its loyal customers as they are scared into dumping beef from their tables.

Here is the bottom line of every cattleman, processor, restaurant chain and super market that depends on beef must do! Drastic, dramatic action must be taken to reach the consumers with the truth. Consumers, armed with that truth, must become outraged about the real reasons prices are soaring and quality is going down, as the danger to their own health is increasing. Consumers must be warned taught that a force is loose in our country which is robbing them of the freedom of choice for their own dinner plate and especially for their own health. Cattlemen know these facts – but the average American doesn't.

This is a crisis situation which calls for drastic, creative measures. First of all, the image of the great American cowboy that we all grew up with would never submit to roving gangs of marauders who intend to steal their rangelands or rustle their cattle. Those cowboys wouldn't plead for a seat at the table so they could beg for mercy and the right to exist. In fact, their first inclination would be to kick over that table and send these whiny wimps packing!

The only way to stop the brute force of the World Wildlife Fund is to destroy them before they destroy the beef industry! How can that be done? Expose their game. Tell the truth to the public – the consumer. Make the WWF the target – not beef! Refuse to surrender or comply.

The non-election Regional government is the key to just about evrerything. The president, or whatever our majestic ruler is going to be called, will have a phalanx of toadies who will run the regions as order by Washington.. All of the topics below are building toward the regional form of government.

You can use these to explain to 'willing to hear' councilpersons and commissioners why we are seeing these new must-have programs in our towns and counties.

NON-ELECTED REGIONAL GOVERNMENT

Where did all this come from?

In the mid-1960s, author Jo Hindman wrote abou*t* Urban Renewal and metro-planning. In her book, *Blame Metro*, she said, "Much is written about the incognito warfare on United States soil which public officials and their accomplices are waging to wrest private property from landowners. The strategy is to make property ownership so unbearable by harassment through building inspections, remodeling orders, fines and jailings, that owners give up in despair and sell to land redevelopers at cut-rate prices. *Positive municipal codes are the weapons in the warfare.*"[1]

Note, Hindman **wrote that in 1966,** yet it fully applies to today's attacks on private property; many of the same strategies are being used, they just "changed the names to protect the guilty."

She writes, "'Strengthening county government' is a hackneyed Regional phrase indicating that the Regional take-over has begun. . ... Planning assistance subsidized by Federal money leads small cities and counties into direct obedience under a **regional master plan**. *Land use rights are literally stolen* from landowners when zoning is applied to land."

In 1949, the Communitarian forebears of today's planners wrote the original plans that were designed to free us of our property under the National Housing Act. Back then it was the American Society of Planning Officials, the American Institute of Planners, and the National Planning Association. Today it is the American Planning Association (APA), which was formed in 1978 by combining the American Institute of Planners and the Society of Planning Officials. As you can see by this footnote, the APA brags that **they were meddling in our private affairs since 1909**, in fact here are the exact words, "On May 21-22, **1909,** 43 planners met in Washington, D.C., at the first National Planning Conference. This event is considered to be **the birth of the planning movement in America.**" A sad day for the American republic.

Mimicking today's ICLEI V.P. Harvey Ruvin, the 60s' American Institute of Planners "makes no bones about its socialist stance regarding land; its constitution states AIP's '**particular sphere of activity shall be the planning of the unified development of urban communities and their environs and of states, regions, and the nation as expressed through determination of the comprehensive arrangement of land uses and land occupancy and the regulation thereof.**" Hindman says, "The present-day (1960s) crew of planners, **drawing no line between public and private property, believe that land-use control should be vested in government and that public planners should have sole right to control the use of all land.**"

That is not just similar to what is going on today; that is exactly what is happening. Why? Because the sons, daughters and cronies of the puppeteers that were pulling the strings back at the beginning and middle of the 20th Century are pulling the strings of today's planners. We just have a new generation of the same treacherous, thieving scheme updated with new-fangled, high-tech sounding names for the same old land (**and people**) control mechanisms.

THE TRANSECT

A 2002 APA Journal article gives the original meaning of transect as: <u>a cut or path through part of the environment showing a range of different habitats. Biologists and ecologists use transects to study the many symbiotic elements that contribute to habitats where certain plants and animals thrive.</u>

Planners took that technique, one that was designed for studying flora and fauna, and tweaked it to apply to humans. In fact, the tweak was more a wrenching, actually it is more in the line of suspending critical thinking to superimpose the artificial and nonsensical process of the transect on humans and their mobilization. Control the land and the water and you control humanity itself.

Under the biological study, a transect shows where certain flora and fauna thrive, exist somewhat readily, or barely subsist in the different habitats from the arctic to tropical areas. With great literary(?) license, planners take the definition of biologic transect and, just like Oliver Stone rewrites history, these planners are rewriting biology; they want to play an active role in the phylogeny of *homo sapiens*, in fact they want to devolve it. One of the problems here is that their fairy tale is being used to take property rights (and thus liberty) from man and make him a slave. Laws should not be based upon make-believe. Yet this country, no the entire world, is being redesigned using Communitarians' far-fetched, pseudo-utopian desires to sate the global elites' desire to control the entire globe.

Look at their definition of transect for people and land planning: "Human beings also thrive in different habitats. Some people prefer urban centers and would suffer in a rural place, while others thrive in the rural or suburban zones. Before the automobile, American development patterns were walkable, and transects within towns and city neighborhoods revealed areas that were less urban and more urban in character. This urbanism could be analyzed as natural transects are analyzed."

To compare humans in differing habitats with flora or fauna is preposterous hubris, and especially because the planners are using apples and orangutans: "some people prefer urban centers and would suffer in a rural place," does not mean the same thing as the biological transect means. The suffering would be a mental fabrication and would be such that to call it suffering in the same sense as plants or animals outside their natural habitat is absurd.

The planners also extol the virtues of the time before the automobile, "*American development patterns were walkable, and transects within towns and city neighborhoods revealed areas that were less urban and <u>more</u>*

urban in character. This urbanism could be analyzed as natural transects are analyzed." **As if what we have today is "unnatural."** What these planners keep forgetting (and want us to forget also) is that we humans are part of nature and thus what we are and what we do _is natural._ Unlike other animals, we humans have a moral and cognitive brain. Our brain is what provides us with the necessary tools we need to survive and prosper, and one of those tools is the automobile.

So we have a convoluted, computer-modeled construct of what the entire ecosystem of the world should be and is called the Transect. But as with everything else in this New World Order NewSpeak, that really isn't the truth. No, they did not sit down with the details of biological transect and translate it _via_ computer modeling to a human/development version. What they did was take _The Ideal Communist City_ (see sources in Appendices) and figured out how to sell it to the American public by superimposing it over their Transect model.

The APA describes the Transect as "a geographical cross-section of a region used to reveal a sequence of environments." For human environments, this cross-section can be used to identify urban character, a continuum that ranges from rural to urban. In transect planning, this range of environments is the basis for organizing the components of the built world: building, lot, land use, street, and all of the other physical elements of the human habitat. Pay close attention to that last sentence, "_the basis for organizing the components of the built world._" In traditional understanding of English, that means telling us where each component of our lives goes; we don't get to choose where we build our homes unless they in the area designated by planners as the same sentence continues, "building, lot, land use, street, and _all of the other physical elements of the human habitat._" _Translation: w_e will be told what and where we may build or even _if_ we may build, and how we will live in that habitat.

To continue from the APA article, "In transect planning, the essential task is to find the main qualities of immersive environments, …. Once these are discovered, transect planning principles are applied **to rectify the inappropriate intermixing of rural and urban elements — better known as sprawl.** This is done by **eliminating the 'urbanizing of the rural'. . . or, equally damaging, the 'ruralizing of the urban'** into discrete categories. This approach is also dictated by the requirement **that human habitats fit within the _language of our current approach to land regulation (i.e., zoning)._**"

The discrete categories of the transect continuum run from Rural Preserve, Rural Reserve, Sub-Urban, General Urban, Urban Center to Urban Core. **Understand that the Rural Preserve is the Wildlands, the area humans will be forbidden to enter**, and the Rural Reserve will be the connecting corridors to the Reserve area, i.e., corridors for fauna movement and human use will be highly restricted.

Remember, as pointed out at the beginning of this article, the Communitarians, or global elites, introduced the zoning and planning systems used in this country. Now that they have gotten the American public inured to "planning," they want to move us to the next step — where they plan every aspect of our lives through planning. To do so, they have to pretend that the original zones and plans came from us, the people, so they can say they need to throw the old ones out and introduce a whole new system. We are told, "_The most important obstacle to overcome is the restrictive and incorrect zoning codes currently in force in most municipalities._ Current codes do not allow New Urbanism to be built, but do allow sprawl. Adopting a Traditional Neighborhood Design (TND) ordinance and/**or a system of 'smart codes' allows New Urbanism to be built easily without having to rewrite existing codes.**"

New Urbanism (transect planning plus) deals with everything but property rights. (Actually property rights are verboten in this not-so-brave new world they are bringing us, so they ignore them because property rights will not exist in the not to distant future if we do not put a stop to this.) It is Sustainable Development written in capitals and boldface. And how do they plan on doing this? **The most effective way to implement New Urbanism is to plan for it, and write it into zoning and development codes. This directs <u>all future development into this form</u>.**

A sample the New Urbanism (Habitat III) planning (in their words):

"The New Urban Agenda presents a paradigm shift based on the science of cities; it lays out standards and principles for the planning, construction, development, management, and improvement of urban areas along its five main pillars of implementation: national urban policies, urban legislation and regulations, urban planning and design, local economy and municipal finance, and local implementation. It is a resource for every level of government, from national to local; for civil society organizations; the private sector; constituent groups; and for all who call the urban spaces of the world "home" to realize this vision.

The New Urban Agenda incorporates a new recognition of the correlation between good urbanization and development. It underlines the linkages between good urbanization and job creation, livelihood opportunities, and improved quality of life, which should be included in every urban renewal policy and strategy. This further highlights the connection between the New Urban Agenda and the 2030 Agenda for Sustainable Development, especially Goal 11 on sustainable cities and communities.

ATTACKS ON PRIVATE PROPERTY

Private property rights represent the greatest gateway to personal independence and wealth of individuals. It's the root of the free market system. So it's no surprise that private property it a major target of the Green New Deal. These are just some of the programs that are attacking private property rights. Keep in mind that, without the right to property, we are slaves. Use these for letters to editors, research for your city and country bureaucrats, and most important – to give to friends and neighbors to educate them on what will be a 'new normal' that won't be worth living in.

BANNING ZONING FOR SINGLE-FAMILY HOMES

We are witnessing a complete transformation of our cities as city councils and county commissions rush to create Smart Growth communities, which create massive high-rise buildings designed to eliminate the need for personal transportation such as cars. Instead, massive federal grant programs are pushing plans for light-rail trains, trolleys and bike lanes. The point is, we can all walk or ride such transportation to work and shopping, thereby reducing the global warming threat, as called for in the Green New Deal.

One of the main indicators used by economists to measure the health of the nation's economy is housing starts – the number of private homes being built around the nation. In 2018 housing starts fell in all four regions of the nation, representing the biggest drop since 2016.

While many economists point to issues such as higher material costs as a reason for the drop in housing starts, a much more ominous reason may be emerging. Across the nation, city councils and state legislatures are beginning to remove zoning protections for single-family neighborhoods, claiming they are racist discrimination designed to keep certain minorities out of such neighborhoods. In response to these charges some government officials are calling for the end of single-family homes in favor of multiple family apartments.

- Minneapolis, Minnesota: the city council is moving to remove zoning that protects single-family neighborhoods, instead planning to add apartment buildings in the mix. The mayor actually said such zoning was "devised as a legal way to keep black Americans and other minorities from moving into certain neighborhoods". Racist, social injustice are the charges.

- Chicago, Illinois: So-called "affordable housing" advocates have filed a federal complaint against the longtime tradition of allowing City Aldermen veto power over most development proposals in their wards, charging that it promotes discrimination by keeping low-income minorities from moving into affluent white neighborhoods. Essentially the complaint seeks to remove the Aldermen's ability to represent their own constituents.

- Baltimore, Maryland: The NAACP filed a suit against the city charging that Section 8 public housing causes ghettos because they are all put into the same areas of town. They won the suit and now the city must spend millions of dollars to move such housing into more affluent neighborhoods. In addition, landlords are no longer permitted to ask potential tenants if they can afford the rent on their properties.

- Oregon: Speaker of the Oregon House of Representatives Tina Kotek (D-Portland) introduced and passed legislation that will end single-family zoning in cities of 10,000 or more. She claims there is a housing shortage crisis and that economic and racial segregation are caused by zoning restrictions.

Such identical policies don't just simultaneously spring up across the country by accident. There is a force behind it. The root of these actions are found in "fair housing" policies dictated by the federal Housing and Urban Development Agency (HUD). The affected communities have all taken HUD grants. There is very specific language in those grants that suggest single-family homes are a cause of discrimination. Specifically, through the HUD program called Affirmatively Furthering Fair Housing (AFFH), the agency is taking legal action against communities that use "discriminating zoning ordinances that discourage the development of affordable, multifamily housing…". The suits are becoming a widely used enforcement tool for the agency.

As the Smart Growth high-rise buildings begin to tower over the cities, a new movement has begun to eliminate single-family neighborhoods. City governments, such as **Minneapolis, have declared that zoning for single-family neighborhoods is racist** as folks who live in these homes are self-segregating themselves from people they don't want to live next to. Their solution is to eliminate such zoning and allow the building of "affordable" apartment buildings in those neighborhoods. In other words, government housing that will have a severe impact on the home value and equity that was to be personal wealth for the owners. **Oregon, using the excuse of a housing crisis, has become the first state to fully ban protections for single-family homes**.

Senator Corey Booker, Julian Castro, and Senator Elizabeth Warren have all called for pressure from the federal government to be placed on local governments to demand more development of affordable housing high-rises in single-family neighborhoods. A UCLA assistant professor of urban planning, Kian Goh, asserts, **"If we want to keep cities safe in the face of climate changes, we need to seriously question the ideal of private home ownership."** Socialist Bernie Sanders has called for "Housing for All" with a $2.5 trillion taxpayer price tag. **The bottom line to such Green New Deal housing policies IS THAT EVENTUALLY ALL HOMES WILL BE GOVERNMENT HOUSING.**

EMINENT DOMAIN

"Philadelphia is currently using eminent domain to take <u>more than 1,300 private properties</u> and develop them into a mix of market-rate and affordable housing units. The move is causing controversy among proponents of private property, but it's the kind of bold action cities will need to turn to more if they want to build the amount of affordable housing needed. Another option would be to do <u>what Hugo Chavez did</u> when he came to power: seize the land owned by the rich, not pay them for it, and give it to the poor." Peter Moskowitz, "Evict the Rich, *The Outline,* 2017

It is vital to note that in the Smart Growth utopias there is a class of people being created that live differently than most of the rest of us – differently at least until Sustainable Development policy drives us all to be equally controlled.

We find them in the inner cities. This class is composed of the ethnic, minority, and lower income communities. There you find raw anger, hate, and a growing sense of hopelessness for generations of people. Why? They are the first to feel the full impact of the top-down control of raging government overreach. They are told where to live, how to live, and how much they will be allowed to live on, all dictated to them by government.

Their neighborhoods are the first to be targeted for "improvement" by Smart Growth policies. These are usually established neighborhoods with older buildings, probably in need of improvement and updating. The planners hunger to get their hands on these areas, so they create the grand "vision" for its "improvement," including new buildings, new shopping, new opportunities.

Yet here is the reality. The folks living there are close to their families and life- long friends. Some do own their property, perhaps handed down from older generations. Some own small businesses -- bakeries, restaurants, perhaps even a few operate small manufacturing companies. They aren't getting rich, but they have their own familiar culture, traditions, and way of life; they are comfortable.

Now come the city leaders who see them just as a specific voter block. And THEY have a plan to save these poor, miserable souls from the ravages they have suffered from the unfair, racist system that has kept them down.

The plan is to bulldoze their neighborhoods, destroying their culture, shutting their businesses and wiping out their homes and private property through the power of eminent domain. These entire neighborhoods will be replaced with brand new condos that reach for the sky, complete with corporate stores, restaurants and even offices.

What happens to the people who used to live there? They can't afford these new condos. Ah… the city leaders have a plan for them -- affordable public housing. Those who have lost their jobs or businesses are now forced onto public welfare programs and all is well. They are well taken care of in our Smart Growth utopia.

The fact is the NAACP was partly correct in their suit against Baltimore when they said Section 8 public housing causes ghettos. Throwing whole communities into huge public housing projects naturally creates high crime rates and hopelessness. Desperate people trying to find ways to get ahead usually are given little choice but to turn to crime.

The welfare system in the United States is at fault as it dictates to the recipients that they are not allowed to earn much money or own any business enterprise while in the system or they will lose that government subsidy. So, instead, an underground economy begins to grow. But forced to be underground, that economy is going to be predominately illegal --drugs, prostitution, stolen goods. Eventually, brutal gangs like MS13 take over the growing crime economy as they threaten and intimidate the locals. Life becomes drudgery and dangerous in the growing blighted areas purposely created by government.

Such is life in the public housing programs where there is hopelessness and despair as these folks see no way out. Government control rather than personal choice and initiative rules the day in more and more neighborhoods in more and more cities as a result of the Smart Growth utopian bulldozers and the weapon called Sustainable Development. That government control was never intended to make these neighborhoods places for the inhabitants to thrive and make something of themselves.

RENT CONTROLS ON LANDLORDS

As noted earlier, as the attack grows on such private homes, most of the high-rise pack and stack Smart Growth buildings are rental properties. The attack on landlords has begun, as city governments demand that these property owners are charging too much for rent. Of course, the landlords are simply trying to earn a profit on their properties after taxes have been raised, and regulations have dictated an endless list of rules that force the owners to spend more and more money. Not fair, say the Green New Dealers. So more communities are forcing rent controls on the landlords. **Baltimore, Maryland says landlords should not be allowed to even ask prospective tenets if they can afford the rent. That, too, is racist.**

Then there is New York, for example, which now requires developers of large housing projects to set aside 20 percent or more for affordable housing. But the pushers of market-friendly solutions, and even most affordable housing activists, miss a central point in the housing debate: we already have enough housing in this country. The problem is not supply. It's just that the supply is owned by the wrong people. From downtowns to suburbs, there's a glut of vacant housing and land owned by the rich. The one neat trick to solving the housing crisis: give the things owned by the rich to the poor. The richest neighborhoods in many cities are also some of the most vacant.

"This is not a new phenomenon — it's one of the central theses of **Frederick Engels'** 1872 treatise, "The Housing Question:" if there's no purposeful depression of prices on land, housing prices have no reason to become cheap. The land at the center of cities will always go up, until they are unaffordable to everyone but the richest."The problem is there's little political will in hyper-capitalist economies to take over privately owned land. But as the housing crisis continues, that's changing," from Moskowitz's article noted above. When someone quotes Engels, you need to grab your wallet and protect your property. Engles, of course, co-created communism with Karl Marx.

After the London public housing project Grenfell Tower in London caught fire, killing dozens, Moskowitz commented that a poll suggested that the apartments of the rich be confiscated to house Grenfell's victims. Moskowitz signified, 'It was a small sign that housing redistribution is becoming politically palatable."

Again, please note: Julian Castro along with Senators Corey Booker and Elizabeth Warren have called for pressure from the federal government to be placed on local governments to demand more development of affordable housing high-rises in single-family neighborhoods. A UCLA assistant professor of urban planning, Kian Goh, asserts, **"If we want to keep cities safe in the face of climate changes, we need to seriously question the ideal of private home ownership."** Socialist Bernie Sanders has called for "Housing for All" with a $2.5 trillion taxpayer price tag. **The bottom line to such Green New Deal housing policies is that eventually all homes will be government housing.**

In a 2018 article by Dan Herriges, in Strong Towns.org., about housing vouchers:

> **Local rent regulation**, including inclusionary zoning (requiring developers to include a share of affordable units in their projects) and rent control (capping allowable rents or rent increases). These are ultimately indirect subsidies, paid not out of a governmental budget, but out of the profit margins of landowners and developers and the rents of market-rate tenants, which are affected by the additional regulation. There's a lot of debate over what and how great the unintended consequences might be -- of particular concern is that if these policies depress the production of new housing, most or all of their benefits might be canceled out. Economies are complex systems, and the indirect consequences of regulation can be wickedly hard to predict.
>
> There's a common misconception that if developers would just settle for a little less profit, they could build working-class housing without subsidy. This is almost never true. The reality is that, much as lower-income people usually buy used cars, lower-income people usually do not live in newly-constructed homes. This was true in 1920, it was true in 1950, it was true in 1980, and it is true today. The primary source of affordable housing is older housing that has "filtered" down from a higher price point.

So it is pretty obvious that the issue is understood. Yet, those wanting to move us to socialism *via* Agenda 21 or the Green New Deal are still going to be pushing for 'reforms' that lead to abolishment of private property.

ALTERNATIVE ENERGY

Recently Michael Moore put out a video that shows exactly what wind and solar energy are doing to the environment – and how useless they are. If Moore is saying it, how Green can they be? These articles are good information for all needs – letters to editor, testimony to bureaucrats, and bringing your friends into 2020 for real and realistically.

HOW EXACTLY DO THEY PLAN TO REPLACE FOSSIL FUELS?

By Paul Driessen

Berkeley, CA, Takoma Park, MD and other cities; California, Connecticut, New York, Virginia and other states; Germany, England and other countries; the European Union – all plan to banish oil, natural gas and coal within 10, 20 or 30 years. A number of US states have joined Regional Greenhouse Gas Initiatives and proudly say <u>We Are Still In</u> … the <u>Paris climate treaty</u>, no matter what President Trump says or does.

Forget the headlines and <u>models</u>, and look at <u>hurricane</u>, <u>tornado</u>, <u>sea level</u> and other historic records. There is no crisis, no unprecedented warming or weather events, certainly nothing that proves humans have replaced the powerful natural forces that have always driven <u>climate changes and weather events</u>.

But for now, let's just examine their zero-carbon plans. How exactly will they make this happen? Where do they plan to get the turbines, panels and batteries? The raw materials to manufacture them? How do they plan to function as modern societies with pricey, erratic energy and frequent power disruptions?

How would they – or America, if the entire USA goes <u>Green New Deal</u> – handle a COVID-27 outbreak? How would they manufacture cars, airplanes, wind turbines, toilet paper, <u>pharmaceuticals</u> or much of anything else with intermittent energy? It hasn't worked in Europe (see below), and it won't work here.

Moreover, it's not just replacing today's coal and gas power plant megawatts. It's doubling today's electricity generation, because Green New Dealers want to replace all fossil fuel use: gasoline and diesel <u>cars, trucks and buses</u>, home and water heating, factory power, hospital emergency power, and more.

It's tripling current megawatt generation, because they don't like nuclear or hydroelectric power either, and they'll need far more electricity to charge enough batteries to ensure backup power for all the fossil and other power they want to eliminate. That will require a lot of wind turbines, solar panels and batteries.

Where do they plan to put all of them? Some of those states and countries have lots of rural land, wildlife habitats and shallow waters off their coasts that they can turn into huge industrial energy zones. But what are those self-righteous cities going to do? Where within their city limits do they plan to put dozens of 650-foot tall turbines and tens of thousands of panels? Or do they plan to just impose those facilities on their rural neighbors? Or tap into regional power grids and use electricity that someone else is generating – with coal, gas, nuclear, hydro, and maybe wind or solar? How will they separate "good" and "bad" electrons?

All of these GND cities and states will have to deal with <u>frustrated rural families</u> who don't want the ruined scenery, desecrated ridge lines, <u>dead birds and bats</u>, <u>maddening light flicker</u> and <u>excruciating infrasound</u> that towering turbines would bring. Don't want millions of rural acres blanketed with solar panels. Don't want hundreds of miles of new high voltage transmission lines crossing their backyards. Don't want their lands seized via eminent domain, virtually at the point of a gun if they still resist.

They don't want the 25-50-100% higher household electricity bills, the soaring price tags for products and services that go with soaring electricity costs for every business, farm, factory and hospital. They don't want more good manufacturing jobs destroyed by skyrocketing energy prices – and sent overseas.

Do Green New Deal politicians have the foggiest idea how many turbines, panels, batteries and miles of transmission lines they will need to replace all fossil fuels? How few years those energy systems last before they have to be replaced? Do they have any idea what they're going to do with the defunct turbine blades and solar panels that can't be recycled or burned? How many cubic miles of landfills they will need? Will communities want those landfills? Will urban pols just employ more eminent domain?

It would take hundreds of 850-foot-tall 12-MW offshore turbines to supply the green new world electricity demands of a major city – or thousands of 2- or 3-MW onshore turbines. Tens of millions of solar panels.

Millions of acres of former crop, scenic and wildlife habitat land would be impacted. They'd need millions of half-ton 85-kWh Tesla battery packs as backup for a week of windless or sunless days.

Where do they intend to get the millions of tons of steel, copper, cobalt, lithium, aluminum, rare earths, carbon-fiberglass-plastic composites, limestone and other raw materials to build all those electricity generation and storage systems, and all the new transmission lines? Will they now support opening more US lands to mining? How do they plan to mine and process the materials without fossil fuels?

If the mining is not to take place here in United States, under our tough laws and regulations – then where exactly will it be done? In China and Russia? or maybe in Africa and South America, where many mines are operated by Chinese and Russian companies that don't give a tinker's damn about child labor, slave labor, workplace safety, air and water pollution, toxic and radioactive wastes, mined land reclamation – or the soaring rates of lung, heart, skin and intestinal diseases, osteoporosis, cancers and other maladies.

All these squalid places and horrific stories are far away – out of sight, out of mind. Environmentalists love to say: Think globally; act locally. This would be a good time to start practicing that ethical code.

The more honest politicians promoting a GND future admit it would eliminate a lot of oil, gas, coal, petrochemical, manufacturing and other high-paying jobs. But, they claim, their (pseudo-)renewable energy world would create millions of new jobs. A look behind The Great Oz's curtain is very revealing.

Coal-fired power plants generate 7,745 megawatt-hours of electricity per mine and power plant worker; natural gas generates 3,812 MWh per oil and gas field and utility worker. That super high efficiency and resultant low-cost electricity sustain millions of jobs in manufacturing and countless other industries.

In stark contrast, wind turbines produce a measly 836 MWh for every employee, while solar panels generated an abysmal 98 MWh per worker. Put another way, it takes 79 solar workers to produce the same amount of electricity as one coal worker or two natural gas workers. Not only will this expensive, intermittent, weather-dependent electricity kill millions of good American jobs; the GND wind and solar jobs will mostly be lower-wage positions installing, maintaining, repairing and replacing turbines and panels, and hauling huge dilapidated blades, panels, hulks and concrete foundations to monster landfills.

Residential electricity prices are already outrageous in New York (17¢ a kilowatt-hour), California (19¢ per kWh), Connecticut (20¢) and Hawaii (31¢) – versus 9¢ a kWh in Arkansas, Georgia and Oklahoma. Going 50-100% wind and solar would send family rates skyrocketing to German levels: 37¢ per kWh.

At the 8¢ per kWh in 2019, Virginia's Inova Fairfax Women's and Children's Hospital pays about $1.6 million annually for electricity (based on typical hospital costs per square foot). At California's (15¢ per kWh), or Germany's business rate (22¢), Inova would have to shell out an extra $1.4-2.8 million a year for electricity. That would mean employee layoffs, higher medical bills, reduced patient care, more deaths.

How is the vaunted transition to wind and solar actually working in Europe and Britain? In 2017, German families and businesses were pummeled by 172,000 localized blackouts. Last year, some 350,000 German families had their electricity cut off because they couldn't pay their power bills. In Britain, millions of elderly people have to choose between heating and eating decent food; many spend their days in libraries to keep warm; and more than 3,000 die every year because they cannot heat their homes properly, making them more likely to succumb to respiratory, heart, flu or other diseases.

Across Europe, 11 million jobs are "at risk" because of an EU "green deal" that many say is suicidal. Meanwhile, China and India are still building coal and gas power plants, making products for the USA and Europe, creating jobs, building airports, and sending billions of tons of CO2 into the atmosphere.

GND politicians have dodged these issues for years – while steering billions of taxpayer dollars to the green activist groups, crony capitalists and industrialist rent seekers that help keep them in office.

Even worse, they and their media allies neatly dodge the most glaring reality. The only way this energy and economic transformation will happen is through totalitarian government at the local, state and federal level: liberal urban voters and politicians against the rest of America. Those are the seeds of resentment, anger, societal division, endless litigation, and violence. We need to head that grim future off at the pass.

WIND POWER
THE GIGA AND TERRA SCAM OF OFFSHORE WIND ENERGY

By Paul Driessen

Can anti-fossil fuel policies based on climate crisis alarmism possibly get any more insane than this?

In what might be described as a pre-Halloween trick of ginormous proportions, the International Energy Agency (IEA) now asserts that "renewable, sustainable" energy output will explode over the next two decades. Certainly for onshore wind and solar energy – but especially for offshore wind, says the IEA.

"Offshore wind currently provides just 0.3% of global power generation," IEA executive director Fatih Birol noted. But "wind farms" constructed closer than 37 miles from coastlines around the world, where waters are less than 60 meters (197 feet) deep, could generate 36,000 terawatt-hours (36 million gigawatt-hours or 36 billion megawatt-hours) of electricity a year, he assures us. That's well above the current global demand of 23,000 terawatt hours, Birol and a new IEA report say.

In fact, the potential for offshore wind energy is so great, the IEA asserts, that 20 years from now the industry will be 15 times bigger than in 2019 – and will attract $1 trillion a year in investments (riding the coat tails of government mandates and subsidies). The boom will result from lower costs per megawatt, larger turbines, and technological developments like floating platforms for turbines, says the IEA.

Wind "farms"? Like some cute, rustic Old McDonald family farm? Are you kidding me? These would be massive offshore electricity factories, with thousands, even millions, of turbines and blades towering 500-700 feet above the waves. Only a certifiable lunatic, congenital liar, complete true believer, would-be global overseer or campaign-cash-hungry politician could possibly repeat this IEA hype – or call these wind energy factories renewable, sustainable or eco-friendly.

They all clearly need yet another bucket of icy cold energy reality dumped over their heads – in addition to this one, this one and this one. If the world buys into this crazy scheme, we all belong in straitjackets.

As I have said many times, wind and sunshine may be free, renewable, sustainable and eco-friendly. But the turbines, solar panels, transmission lines, lands, raw materials and dead birds required to harness this widely dispersed, intermittent, weather-dependent energy to benefit humanity absolutely are not.

A single 1.8-MW onshore wind turbine requires over 1,000 tons of steel, copper, aluminum, rare earth elements, zinc, molybdenum, petroleum-based composites, reinforced concrete and other raw materials. A 3-MW version requires 1,550 tons of these non-renewable materials.

By my rough calculations (here and here), replacing just the USA's current electricity generation, backup coal and natural gas power plants, gasoline-powered vehicles, factory furnaces, and other fossil fuel uses with wind turbines and backup batteries would require: some 14 million 1.8-MW onshore turbines, sprawling across some 1.8 billion acres, some 15 billion tons of raw materials, thousands of new or expanded mines worldwide, and thousands of mostly fossil fuel-powered factories working 24/7/365 in various foreign countries (since we won't allow them in the USA) to manufacture all this equipment.

Those overseas mines now "employ" tens of thousands of fathers, mothers and children – at slave wages.

Can you imagine what it would take to build, install and maintain 36 billion megawatt-hours of offshore wind turbines ... in 20 to 200 feet of water ... many on floating platforms big and strong enough to support monstrous 600-foot-tall turbines ... in the face of winds, waves, salt spray, storms and hurricanes?

The impacts on terra firma ... and terra aqua ... would be monumental, intolerable and unsustainable.

Moreover, a new study – by the company that has built more offshore industrial wind facilities than any other on Earth – has found that offshore turbines and facilities actually generate much less electricity than previously calculated, expected or claimed! That's because every turbine slows wind speeds for every other turbine. Of course, that means even more turbines, floating platforms and raw materials. Using 3, 9 or 10-MW turbines would mean fewer of the beasts, of course, but larger towers, bases and platforms.

More turbines will mean countless seagoing birds will get slaughtered and left to sink uncounted and unaccountable beneath the waves. The growing jungle of fixed and floating turbines will severely interfere with surface and submarine ship traffic, while constant vibration noises from the towers will impair whale and other marine mammals' sonar navigation systems. Visual pollution will be significant. And there'd be thousands of miles of submarine cables bringing electricity to onshore transmission lines.

Maps depicting the USA's best wind resource areas show that they are concentrated down the middle of the continent – right along migratory flyways for monarch butterflies, geese, endangered whooping cranes and other airborne species; along the Pacific Coast; and along the Atlantic Seaboard.

Coastal states, especially their big urban areas, tend to be hotbeds of climate anxiety and wind-solar activism. Indeed, many Democrat Green New Deal governors and legislators have mandated 80-100% "clean, renewable, sustainable, eco-friendly" energy by 2040 or 2050. California, Oregon and Washington in the West ... and Maine, New York, New Jersey, Connecticut and Virginia in the East ... are notable examples. So the IEA's love affair with offshore wind energy is certainly understandable. Of course, Blue State Great Lakes would also be excellent candidates for fixed and floating turbines.

Pacific Ocean waters typically get deep very quickly. So thousands of huge floating platforms would be needed there, although Puget Sound is also windy and could be partially denuded for turbines, as they've done in West Virginia's mountains. California prefers to import its electricity from neighboring states, rather than generating its own power. However, as Margaret Thatcher might say, pretty soon you run out of other people's energy. So homegrown wind energy will soon be essential – and inland Golden State and Middle America voters would almost certainly support putting turbines straight offshore from Al Gore's $9-million mansion in Montecito and the Obamas' $15-million cottage in Rancho Mirage.

When it comes to actually implementing these ambitious "renewable energy goals," resistance and delays grow exponentially. A Massachusetts wind project for 170 offshore wind turbines was originally proposed around 2001. It's now down to 130 3.6-MW behemoth turbines, with the US Interior Department delaying permits yet again, pending "further study." The reaction of coastal residents to the reality of endless thousands of turbines could well turn into Fossil Fuels and Nuclear Forever.

Actual electricity output is rarely as advertised. It often hits <u>20% or lower</u>, depending on locations – and fails completely on the hottest and coldest days, when electricity is most urgently needed. During the July 2006 California heat wave, turbines generated only 5% of nameplate capacity. In Texas, wind capacity factors are generally <u>9% to 12%</u> (or even down to 4% or zero) during torrid summer months. Offshore, echoing Samuel Taylor Coleridge, they'd be as idle as a fleet of painted turbines upon a painted ocean.

Actual wind turbine electricity output <u>declines by 16% per decade</u> of operation – and worse than that offshore, because of storms and salt spray. Removing obsolete offshore turbines requires huge derrick barges and near-perfect weather. Costs and difficulties multiply with turbine size, increasing distance from shore, and whether concrete bases and electrical cables must be removed and seabeds returned to their original condition, as is required today for offshore oil and gas operations.

Cutting up 300-foot (or taller) towers and 200-foot (or longer) blades from offshore turbines, and hauling the sections to onshore landfills and scrap yards, is no piece of cake. <u>Recycling blades is also difficult</u>, because they are made from fiberglass, carbon fibers and petroleum resins; burning blades releases hazardous dust and toxic gases, and so is (or should be) prohibited.

Dismantling and disposal costs could easily reach millions of dollars per offshore turbine, and many billions for every industrial-scale wind "farm." But wind energy operators should not be allowed to simply leave their derelicts behind, as they have done with smaller turbines in Hawaii and California.

Bottom line: From any economic, environmental, raw materials or energy perspective, offshore wind energy is simply unsustainable. It's time for politicians, environmentalists and industry promoters to stop selling offshore wind (and onshore wind and solar power) as magic pixie dust to replace fossil fuels.

WIND POWER OR WILDLIFE: IT'S YOUR CHOICE!

By <u>Paul Driessen</u>

The latest justification for extending the industrial wind electricity production tax credit (PTC) is that we need an "all of the above" energy policy. The slogan falls flat, even when it's expanded to "all of the above and below" – which is rarely the case with radical environmentalists and "progressive" politicians, who steadfastly oppose "any of the below" (ie, hydrocarbons).

America needs an "all of the sensible" energy policy. If an energy option makes sense – technically, economically and environmentally – it should be implemented. If it flunks, it should be scrapped.

Industrial wind energy mandates, renewable portfolio standards, subsidies, feed-in tariffs and production tax credits fail every test. They flunk environmental standards disastrously. In fact, they are subsidizing the slaughter of countless eagles, hawks, falcons, owls, herons, cranes, egrets, other birds and bats.

The wind PTC epitomizes "you didn't build it." If any business "didn't get there on your own," or was "successful because, along the line," somebody (in government) "gave you some help" – it is Big Wind.

Industrial wind energy has been mandated, propped up, subsidized, built and protected by government. Elected and unelected officials at the federal, state and local levels have given it every unfair advantage that taxpayer and ratepayer money, legal favors and exemptions, and crony corporatism could bestow upon it. Meanwhile, in numerous cases, the same legislative, regulatory, environmentalist and industrialist cronies have penalized and marginalized Big Wind's hydrocarbon and nuclear competitors – often for the same reasons that are ignored with wind energy.

Industrial wind is actually our least sustainable energy resource. It requires perpetual subsidies to survive. The tax revenues it takes from productive sectors of the economy, the insufficient and unreliable nature of wind electricity, and the exorbitant electricity rates that wind turbines impose on factories and businesses, kill two to four jobs for every "green" job created. Wind is a net job loser.

Big Wind also imposes excessive environmental impacts. It requires vast amounts of raw materials and land for turbines, backup power and long transmission lines. The extraction and processing of rare earth metals and other materials devastates large agricultural, scenic and wildlife habitat areas and harms people's health, especially in China. Worst, the turbines are returning numerous bird and bat species to the edge of extinction, after decades of patient, costly efforts to nurse them back to health.

These are not sparrows and pigeons killed by housecats. They are bats that eat insects and protect crops. They are some of our most important and magnificent raptors, herons, cranes, condors and other majestic sovereigns of our skies. They are being chopped out of the air and driven from numerous habitats.

The US Fish & Wildlife Service (FWS), American Bird Conservancy (ABC) and other experts estimate that well over 500,000 birds and countless bats are being killed annually by turbines. The subsidized slaughter "could easily be over 500" golden eagles a year in our western states, Save the Eagles International biologist Jim Wiegand told me. Bald eagles are also being butchered. The body count for the two species could soon reach 1,000 a year.

In the 86-square-mile area blanketed by the Altamont Pass wind facility, no eagles have nested for over 20 years, and golden eagle nest sites have declined by half near the actual facility, even though both areas are prime eagle habitat, says Wiegand. Wildlife expert Dr. Shawn Smallwood estimates that 2,300 golden eagles have been killed by Altamont turbines over the past 25 years.

The wind industry keeps the publicly acknowledged death toll "low" and "acceptable" by employing deliberately flawed methodologies, says Wiegand. Companies have crews search around turbines that are not operating; search only within narrow radiuses of turbines, thus missing birds that were flung further by the impact or limped off to die elsewhere; search for carcasses only every 2-4 weeks, allowing scavengers to take most of them away; avoid using dogs to sniff for bodies; not count disabled or wounded birds and bats; and pick up carcasses, under the guideline of "slice, shovel and shut up."

High security at most wind turbine sites makes independent analysis almost impossible, adds ABC wind energy coordinator Kelly Fuller. Even the faulty (fraudulent?) raw bird kill data are rarely made public and are difficult to access even through the Freedom of Information Act. Amazingly, Fish & Wildlife does not require that the information be made public. What little does get released is too often filtered, massaged and manipulated – and now the FWS may allow the industry to put even these suspect body counts into private data banks that would not be subject to FOIA.

The FWS and Justice Department prosecuted and fined oil companies for the unintentional deaths of just 28 small migratory birds (no raptors and no rare, threatened or endangered species) over several months throughout North Dakota. They fined ExxonMobil $600,000 for accidentally killing 85 birds over a five-year period in five states. But they have never prosecuted or penalized a single wind turbine company for its eco-slaughter. Now they are going much further.

The Service has proposed to grant "programmatic take" permits that would allow wind turbine operators to repeatedly, systematically, legally and "inadvertently" injure, maim and kill bald and golden eagles –turning what has been outrageously selective (non)enforcement of endangered species laws into a 007 license to kill. While the new rule "is not specifically designed for the wind industry" (as an industry spokesman helpfully pointed out), Big Wind will be by far the biggest beneficiary.

The FWS says it can do this based on illusory "advanced conservation practices" that are "scientifically supportable," approved by the Service, and "represent the best available techniques to reduce eagle disturbance and ongoing mortalities to a level where remaining take is unavoidable and incidental to otherwise lawful activity." The Service also claims "mitigation" and other "additional" measures may be implemented where necessary to "ensure the preservation" of eagles as a species.

When its goal is to restrict development, the FWS frequently defines species, subspecies or "distinct population segments" for sage grouse, spotted owls, "jumping mice" and other wildlife – or labels a species "imperiled" in a selected location, even when it is abundant in nearby locations. With eagles, the proposed "take" rules strongly suggest that the Service could easily say the presence of eagles in some parts of the Lower 48 States or even just Alaska would mean their preservation is ensured, even if they are exterminated or driven out of numerous habitats. (Ditto for other species imperiled by wind turbines.)

Attempts to "mitigate" impacts or establish new population segments will almost certainly mean imposing extra burdens, restrictions and costs on land owners and users outside of turbine-impact areas.

Another vital, majestic species being "sliced" back to the verge of extinction is the whooping crane, North America's tallest bird. Since 2006, installed turbine capacity within the six-state whooping crane flyway has skyrocketed from 3,600 megawatts to some 16,000 MW – and several hundred tagged and numbered whooping cranes "have turned up missing and are unaccounted for," says Wiegand. And yet, another 136,700 MW of new bird Cuisinarts are planned for these six states!

The Service knows this is happening, and yet turns a blind eye – and Big Wind is not about to admit that its turbines are butchering whooping cranes, bald eagles, Peregrine falcons, bats and other rare species.

This subsidized slaughter and legalized carnage cannot continue. Every vote to extend the PTC, or approve wind turbines in or near important bird habitats and flyways, is a vote for ultimate extinction of majestic and vital species in numerous areas all over the United States.

Wind energy is not green, eco-friendly, sustainable or sensible. Extending the subsidized slaughter is not something any members of Congress, state legislatures or county commissions – Republican or Democrat – should want to have on their conscience.

SOLAR POWER
THE SOLAR PANEL TOXIC WASTE PROBLEM

By Duggan Flanakin

For decades, the solar industry benefited from generous federal, state, and local subsidies to increase its footprint. Yet these generous subsidies ignore the costs of disposal of solar panel waste.

Things may be changing. In May 2018, Michael Shellenberger, a Time Magazine "Hero of the Environment" and Green Book Award Winner, wrote in Forbes that the problem of solar panel disposal will explode with full force in two or three decades and wreck the environment because it is a huge amount of waste which is not easy to recycle.

Shellenberger was citing comments, published in the South China Morning Post, from Chinese solar expert Tian Min, general manager of Nanjing Fangrun Materials, a recycling company in Jiangsu province that collects retired solar panels. Tian called his country's solar power industry "a ticking time bomb."

This is not really news. The Associated Press had reported in 2013 that the heavily subsidized solar industry was creating millions of pounds of polluted sludge and contaminated water that is often shipped landfills often hundreds of miles away.

The now-defunct, bankrupted Solyndra used its $535 million in guaranteed federal dollars to generate about 12.5 million pounds of hazardous waste, much of which was carcinogenic cadmium-contaminated waste, during its four years of operations.

But, you say, solar energy is clean, green, and mean – and taking over the world one massive array at a time. Isn't that what we have all been told?

The truth can be brutal. The average lifespan of a solar panel is about 20 years, but high temperatures (as in the Mojave Desert) can accelerate the aging process for solar cells, and snow, dust, and other natural events (tornadoes, earthquakes),can cause material fatigue on the surface and in the internal electric circuits – gradually reducing the panel's power output.

Solar panels generate 300 times more toxic waste per unit of energy than nuclear power plants. They also contain lead, cadmium, and other toxic (even carcinogenic) chemicals that cannot be removed without breaking apart the entire panel. Worse, rainwater can wash many of these toxics out of the fragments of solar modules over time.

Another real concern is the vast increase in the use of nitrogen trifluoride (NF3) in the construction of solar panels – up 1,057 percent over the past 25 years. The UN Intergovernmental Panel on Climate Change deems NF3 to be 17,200 times more potent than carbon dioxide as a greenhouse gas – meaning that even relatively minor quantities can have major impacts.

While the European Union has long required solar panel manufacturers to collect and dispose of solar waste, in the U.S. until very recently only Washington State had any recycling requirements. Yet even their standards did not address costs.

Proponents like to cite the small size of the industry to date as a reason to ignore recycling requirments and costs in their business plans. But the deeper truth is that the costs for solar waste disposal can be huge. As Cara Libby, senior technical leader of solar energy at the Electric Power Research Institute (EPRI), put it, "I've heard that [recycling] will have to be mandated because it won't ever be economical."

Japan is also facing a growing solar waste problem. In a November 2016 article, Osamu Tomioka stated that Japanese solar panel waste will likely grow from the current 10,000 tons a year to 800,000 tons a year – and that just to recycle all of the waste produced through 2020 will take 19 years. How long will it take, and at what cost, to recycle 80 times that amount?

A 2018 report from the Institute of Energy Research suggests imposing a recycling fee on solar panel purchases. A federal disposal and decommissioning fund would then dispense funds to state and local governments to help pay for removal and recycling or long-term storage of solar panel waste. [Similar fees help recover costs for nuclear waste disposal and coal mine reclamation for bankrupt facilities.]

But how much of a fee would be needed? IER admits that recycling costs are generally more than the economic value of the materials they recover. And bankruptcies have been all too common in an industry that has relied so heavily on disappearing subsidies.

The simple truth is that it is past time for a real accounting of the overall costs to the public and to the environment of a massive increase in the use of solar panels as compared, for example, of increased reliance on non-intermittent technologies like nuclear energy and natural gas.

WATER CONTROLS

Shortly after Agenda 21 was written, NGOs, government departments, and every green group in the world were jumping in to help destroy property rights in their areas of 'expertise'. I got to experience it first hand. In the mid-90s, before the Internet, the U.S. government held a meeting *via* satellite link between Washington, D.C., and cities and towns across western Montana, Idaho, eastern Washington, and Oregon. The subject was the Columbia River Basin.

I was living in Helena, Montana. The meeting was held in a school or some building like a school on a Saturday morning. The room had about a dozen round tables with six chairs each, and we all watched the presentation on a screen. In attendance were the press, people from farming and Ag organizations, local officials and other regular citizens like me – wanting to know what was afoot. After the viewing, we had one of those infamous consensus meetings.

The major point of that meeting was that the Columbia River Basin needed to be returned to the state it was before Columbus. Actually, they wanted to go beyond that. Not just the unspoken words, NO WHITE MAN, that were implied, but the eventual goal was NO MAN. Understandably, the global elite want that area to be re-wilded, to be part of the Wildlands Project. How would they start? By getting rid of all the damned dams.

GREEN INSANITY IS FLOODING TOWNS AND DESTROYING LIVES

By Joe Herring, *New American*

Having written extensively on the catastrophic flooding of the Missouri River basin in 2011, I believe that the occasion of this present flood disaster plaguing Nebraska, Iowa, and South Dakota has given rise to many questions. Foremost, I have been asked if there is an environmentalist element, as there was in 2011, when the Corps of Engineers intentionally permitted the flooding of eight states in order to further their highest priority (as per the Master Water Control Manual) of "habitat restoration for riverine wildlife" at the expense of the original top priority, flood control, and the preservation of human life and property.

Green "deism" does play a role in our current woes, but not as directly as it did in 2011. More of a "Best supporting Actor," in this case.
The Master Water Control Manual is the bible of the Missouri River basin dam system. It defines the duties and protocols to be followed in order to best meet the various needs represented in the list of priorities.

From the completion of the dam construction (in 1967) until 2004, the Master Water Control Manual listed the priority functions in order of importance, with flood control being number one.
1) flood control
2) irrigation and upstream beneficial uses
3) downstream water supply
4) navigation and power
5) recreation and wildlife

In 2004, under pressure from environmentalist organizations who had been lobbying hard for the previous decade, Congress approved a revision to the manual that no longer specifically prioritized the uses of the system, leaving the order of the functions to the discretion of the Corps of Engineers.

The previous list was then essentially upended, with wildlife (habitat restoration, preservation, and imitation of natural cycles) becoming the top priority, and all the others swapping places back and forth depending on the year.
Flood control slipped lower and lower on the ladder as the Green movement grew in strength, demanding a return to the "wild rivers" that, in their sainted opinions, man should have never attempted to control.

This led the Corps to utilize the dams in a way for which they were never designed — to attempt to mimic the natural cycles of the river through the seasons.
In spring, the pre-dam river rose and flooded with the snow melt and spring rains. In the summer, flows slowed, and levels dropped until fall and early winter, when rains and sporadic snow-melt cycles increased the flow prior to hard freezing.

The "engineers," guided by the Endangered Species Act, not the Flood Control Act, bank water throughout the fall and winter, preparing to release it in spring to mimic nature with a sort of controlled flood.

Sometimes they get away with the gamble, but other times nature intrudes on their Gaia-worshiping skit and provides a stark reminder that "playing God" and "being God" are quite different things, indeed. Nature lets loose with the real thing in the form of heavy snowfalls, heavier than normal rains, or a super-thaw from a rapid increase in temperatures and a wind-driven warm rainfall that rid thousands of square miles of an average three feet of snowpack in roughly 36 hours, as happened last week. And once again, the faux gods were caught short.

Did the Corp cause the current flooding? In my opinion, no. However, it greatly contributed to its severity in numerous ways, not the least of which is its influence on the management of smaller tributary rivers and streams throughout the basin — the very rivers and streams that are presently roaming miles from their banks. The primary reason the Corps deserves a major share of responsibility is its mismanagement of the dam system. Had they been drawing down water throughout the early winter in anticipation of a higher than normal runoff due to higher than normal snow accumulations in the lower reaches of the basin, then the tributaries presently flooding would have had more room to drain through their natural outlet, the mighty Missouri river.

Would it have eliminated the flooding we see destroying farms, homes, and roads on our televisions (or right outside our own windows!)? Not entirely, no. However, it is unarguable that managing the Missouri River mainstem dams with an eye toward flood control above all else would have greatly minimized the severity of the event.

Don't forget: we still have all the mountain and plains snowmelt in the upper reaches of the basin yet to come, as melting in that region doesn't begin in earnest until late April and early May. Fortunately, the accumulated snowpack levels in the upper basin are roughly normal, unlike in 2011, when they averaged 275% of normal — a circumstance of which the Corps was repeatedly made aware, and one it chose to ignore.

After the 2011 flood and my subsequent exposure of the Corps's liability through the series of articles (linked above), a congressional investigation was launched into the management of the system. A civil lawsuit on behalf of affected landowners was also filed.

The congressional investigation found precisely what I had described: that the disordered priorities rendered millions of people vulnerable to the very circumstances the dam system was built to prevent.

However, under pressure from extremely well funded environmentalist organizations, Congress stopped short of ordering the Master Water Control Manual to be revised, failing to order flood control to again be the top priority. Instead, legislators settled for the Corps of Engineers promising to do better next time.

The civil suit fared better, as politics and intimidation were largely removed from those proceedings. They won their case against the Corps and a 375-million-dollar judgment as damages.

However, the Master Water Control Manual remains untouched to this day, and the people's safety remains suborned to the fevered dreams of wild-eyed greeniacs populating the agencies charged with management of our natural resources. As of this writing, 74 cities, four tribal areas, and 65 counties in Nebraska alone were under declarations of flood emergency, with the bulk of those towns cut off from the rest of the state entirely by standing flood water or destroyed roads and bridges. South Dakota and Iowa both tell similar stories of disaster.

Hamburg, Iowa, a small town southeast of Omaha, experienced terrible flooding in 2011. The town bolstered and raised the levee that protected their town and managed to save some of it from further ravages during that months-long catastrophe. Always eager to help, the Corps of Engineers informed the city of Hamburg that its levee had to be "brought up to standard" or reduced to its original height.

The cost of such a project, 5.5 million dollars, was simply too expensive for such a small town, still reeling from the flood aftermath. Sadly, they acceded to the Corps's demands and removed the portion of the levee that had saved them in 2011.

Hamburg is now almost entirely underwater — not a few inches, mind you, but several *feet* underwater, across the town. It is entirely likely that Hamburg will simply fade into memory once the waters recede, a victim of environmentalist hubris and bureaucratic formality, a footnote in the Corps's grand march to restore the mighty river to its once untamable self.

There is no way to eliminate the possibility of flooding. The best we can do is to prevent flooding to the greatest extent possible. There is only one way to accomplish that: revise the Master Water Control Manual and make flood control the highest priority once again. Then ensure that the Corps follows it to the letter — under penalty of law.

Having written extensively in these pages (read here, here, and here) on the catastrophic flooding of the Missouri River basin in 2011, I believe that the occasion of this present flood disaster plaguing Nebraska, Iowa, and South Dakota has given rise to many questions. Foremost, I have been asked if there is an environmentalist element, as there was in 2011, when the Corps of Engineers intentionally permitted the flooding of eight states in order to further their highest priority (as per the Master Water Control Manual) of "habitat restoration for riverine wildlife" at the expense of the original top priority, flood control, and the preservation of human life and property.

Green "deism" does play a role in our current woes, but not as directly as it did in 2011. More of a "Best supporting Actor," in this case.

The Master Water Control Manual is the bible of the Missouri River basin dam system. It defines the duties and protocols to be followed in order to best meet the various needs represented in the list of priorities.

From the completion of the dam construction (in 1967) until 2004, the Master Water Control Manual listed the priority functions in order of importance, with flood control being number one.
1) flood control
2) irrigation and upstream beneficial uses
3) downstream water supply
4) navigation and power
5) recreation and wildlife

In 2004, under pressure from environmentalist organizations who had been lobbying hard for the previous decade, Congress approved a revision to the manual that no longer specifically prioritized the uses of the system, leaving the order of the functions to the discretion of the Corps of Engineers.

The previous list was then essentially upended, with wildlife (habitat restoration, preservation, and imitation of natural cycles) becoming the top priority, and all the others swapping places back and forth depending on the year.

Flood control slipped lower and lower on the ladder as the Green movement grew in strength, demanding a return to the "wild rivers" that, in their sainted opinions, man should have never attempted to control.

This led the Corps to utilize the dams in a way for which they were never designed — to attempt to mimic the natural cycles of the river through the seasons.
In spring, the pre-dam river rose and flooded with the snow melt and spring rains. In the summer, flows slowed, and levels dropped until fall and early winter, when rains and sporadic snow-melt cycles increased the flow prior to hard freezing.

The "engineers," guided by the Endangered Species Act, not the Flood Control Act, bank water throughout the fall and winter, preparing to release it in spring to mimic nature with a sort of controlled flood.

Sometimes they get away with the gamble, but other times nature intrudes on their Gaia-worshiping skit and provides a stark reminder that "playing God" and "being God" are quite different things, indeed. Nature lets loose with the real thing in the form of heavy snowfalls, heavier than normal rains, or a super-thaw from a rapid increase in temperatures and a wind-driven warm rainfall that rid thousands of square miles of an average three feet of snowpack in roughly 36 hours, as happened last week. And once again, the faux gods were caught short.

Did the Corp cause the current flooding? In my opinion, no. However, it greatly contributed to its severity in numerous ways, not the least of which is its influence on the management of smaller tributary rivers and streams throughout the basin — the very rivers and streams that are presently roaming miles from their banks. The primary reason the Corps deserves a major share of responsibility is its mismanagement of the dam system. Had they been drawing down water throughout the early winter in anticipation of a higher than normal runoff due to higher than normal snow accumulations in the lower reaches of the basin, then the tributaries presently flooding would have had more room to drain through their natural outlet, the mighty Missouri river.

Would it have eliminated the flooding we see destroying farms, homes, and roads on our televisions (or right outside our own windows!)? Not entirely, no. However, it is unarguable that managing the Missouri River mainstem dams with an eye toward flood control above all else would have greatly minimized the severity of the event.

Don't forget: we still have all the mountain and plains snowmelt in the upper reaches of the basin yet to come, as melting in that region doesn't begin in earnest until late April and early May. Fortunately, the accumulated snowpack levels in the upper basin are roughly normal, unlike in 2011, when they averaged 275% of normal — a circumstance of which the Corps was repeatedly made aware, and one it chose to ignore.

After the 2011 flood and my subsequent exposure of the Corps's liability through the series of articles (linked above), a congressional investigation was launched into the management of the system. A civil lawsuit on behalf of affected landowners was also filed.

The congressional investigation found precisely what I had described: that the disordered priorities rendered millions of people vulnerable to the very circumstances the dam system was built to prevent.

However, under pressure from extremely well funded environmentalist organizations, Congress stopped short of ordering the Master Water Control Manual to be revised, failing to order flood control to again be the top priority. Instead, legislators settled for the Corps of Engineers promising to do better next time.

The civil suit fared better, as politics and intimidation were largely removed from those proceedings. They won their case against the Corps and a 375-million-dollar judgment as damages.

However, the Master Water Control Manual remains untouched to this day, and the people's safety remains suborned to the fevered dreams of wild-eyed greeniacs populating the agencies charged with management of our natural resources. As of this writing, 74 cities, four tribal areas, and 65 counties in Nebraska alone were under declarations of flood emergency, with the bulk of those towns cut off from the rest of the state entirely by standing flood water or destroyed roads and bridges. South Dakota and Iowa both tell similar stories of disaster.

Hamburg, Iowa, a small town southeast of Omaha, experienced terrible flooding in 2011. The town bolstered and raised the levee that protected their town and managed to save some of it from further ravages during that months-long catastrophe. Always eager to help, the Corps of Engineers informed the city of Hamburg that its levee had to be "brought up to standard" or reduced to its original height.

The cost of such a project, 5.5 million dollars, was simply too expensive for such a small town, still reeling from the flood aftermath. Sadly, they acceded to the Corps's demands and removed the portion of the levee that had saved them in 2011.

Hamburg is now almost entirely underwater — not a few inches, mind you, but several *feet* underwater, across the town. It is entirely likely that Hamburg will simply fade into memory once the waters recede, a victim of environmentalist hubris and bureaucratic formality, a footnote in the Corps's grand march to restore the mighty river to its once untamable self.

There is no way to eliminate the possibility of flooding. The best we can do is to prevent flooding to the greatest extent possible. There is only one way to accomplish that: revise the Master Water Control Manual and make flood control the highest priority once again. Then ensure that the Corps follows it to the letter — under penalty of law.

HERE'S THE DAM DEAL: BUILD MORE DAMS

By David Wojick | CFACT

"*Green Insanity Is Flooding Towns and Destroying Lives*" is an important article in *American Thinker* by columnist Joe Herring. His article is about perverse green practices in the operation of America's existing system of flood control dams, but it also applies to the need for new dams.

Our national flood control system is only half built and we need to finish it. Flood control dams took one of the first hits from the tragic rise of radical environmentalism. The infamous National Environmental Policy Act (NEPA) was passed in large part to stop the federal flood control program, on the green grounds that reservoirs "drowned" rivers. It has been unfortunately successful in that regard.

NEPA requires formal Environmental Impact Assessments (EIA) for all federal water projects (and many other federal actins as well). Its requirements are open ended, which creates what I call the "black hole of environmental assessment."

Here is how the black hole of environmental assessment works. The agency does its EIA, but opponents of the project challenge it in Court, on the grounds that some aspect has been overlooked. The Court then orders the agency to expand the EIA to include this new feature, which is likely to be time consuming and expensive.

Since there is no end to possible (and speculative) environmental impacts, this delaying tactic can be used over and over again against a given project. In effect it creates a procedural black hole that the agency can never get out of. The Court never actually rules against the project, they just make building it impossible.

That when rivers flood, they kill people and destroy their homes was deemed irrelevant under NEPA. As a result, destructive flooding continues. In fact it gets worse over time because of economic growth and development (which the greens also object to). It is time for this green tyranny to end.

Flood control dams capture otherwise destructive flood waters, then release them slowly at a later time. Releasing this retained water can provide a number of useful services, including municipal water supply, irrigation and hydropower. Plus the reservoirs provide habitat and recreation.

Many places that are subject to destructive flooding also see destructive droughts and dams can mitigate both in combination. For example, California has been in a major drought. Now there is tremendous snowpack in the Sierra Nevada Mountains. If this runs off too quickly it will cause serious flooding. Nor does California have the reservoir capacity to hold it all for drought relief. More dams would clearly be great under these combined flood and drought conditions, which are not unusual.

We can argue all day over whether climate change will cause an increase in floods and droughts (I say not). But we all agree that there will be a lot of both to come. For those that do believe in serious climate change, some of the models project massive increases in both floods and droughts, which certainly calls for a lot more dams.

On the hydropower side, flood control dams are often built in series. In such cases the water released by upstream dams then flows over those downstream. Thus the same water can generate renewable electricity several times.

Many of the needed dams have already been designed. In fact many were authorized by Congress before the greens stopped them from being built. Most of these authorizations have expired but the plans are still on the drawing boards of the agencies. They need to be reauthorized. It would also help if NEPA were brought under control.

Let's build these dams and finish America's flood control program. Then we can stop a lot of floods, cure a lot of droughts, save lives and property, and generate needed power along the way.

AGENDA 21/NEW GREEN DEAL IN OUR SCHOOLS AND CHURCHES
TEACHERS, PREACHERS, AND GREENS, THE UNHOLY ALLIANCE TO TRANSFORM AMERICA

When Communism "fell" in the late 1980s, those who were busy scheming to impose global governance on the sovereign nations had a problem. Suddenly, the only super power in the world was the United States – the only nation on Earth based on the ideals of limited government, individual liberty and free enterprise. If American bedrock ideals of freedom took hold in the emerging nations of the old Soviet Empire, global governance was impossible.

What to do? The answer was obvious. Change America. Get her to join the community of nations with a proper attitude. Force her to learn her proper place. Target: America's attitudes, values and beliefs. And to force us to quickly question those American ideals, elements of guilt and fear would be essential.

Two specific targets were identified: the American public school system and America's Christian churches. These were the breeding grounds for the out-of-step American ideals. The schools taught us of the Founding Fathers and their courageous battle to recognize that we are all born with our rights as free individuals. And they taught us that its government's job to protect those rights. Moreover, the very source of those ideals, as stated by the Founders, over and over again, came from Christian teachings. In short, Christianity is the root of American culture.

The guilt and fear elements of the scheme were to come from a campaign that told us that American selfishness and mass consumption were destroying the planet. Specifically, the modern environmental movement was chosen as the shock troops to scare, and thus compel, America into the global village. Over the next three decades these forces combined to rapidly and drastically change America in a very significant way. As Ronald Reagan said, "*We are but one generation away from losing our liberties.*" Change the attitudes, values, and beliefs of just one generation and America will forget its founding principles and fall in line with the globalist worldview.

They can Stop Knowledge By Banning it! Globally Acceptable Truth

SCHOOL REFORM = INDOCTRINATION

Throughout American history parents took on the role of teaching children boundaries, without which a free society cannot function. Children were taught at a young age to respect the rights of others; they were taught the rules of games, without which they could not be played; they were taught to not go into a neighbor's yard without permission; they were taught modesty and loyalty and pride in their school, town, and nation. They were taught to be independent and take care of their own, without expecting someone else to do it for them. And they were taught that their property, ideas, and dreams are their own, to control and pursue. These are attitudes, values, and beliefs that make a free society possible. To get America to fall in line and accept the concept of global governance, these things needed to be changed – and fast.

It is fairly well known what has happened to American schools since the 1990s, when massive "reform" took place through the establishment of the federal Department of Education and programs with names like Goals 2000, School to Work, Workforce Development and later, No Child Left Behind, and now Common Core. Local control of American schools disappeared and a federal curriculum based on behavior modification, focusing on a global outlook, replaced basic academics and true American history. A psychology-driven curriculum, instead, focused on breaking down the structure of American society.

Parents were virtually eliminated from the education process, kept from visiting classrooms, participating in homework assignments, and banned from seeing copies of tests and evaluation exams. In time, Americans began to notice that their children changed after entering school. Children were not learning to read and write. Math skills declined. Knowledge of basic American and World history was near non-existent.

But children suddenly announced that they were now vegetarians (usually at about the third grade). Parents began to notice that environmental questions or statements started popping up in math, language, and history textbooks. Children were obviously learning little about America's unique history or the ideals of the Founders.

Today, in the classroom, rather than basic academics, the children are fed a steady stream of pictures and stories of environmental destruction, supposedly caused by man. The textbooks speak of the earth only as a fragile victim of man's development. The students are taught that the earth is their "mother" for which all good derives.

A fourth grade math book called Quest 2000 contains "math" questions like this one: Mindy read that a typical goldfish lives for six years. Mindy has a goldfish six years old. Should Mindy continue to buy goldfish? Explain your thinking.

Representatives of groups like the Sierra Club and People for the ethical Treatment of Animals (PeTA) are brought into the classroom for days on end to talk to the children and indoctrinate them in the "green" message. There are no opposing views introduced (because that would interrupt the behavior modification process). Some children have been forced to watch Al Gore's film, "An Inconvenient Truth" as many as four times during their school days. And now, they are being introduced to sexual deviancy in kindergarten, and read to by transvestites in costumes.

The children, after being fed a constant diet of such dribble, are then assessed and evaluated on the progress of their behavior modification. Parent's think those tests are about testing for academic ability. If children fail to respond with the proper attitudes, they are given special courses and "personalized" computer programs to help them along the way. And then they are tested again and again until they submit.

After twelve years of this indoctrination your children will certainly have all of the proper environmental attitudes, unable to think or reason for themselves, ready to accept and support whatever message those in charge hand down. In other words, your child has become the perfect anti-property, anti-technology, anti-industry, unquestioning, simple-minded, global village idiot.

And the indoctrination is taking its toll. Children have been known to break out into tears when meat is served for dinner because they've been assaulted by PeTA in the classroom – told that animals are our friends, and we don't eat our friends. One six year-old girl refused to sleep in a beautiful old four-poster bed inherited from her grandmother. When asked why, sobbing, she told her mother, because they had to kill trees to make it. Another young boy compared lumberjacks to rapists and murderers.

The American public education system has become a major tool in the drive to destroy **from within the American ideal.**

GREEN INVASION OF CHRISTIAN CHURCHES

Some worried and concerned parents try to find comfort that their children are at least safe in their church Sunday school, where they will at least learn the proper attitudes, values, and beliefs from a solid Christian view. They are about to be shocked out of that comfort zone.

The lesser noticed and perhaps more covert effort to modify American society has been the assault on Christian churches. It's an invasion specifically designed to change the very root of Western culture.

Beginning in 1993, 67,000 Christian congregations were targeted by a highly organized and well-funded effort to change, and ultimately remove Christianity as a threat to the Green agenda.

The driving force behind the assault on Christian churches is called the National Religious Partnership for the Environment (NRPE). The Partnership is a formal agreement among four of the nation's largest religious organizations, including the U.S. Catholic Conference, National Council of Churches, Coalition on the Environment and Jewish Life, and the Evangelical Environmental Network. In addition, The Union of Concerned Scientists (UCS) holds a special "consultative" relationship with the Partnership. Funding comes from (among others) Pew Charitable Trusts, Stephen C. Rockefeller, the Turner Foundation, W. Alton Jones Foundation and the New World Foundation.

The Partnership operates out of an Anglican church in New York City called St. John, the Divine. The Cathedral is also the home of the Gaia Institute and the Temple of Understanding. The Temple is an official United Nations Non-Governmental Organization (NGO).

The former Executive Director of the Partnership, Paul Gorman, said, "…*how people of faith engage the environment crisis will have much to do with the future well-being of the planet, and in all likelihood, with the future of religious life as well.*"
But don't be misled into thinking these are just good Christians seeking to address environmental issues. The exact opposite is the case. The programs of the Religious Partnership for the Environment seek to steer churches away from Christian teachings and, instead engage in spreading the worship of the earth – "*Gaia*" – in the name of the Christian religion. Worship of Gaia, in fact, calls for man to worship the creation rather than the creator – the exact opposite of Christian teachings.
Today's environmental movement promotes a social order for a global society organized around the notion that the earth, itself, is the giver of life. They advocate that man is not part of the ecology, but, in fact, is the destroyer of it. Disciples of the Gaia hypothesis believe that all living things (except for man) are interconnected and, to damage or destroy even a tiny insect, is to damage whole ecological systems.

Such a position is the basis for the **Wildlands Project** that calls for "rewilding" 50% of all the land in every state, a massive assault on the concept of private property and state and national sovereignty. That idea, created by the radical Earth First group, quickly made its way into a major UN document called the Biodiversity Treaty, and though never ratified by the US Senate, is now being implemented across the nation, with millions of acres of land being locked away from human use. It is also the basis behind wolf and bear reintroductions; behind the destruction of dams; behind the blocking of building projects for the sake of flies and sucker fish; and it's the *very root of Agenda 21 and Sustainable Development that is now dictating development policy and so-called social justice in nearly every city and county in the nation.*

Meanwhile, the Religious Partnership for the Environment is moving to bring all of the world's religions in line to spout from their pulpits the Gaia position as the true source of life and spirituality and, therefore, the only relevant object of worship. They are, in short, changing Christianity to match their worldview.

Regularly, the Partnership sponsors conferences and seminars to bring pastors, priests, and rabbis together for instruction. They prepare sermons, issue papers and Sunday school materials to carry the Gaia message into the churches. The documents are carefully written in the language or style of each religion so the church leader can easily incorporate them into church policy. Shortly after attending such a meeting, it is not surprising to hear a pastor suddenly preaching carefully worded sermons, which, upon investigation, are found to contain earth-worshiping paganism – a fact the minister would no doubt be shocked to learn.

In May, 1992, the Partnership issued a Declaration of the "Mission to Washington." The document was a statement of purpose on how the Partnership intended to deal with our nation's environmental policy. The final line of the document stated, *"Understanding that the world does not belong to any one nation or generation, and sharing a spirit of utmost urgency, we dedicate ourselves to undertake bold action to cherish and protect the environment of our planetary home."* The language is straight out of the scriptures of Agenda 21, the Biodiversity Treaty, Gaia, Al Gore's book, "Earth in the Balance," and the Sierra Club.

The document was then signed by a wide array of religious leaders including Reverend Theodore M. Hesburgh, President, University of Notre Dame; Reverend Gilbert Horn, Ex. Dir. Colorado Council of Churches; Mrs. Annette Kane, Ex. Dir, National Council of Catholic Women; Dr. C. William Nichols, Pres. Christian Church (Disciples of Christ); The Reverend Dr. William Phillippe, Ex Dir, General Assembly Council, Presbyterian Church, USA; Rev. Tyrone S. Pitts, Sec Gen, Progressive National Baptist Convention; Dr. Howard Ris, Ex. Dir. National Baptist Convention; Dr. Foy Valentine, former Ex Dir. Christian Life Commission of the Southern Baptist Convention; and Dr. Richard Land, Ex. Dir. Christian Life Commission of the Southern Baptist Convention.

Also signing the document were such notorious environmental leaders as Mr. George Frampton, President, the Wilderness Society; Chief Global Warming alarmist Dr. James Hansen, Director, Goddard Institute for Space Studies; The Rev. Thomas Berry, Director, the Temple of Understanding; and Dr. Howard Ris, Ex. Dir. Union of Concerned Scientists.

In short, these respected Christian leaders locked arms with some of the most radical environmentalists in a document that declared its determination to enforce radical environmental policy based on pagan earth worship and anti-American, anti-free enterprise policy.

Here, these radicals speak for themselves: Helen Caldicott, of the Union of Concerned Scientists: *"Capitalism is destroying the earth."* Please note that the UCS was started in the late 1980s as a part of the Nuclear Freeze movement, which was proven to be funded in part by the Soviet KGB. The membership of the UCS has always consisted of less than 10 percent scientists and more than 90 percent generic America-bashers.

Father Thomas Berry, a dissident Catholic Priest, is a prime spokesman for Gaia. Father Berry contends that Christianity promotes a "deep cultural pathology of human greed and addiction." He advocates that the earth is disintegrating and that Christianity is to blame. In his book, "Dream of the Earth," (published by Sierra Club Books) Berry never uses the word "God" but speaks of a supernatural force in the universe. He says that, *"we should place less emphasis on Christ as a person and a redeemer. We should put the Bible away for twenty years while we radically rethink our religious ideas."*

Also part of the Temple of Understanding was Maurice Strong, Secretary General of the UN's Earth Summit, which produced the Biodiversity Treaty and Agenda 21. Strong owns a ranch in Colorado where he has built a Babylonian sun god temple. Strong told the Earth Summit, "Isn't the only hope for the planet that the industrialized civilizations collapse? Isn't it our responsibility to bring that about?"

Mathew Fox, a former member of the Dominican Order and a self-proclaimed New Age leader and Gaia spokesman, said, *"the world is being called to a new post- denominational, even post Christian believe system that see the earth as a living being – mythologically, as Gaia, Mother Earth – with mankind as her consciousness."*

How does all of this pagan earth worship affect American society and, moreover, affect the average Christian

American in their church pew? Are the efforts of the Partnership and its supporters reaching their goal of changing the attitudes, values and beliefs of American society to fit into the global village? You be the judge. Following are a few actual events that have taken place around the nation in recent years.

ITEM: As the congregation sit in their church pews in the great Cathedral of St. John, the Divine in New York City, the priest stands at the alter, ready to receive a procession of animals for the annual Feast of Saint Francis blessing. Down the aisle comes a procession of elephants, camels, donkeys, monkeys and birds. These are followed by members of the congregation carrying bowls of compost and worms. Next, to the sounds of music, come acrobats and jugglers. In the pulpit, former Vice President Al Gore delivers a sermon, saying, "God is not separate from the Earth."

ITEM: Meanwhile, in Kansas City, at the Westin Crown Center Hotel, in an event sponsored by the Episcopal Diocese of Kansas, a North American native Indian prays to the grandfather spirit. And he prays to the spirits of the Four Directions. He prays for these spirits to bless the Earth and oversee the conference.

Then, former California State Senator Tom Hayden, a founder of the radical Students for a Democratic Society (SDS), offers an earth prayer, claiming the earth was speaking through him as he said, "*On this Earth Day let us say an earth prayer and make an earth pledge.*" "In the Bible," Hayden says, "*Ruah means both wind and spirit, so let us take time to breathe with the universe, connect with the earth and remember what we need to know and do.*" Hayden continued his prayer by saying, "*Celebrate that ancient spirits are born again in us, spirits of eagle vision, of coyote craft, of bear stewardship, of buffalo wisdom, of ancient goddesses, of druids, of native people, of Thoreau and Sitting Bull – born again and over again in John Muir and Rachel Carson and David Brower and Alice Walker.*" Hayden then asked the congregation to commit to carry the written word of Al Gore into official deeds.

Then, musician Paul Winter entertained the congregation with his saxophone. He explained that he had gone into the Superior Forest and taped exchanges of howls between his saxophone and a wolf. He then asked the congregation to join him in a "Howl- le-lu-ia Chorus." He made a wolf sound, and nearly 200 Episcopalians from Kansas howled back, expressing their oneness with the wolf.

ITEM: On a hillside, just outside Boulder, Colorado, 200 Americans "found their own space" and began meditating and resonating – using vibrating sounds that sounded something like locusts. Leader of the meeting was Jose Arguelles, leader of PAN (Planet Art Network) and New Age Transformation. Arguelles is the man who claims to have "decoded" the Mayan calendar and predicts great catastrophe for the world by 2012, unless we reject our current calendar and adopt the natural time Thirteen Moon 28-day calendar.

Addressing the gathered crowd, Arguelles presented them with a new idea – that of seeing the earth as a living, spiritual being that could feel pain. The group was asked to tune into the crystal matrix frequency – what he called Mother Earth's heartbeat. He told them to relax. Many went into a trance-like state. As people felt they were being filled with the Earth's energy, they became vocal, with sounds rising and falling rhythmically. Some swayed and some fell down on the ground and began writhing.

Then Jose Arguelles stood before them and brought them to silence. Arguelles told the group to concentrate on a cloud floating over head, just drifting, and then he told them to invite the cloud in to fill the empty spirit, the empty soul. He then said to invite PAN in – to accept Pan as the leader and guide for their lives.

Jose explained that Pan was the first son of Mother Earth and used to live close to his mother in the primeval forest with his brothers and sisters. Pan's brothers and sisters, he said, were the ones who went out and founded the temple-building societies. He meant the Aztecs and the Egyptians, etc.

But when Pan refused to join his siblings in the cities, they called him evil and "Satan." The siblings, Jose said, invented their own selfish religion – Christianity, which, he said, must be removed because it includes a vision of an Apocalypse.

The Boulder audience was told that right now, Mother Earth is bringing Pan back to save us and lead us into the New Age. The audience was told it could help by surrendering to Pan, tuning into the crystal matrix frequencies and carrying out the directions while tuned in. Arguelles then explained this might included the physical removal of Christians because they are the biggest obstacle to transformation.

Can Americans have any doubt as to where the Earth worshipping, radical environmental movement intends to take American society? Why are "Christian" leaders and officials locking arms with such foes of the American ideal of freedom, and to help them destroy the very religion they profess to lead?

America is in a life or death battle for its very soul, both in its public school classrooms and in its Christian church pews. Freedom is in the balance.

Moral Absolutes = Liberty!

WHAT DO I MEAN BY A FREEDOM POD?

By Tom DeWeese

How do we effectively fight to restore liberty in America? Most think that just getting a president elected is the answer, but what if we lose that race? Or, what if we win the Presidency but lose the House of Representatives and the Senate? What chance do we then have to make any progress in restoring liberty? We have to live in the days after an election. We have to make our way forward in our lives. So, do we simply surrender and accept our fate? Or do we create a new path to protect and promote the ideals of freedom?

The first step to answer that question is to stop depending on one person, one icon to lead us forward. We must take the responsibility ourselves to assure that government does not move forward unattended. We need to be directly involved at every level, especially on the local level. Change the debate to attack anti-freedom policies, expose non-governmental (NGO) carpetbaggers hiding in the shadows dictating policy, force elected officials to be personally responsible for their actions, and organize to assure the election of leaders who promote and defend the principles of freedom.

Picture how different our nation would be if we dug in to create a majority of governors across the nation who understood and operated under the Tenth Amendment which gives the States the power to stand against Federal overreach. What if you had a county commission that refused to participate in non-elected regional government? How would your life change if your city council was made up of individuals who guided your community under the three pillars of freedom, including protection of private property, encouragement and support for local businesses to operate and compete in free enterprise, and the lifting of rules and regulations that stifled personal choices in your individual life? How do we make all of that a reality? Set a goal to turn your local community into a Freedom Pod.

Simply focus on making these goals a reality in your community and, if successful, as prosperity spreads, the idea will certainly spread to a neighboring community, and then to the next. The challenge is to create a successful blueprint and a cadre of dedicated elected representatives that will begin to move into the state level of government. That will set the stage for effecting a federal government as conceived by our forefathers. The result will be the establishment of Freedom Pods across the nation.

For several decades the radical Left has been dedicated in its efforts to organize at every level of government while advocates of limited government failed to do the required "dirty work" of local organization and activism to protect our freedoms. We gave the Left a pretty clear playing field to organize and seize control, and now we are suffering under the result. For the dedicated Left, no position was too small. No appointed board was ignored. When was the last time local Conservative activists cared about positions like City Attorney? Yet these are the very officials who are enforcing the COVID-19 lockdown policies, dictated by governors and mayors. After witnessing this current election crisis, don't you wish people with Conservative values had been interested in gaining positions on the local Board of Elections? Local government is now infested with Planners, NGOs, and federal agencies dictating policies. And the only reason they have power and influence now is because the Left fought to elect representatives who then gave it to them. So, if you want to transform your community into a Freedom Pod you must start from scratch.

HOW TO BUILD A FREEDOM POD IN YOUR COMMUNITY

Here is a brief outline on how you can get started building your community into a Freedom Pod. And remember, the first rule is to focus on the local level. The rest will follow.

1. Start with Research: You need to know your enemy. Who are the players down at City Hall? Most of these planning groups and NGOs are operating in cities all over the nation. They have a history. What programs have they promoted, how are they funded, who are their leaders? In addition, look at your city's comprehensive plan. What programs does it contain? Here's a major hint to look for; Is there a specific part of the city that will be affected by the plan? Where is the money to come from for enactment of the plan? In any part of the comprehensive plan do the words "protection of property rights" appear?

2. Build a Team: To begin to push back, every public movement needs a team. Your team should include 8 parts. 1. Research as described above. 2. The Watchers – this is a team of three or four who volunteer to attend every single public meeting, to record what is said and who said it, determine who are the main movers in the meetings – the leaders pushing the agenda. The Watchers will soon see how the NGOs and Planners operate and note the influence they wield. This is how you determine the players. 3. The Strategist. This will be the main leader for your efforts. The Strategist looks over the research, the comprehensive plan and the players and begins to develop your approach to fight. 4. The Agitators. These are the people who will be your spokesmen to address public meetings, and present your oppositions and your case. They will coordinate as a team to assure their position is presented in a powerful and effective manner. 5. The Victims. These are the people whom the promoters of these policies fear most. The people who will be most affected and perhaps damaged by those policies. Get them in front of elected officials with a compelling story or their plight. 6. The Media Team. Two or three people to stay in constant touch with your local news media. You must build a relationship with local reporters so that they will come to rely on your information for stories. Don't fear the media. Talk openly with them. This can also include helping citizens to write effective letters to the editor. Make your side heard. 7. The Team of Activists. These are the people who will show up to do the grunt work, rally, carry signs, protest in front of City Hall or pack the Council Chamber when you need a show of support.

8. Social Media Team. If you've got some young people on your team this is right up their alley. Develop a website where you can get the word out. Start an online petition concerning a policy you are targeting. You may find that local officials are watching to see if it grows.

3. Take Legal Action: The reason so many local officials ignore our position is because they receive no consequences for their actions. Even if a victim successfully sues the city over a damaging policy, your elected representatives pay no fines or, legal fees nor do they face jail time. But, if handled properly, they are not immune to being held personally responsible. One legal tool to this end is Section 1983 of the 1964 Civil Rights Act. Planning meetings carried out in secret in backrooms of City Hall, often including non-elected NGOs that result in takings of private land, closing of businesses and enforcing arbitrary rules may violate your civil rights. And under that situation, the offending officials, who took an oath to defend the Constitution, may be held personally liable. Just the threat of filing such a suit could have incredible impact. Another possible tool is Section 3 of the 14th Amendment to the Constitution. Research can lead you to the appropriate action. It is just important to know that these tools are there to help you wipe the smirk off the faces of arrogant officials who think they are above the law.

4. Build a Campaign: The most effective way to take control of policy is to elect representatives who support your positions. Many times these people will be found in your organization – the ones who have become the most effective leaders or spokesmen for your cause. To assure you can run an effective campaign, the very first task required is to build an effective Precinct organization in every neighborhood. To begin, make a chart of every single elected position in your community, no matter how small. Begin to find candidates to run for every one of them. Appoint a Precinct Captain for every single precinct and assign them the task of getting to know all of their neighbors. List who is a likely supporter for your cause and make sure they are registered and will get out to vote. The Precinct Captain is like the trail boss getting the herd to market. Organize effectively and candidates, even governors and presidential candidates, will seek you out to help them. You will affect the outcome.

5. Build a Grading System to Reveal How Well Elected Officials Are Defending Liberty: It's a scorecard. Select specific issues dealing with laws and regulations that have been passed or at least voted on in City Council. Set up the scorecard based on a 1 – 10 grade with 1 being the lowest score – or tyrannical. 10 is the highest – a Freedom's Hero. How did these policies affect the three pillars of Freedom? Did they cause needless regulations on local enterprise? Did they take or control private property? How about controls on your energy use or travel restrictions? Put together a report, describing each bill or regulation and then give your local officials an individual grade for each one and then an overall grade. Praise the heroes and attack the tyrants. Send the scorecard to the news media and to social media. You will definitely get the officials attention and it will give you major influence in the community.

These are some very basic guidelines to help start your drive toward building a Freedom Pod in your community. There is obviously much more to be done to create a powerful organization, but these are the baby steps necessary to begin.

The main point is not to fear speaking out. Don't wait for some iconic face to represent you. If they lose so will you. For too long that's what we have done. Now it's time for you to stand up, speak out, take the lead and others will join you. If you don't take these steps then your government will be in someone else's hands, controlling you just as the Left has already done.

Here is the end game for the forces of freedom. No matter who is president, we must take control of our cities, counties, state legislatures, and governors. Only then can we stand up the potential tyranny from Washington, DC. To live your life as YOU choose, start to grow your Freedom Pod today.

AGENDA 21 TO GREEN NEW DEAL - THE WAR ON HUMAN SOCIETY

By Tom DeWeese

For nearly thirty years, as some of us have attempted to sound the alarm over plans to reorganize human society into global governance, we have been mercilessly attacked and labeled as radical conspiracy theorists.

Now, as those very plans move ever closer to enforcement, many are beginning to ask questions about the origins of the plans. Who stands behind them, and where will it all lead? Will life be better? Will there be more freedom and happiness? Are we finally going to create a society free of war and strife, as promised by the promoters? Who's right, the conspiracy theorists or the promoters?

First, a little history. One of the direct results of World War II, which had affected every nation, was the desire to find a way to prevent war. Most of all, the threat of nuclear war truly terrified everyone. This led to the creation of the United Nations as a way to provide a forum where nations could work out their problems in a public forum instead of on a battlefield. That was the selling point, at least.

The fact of the matter is, the United Nations is a club in which nations join voluntarily and pay dues for the privilege. However, from its very beginning, some envisioned a much larger role for the club. They envisioned the end of independent sovereign nations in which they charged were the root of war, strife and poverty. They claimed that for true freedom to exist, everything must be equal, including food, possessions, and opportunity. To achieve that, individual nations must surrender their sovereignty to the greater good – global governance overseen by the United Nations.

Right away, many socialist and communist-run nations grabbed hold of the concept. These were nations where the rights of the people were already determined by those in charge. In short, where government granted rights.

But there was one nation, in particular, that openly opposed this concept, because that nation had been created under the idea that every person possessed their rights from birth and that it was government's job to protect those rights. Such a concept was completely antithetical to the growing determination to give the United Nations central power over the Earth. The United States was soon seen as the major obstacle to the globalist agenda.

Over time, a "cold war" between the totalitarians of the communist nations and the advocates of free nations erupted and the United States found itself the designated leader of the "Free World." As a member of the UN's Security Council, the United States used its single-nation veto power to foil many of the efforts by the communist nations to build a UN power structure. This caused major frustration to those behind the goal of global governance. A solution had to be found to bring the United States into compliance.

Finally, in the 1970s a novel tactic emerged in the form of the illusion of environmental Armageddon by way of the illusion of "Climate Change." It was the perfect tool to propel the argument for independent nations. "It doesn't matter what rights you think you have if you don't have a planet to stand on!" The drive for global governance took hold, full speed ahead. One of the main proponents of the global governance movement, the Club of Rome said, "The common enemy of humanity is man. In searching for a new enemy to unite us, we came up with the idea that pollution, the threat of global warming, water shortages, famine and the like would fit the bill. All of these dangers are caused by human intervention, and it is only through changed attitudes and behavior that they can be over come. The real enemy then, is humanity itself." There it was! The answer. The environment doesn't recognize political or national boundaries. Just grab control of the land, water and air, and control every nation and every human life.

It didn't take long for the globalist forces to jump onto the concept. Again, the Club of Rome laid out the party line necessary to grab control: "Democracy is not a panacea. It cannot organize everything and it is unaware of its own limits. These facts must be faced squarely. Sacrilegious though it may sound, democracy is no longer well suited for the task at hand. The complexity and the technical nature of many of today's problems do not always allow elected representatives to make competent decisions at the right time." So, according to this concept, in order to replace these leaders which were elected by the people, we are going to enforce global policy created by forces unseen, unknown, and equipped with their own agenda. Yep - that will solve the world's problems!

It didn't take long for the communists to grasp the idea. Former Soviet dictator, Mikhail Gorbachev, after the collapse of his socialist paradise, quickly set himself up as an environmentalist to promote this new world order. He explained to the State of the World Forum, "The emerging 'environmentalization' of our civilization and the need for vigorous action in the interest of the entire global community will inevitably have multiple political consequences. Perhaps the most important of them will be a gradual change in the status of the United Nations. Inevitably, it must assume some aspects of world government." And there is was -- the real goal, out in the open.

The UN's Commission on Global Governance went further to explain how it would all come about as it reported, "The concept of national sovereignty has been immutable, indeed a sacred principle of international relations. It is a principle which will yield only slowly and reluctantly to the new imperatives of global environmental cooperation." Now, how to set it all into place...?

The UN began to sponsor a series of international meetings, specifically focusing on the environment and how to "save planet Earth." After a series of such meetings where private, non-governmental organizations (NGOs), officially recognized and sanctioned by the United Nations, met with government leaders, diplomats, and various bureaucrats, began to draw up a plan for using environmental issues as the basis for regulating human activity – all through the noble guidance of the United Nations, of course. Finally, in 1992, more than 50,000 NGOs, diplomats, and 179 world leaders, including U.S. President, George, H.W. Bush, met in an "Earth Summit," in Rio de Janeiro, Brazil. Here, they introduced a series of four documents and treaties for the world to accept as guidelines for UN-led reorganization to save the planet.

Most significant of these plans was one designed to create a global plan of action for the 21st Century. It was named Agenda 21, and its supporters promoted it as a "Comprehensive blueprint for the reorganization of human society." All 179 world leaders signed onto the document, including President Bush, and promised to bring its goals into national policy.

Here's a quick overview of the Agenda 21 plan:

There are four parts: Sections 1 is titled Social and Economic Dimensions. Details include, international cooperation to accelerate sustainable development policies, combat poverty, changing consumption patterns, protecting and promoting human health conditions, and promoting sustainable development by integrating environment policy into development plans.

Section 2: is titled Conservation and Management of Resources for Development. This section outlined plans for promoting sustainable agriculture and rural development, integrating those policies into planning and management of land resources, enforcing sustainable policy into every body of water from seas to rivers and lakes, waste management, and conservation of "fragile" ecosystems, .

Section 3: is titled "Strengthening the Role of Major Groups. Here we get into who was going to promote these policies in a divide and conquer tactic. First, the infamous NGOs who wrote the document gave themselves a major role under the chapter entitled "Strengthening the role of non-governmental organizations: partners for sustainable development." But we were also to have "global action for women towards sustainable and equitable development." Next, children were specifically targeted to be promoters of sustainable development. Another chapter outlined how to pull in local elected officials to promote support for Agenda 21 initiatives. Each chapter in this section of the Agenda 21 document focuses on more and more individual interest groups needed to push the agenda, from business and industry, to science and technology to farmers. No stone was left unturned in this outline to reorganize human society.

Section 4: titled Means of Implementation. Here, finally, are the details on how it was to be accomplished. As all of the individual groups are brought under the umbrella, now the enforcers would focus on the necessary financial resources, transferring environmental technology into decision making, and focusing on education process, not only for schools, but also for "public awareness and training." And then, of course, there are the necessary "International legal instruments and mechanisms."

Here it is, a complete and comprehensive outline for the agenda to completely transform all of humanity under the umbrella of globalism. And of course, it was urgent that the agenda be enforced as quickly as possible because, we were facing an environmental Armageddon caused by selfish, uncontrolled, ignorant humans, unfettered in unenlightened nation-states.

First Global Warming, and then later Climate Change became the focus of the looming disaster. And it simply did not matter if there was no true science to back up the scare tactic. As the Canadian Minister of the Environment, Christine Stewart, openly admitted, "No matter if the science of global warming is all phony... climate change provides the greatest opportunity to bring about justice and equality in the world." There is was! The truth. This whole charade wasn't about saving the environment, but about changing the world order with a new gang in charge.

Timothy Wirth, President of the UN Foundation, further enforced that fact when he said, "We've got to ride this global warming issue. Even if the theory of global warming is wrong, we will be doing the right thing in terms of economic and environmental policy." There it is again – "economic policy!"

And finally, there was Paul Watson, a co-founder of the radical Green NGO called GreenPeace. He summed it all up very nicely, saying, "It doesn't matter what is true, it only matters what people believe is true." No muss, no fuss, just get in line and don't question us!

However, there was still a skeptical world that had to be indoctrinated to follow the party line. So, it was important that the language, while keeping the urgent tension of environmental crisis in the forefront, used soft-peddle words to promote the policies. For example, soothing, reassuring comments such as, "we are just concerned about the environment, aren't you?" "We want to help those less fortunate, living in poverty. Don't you?" "Imagine all the people sharing all the world." Nothing to worry about here, just a giant, loving, worldwide group hug. So, the agenda moved forward, with few questioning its details, motives, and true goals.

Meanwhile, forces inside the UN were determined to hurry along the real agenda --- global governance. As we moved closer to the year 2000, many insiders saw the start of the new Millennium as the perfect opportunity to launch a full-scale framework for global politics. In preparation, the UN planned to sponsor a Millennium Summit to plan the future for the world. A document was prepared for presentation at the Summit called the Charter for Global Democracy. In the UN's words, the document contained "detailed, practical measures which set out an ambitious agenda for democracy in international decision-making, now increasingly known as 'global governance.'"

The Charter contained 12 principles or goals. It would consolidate all international agencies under the direct authority of the United Nations. In addition, the UN would regulate all transnational corporations and financial institutions, along with the establishment of a new institution to establish economic and environmental security by insuring sustainable development. The Charter called for a declaration that Climate Change is an essential global security interest that requires a "high level action team" to control carbon emissions. And, the Charter called for the cancellation of all debt owed by the poorest nations, global poverty reductions, and for "equitable sharing of global resources," including land, air and sea, plus various wealth redistribution schemes. Under the Charter for Global Democracy there would be no independent, sovereign nations, no private property or free enterprise. All would be controlled and regulated by UN edict – all in the name of environmental protection, of course.

But there is more. To establish a government, three main ingredients are necessary; a revenue taxation system, a criminal court system, and a standing army. Principle 3 of the Charter for Global Democracy demanded an independent source of revenue for the UN. Proposed were taxes on aircraft and shipping fuels and licensing the use of the global commons. The "global commons" are defined to be "outer space, the atmosphere, non-territorial seas, and related environment that supports human life." In other words, the UN claimed control of the entire planet, its air and water, even outer space, and the power to tax use of it all.

Principle Number 5 would authorize a standing UN Army. Principle Number 6 would require UN registration of all arms and the reduction of all national armies "as part of a multinational global security system" under the authority of the United Nations.

Principle Number 8 would activate the International Criminal Court, make the International Court of Justice compulsory for all nations, and give individuals the right to petition the courts to remedy what they deemed social injustice, meaning redistribution of wealth based on emotional tirades rather than the rule of law.

There you have it, all the tools necessary to make the United Nations a full- fledged global government, a government over the whole world. But, the Charter for Global Democracy broke one major rule in the UN's plans to dominate the world – it was too honest. It lacked the soft sell and, instead, marched brutally forward, revealing their true agenda. It was never officially presented to the Millennium Summit for world leaders to approve in front of the cameras. However, it remains a shadow agenda, with parts included in other documents. The Criminal Court does exist and there is still a drive for an environmental court. The UN continues to push for full ratification of the Law of the Seas Treaty that would give it full control of the waters of the planet. While the United States has not officially ratified the treaty, Congress has promoted regulations through the Environmental Protection Agency (EPA) to enforce many of the same goals.

Meanwhile, the UN has continued to add more details, a little at a time, through documents released at yet more international gatherings. The Millennium Summit did issue 8 goals, mostly focusing on eradicating poverty, respecting nature, and "Protecting the Vulnerable." The goals are there, just not the direct wording of the Charter. Peace, Brother!

In 2016, the UN issued Agenda 2030, containing 17 goals. They are all the same as Agenda 21 and the Millennium Goals, however each new document issued reveals a little more detail as the UN moves ever closer to enforcing all 12 principles of the Charter for Global Democracy.

Most recently, however, the Sustainable forces again took off the gloves of misdirection, and this time they have gotten away with it. This latest version is called the Green New Deal and it didn't come as a declaration or a suggestion from another summit. This time it came as actual legislation introduced into the U.S. Congress and has been openly accepted as the center of political debate across the nation.

Even though the word "green" is in the title, it, too, is not an environmental policy. The Green New Deal is an economic plan to reorder society away from free enterprise, private property, and limited government. Gee, where have we heard that before? Oh yes, Agenda 21, Agenda 2030, and the Millennium Declaration!

The Green New Deal is divided into four pillars. First is the Economic Bill of Rights, demanding full employment, guaranteeing a living wage, Medicare for all, tuition-free education and the right to affordable housing. Can you find any issue there that is designed to save the planet?

Pillar 2 is labeled the Green Transition. Surely here is where we will find concerns expressed for clean rivers and air, right? Nope. We find money and tax schemes for global corporations who agree to play ball and spread the sustainable propaganda. This helps to fill their pockets as it kills competition from small, independent businesses. There's also the usual attack on cars along with schemes to end shipping of food and products by truck or air. Each community, you see, will be responsible for providing all of its needs for the local population.

Pillar 3 called Real Financial Reform, turns banks into public utilities run by government, doing away with the stock market, all leading to higher taxes and the end of freedom of choice for your financial needs.

Pillar 4 is called a Functioning Democracy. It calls for the creation of a "Corporation for Economic Democracy" that will basically combine government agencies, private associations, and business enterprise into one big corporation, all to be controlled by one, central ruling authority. The last time I checked on such an idea it was called communism.

My colleague, climate change expert Paul Driessen, produced a very clear picture of what life will be like under the Green New Deal. Are you ready America? According to Paul's analysis, the GND would, "control and pummel the jobs, lives, living standards, savings, personal choices and ecological heritage of rural, poor, minority, elderly and working classes." Says Paul, the GND would turn middle America into vast energy colonies. Millions of acres of farmland, wildlife habitat, and scenic areas would be blanketed by industrial wind, solar, and battery facilities. Windswept ocean vistas and sea lanes would be plagued by towering turbines. Birds, bats, and other wildlife would disappear. As you are forced to rip out exiting natural gas appliances from your kitchen, replacing them with electric models, electrical power would only be there when its available, rather that when you need it. And don't forget, as the GND moves to ban petroleum, pharmaceuticals, cosmetics, paints, synthetic fibers, fertilizers, plastics for computers would all be gone, along with millions of jobs. Not to mention that the cost of near non-existent energy would soar.

This, then, is the future offered to us by the power-mad control freaks now plotting every day to "reorganize human society." These policies now dominate political debate and are becoming established in more and more states and communities, yet any attempt to reveal the true goals are immediately labeled "conspiracy theories" and those sounding the alarm are called extremists.

Meanwhile, as we have all suffered through the COVID lockdowns, the forces behind these policies have been busy planning ways to use tactics they have learned from enforcing the pandemic to move forward with a "Green Reset" to tackle the so-called climate crisis. In a recent issue, Time magazine announced the "Great Reset," asserting "The COVID-19 pandemic has provided a unique opportunity to think about the kind of future we want… to share ideas for how to transform the way we live and work."

Bill Gates said that large-scale economic shutdowns are "nowhere near sufficient" to curtail climate change. Rather, we need "to get rid of emissions from all the different sectors." He went on, "Simply shutting down (the economy) is not going to get (us) to our goal. So just like we need innovation for COVID-19, we also need to get rid of emissions from all the different sectors and bring down climate change." Are you ready to live in a cave with no heat or running water to satisfy Bill Gates' demands to reorganize society? What else would be the alternative if we must completely shut down our entire infrastructure of transportation, industry, buildings, electricity, etc?

Green New Deal advocates, like Gates, see the COVID-19 outbreak as a signal to the international community that it is necessary to reform humanity's relationship with nature, pointing to concerns that "as habitat and biodiversity loss increase globally, the coronavirus outbreak may be just the beginning of mass pandemics." That's the new scare tactic – piled on top of climate change. Just as the Club of Rome prediction declared decades ago, the real enemy is humanity itself. So there it is, now facing us like never before – the interconnection of climate change, the Green New Deal, and the COVID-19 pandemic. Step by step, changing and controlling human society.

The COVID-19 lockdown has been the master experiment as to how much manipulation people will accept out of fear. It has been the grand experiment to get us to stop driving, reducing energy use, and change our living habits. All called for in the Green New Deal. Arn Menconi, an environmental activist and recent candidate for the Colorado state senate said, the "coronavirus has proved we can afford the Green New Deal and Medicare for all."

But there is much more planned for the reorganization of human society that few have counted on. Take careful note of the growing manipulation of the free market, a main target of Agenda 21/GND policy. Global corporations, such as Amazon and Walmart, that have agreed to join in Public Private Partnerships (PPPs) with government to promote the Sustainable policies, have been allowed to continue near normal operations and they are thriving in the lockdowns. Meanwhile local, small, independent businesses have been forced to close their doors. As those small business jobs are lost, employees are left with little alternative than to seek positions in the global behemoths or accept government handouts. Soon, we will begin to see the corporations demanding that employees accept Bill Gates' mandatory COVID vaccines or lose their jobs. That means that more and more will have no choice but too march in lockstep with the dictates of their masters. Free thought, free market competition, and free expression will no longer exist anywhere but in the minds of those old enough to remember "when". These are all the enemies of totalitarianism and must be curtailed.

They've managed to find the perfect scare tactic to get us all to "voluntarily" give up our liberties, allow government to shut us in our homes, kill our jobs, stop our schools, and destroy human contact. They have finally achieved the vision of British monarch, Prince Phillip who once said, "If I were reincarnated, I would wish to be returned to Earth as a killer virus to lower human population levels." Never tell these people a joke, because they will eventually turn it into global policy!

How do we stop this drive to destroy our way of life? One thing the COVID lock-down has proven, is that we must regain control of local and state governments. It was mayors and governors who led the way to enforce most of the draconian controls over our ability to move about, go to work and church, see our doctors, and open our businesses. That's why it's imperative that those concerned about stopping this transformation must become active on the local level, organizing, researching, speaking out and running effective local government campaigns.

One major obstacle standing in the way of the forces of freedom to stop this drive for global governance is that too many on the Right have ignored the threat, joining in the chorus against we who have been sounding the alarm. Not one mainstream, Washington, DC-based conservative organization will even mention the words Agenda 21 or the many issues connected to the global agenda. Many Republicans in Congress lamely accept many of the environmental positions, instead offering lighter, "more reasonable" positions. Once they do that, they've already lost the argument. Today's mainstream Conservative movement has changed little of their tactics from those used 50 years ago, when they were fighting Soviet communism. Yet, as the environmental movement takes over the American beef industry and leads the way to destroy private property rights and single-family neighborhoods, little action is taken. We cannot win if we ignore the massive loss of property in cities and farms. We cannot win if we fail to stand with the growing number of Americans who are suffering from the radical environmental assault. We have to change the debate and appeal to the growing legions of victims. And we must learn that the most effective place to begin the fight is on the local level in our communities – not on Capitol Hill.

In 1980, Ronald Reagan beat Jimmy Carter in 49 states. Think about that when you look at today's election results. When that happened, the Left said "never again" and they began to organize. They focused on the local level and not just city council and county commission races. No position was too small or unimportant, including appointed boards, and even city hall jobs. These are the places where policy is decided and regulations, licensing, and government attitudes are prepared and carried out. When was the last time a local Republican group discussed the importance of the office of City Attorney? Yet these are the positions of power that have enforced the COVID lock-downs. After this most recent election don't you wish we had some influence over voter registration and Board of Elections? This is how the Democrats have managed to turn formerly red states blue. Pure determination.

Every freedom-loving American must become vitally aware that we now face the most powerful, determined force of evil to ever threaten humanity. To defeat them we must become equally determined to do the dirty work which our side has ignored for fifty years. This includes, local organization of precincts, finding viable candidates to run, and controlling the debate over issues as they appear, making sure our side is heard. We must decide to relentlessly focus on the three pillars of freedom, including protection of private property rights, taking necessary steps to help small business thrive, and assure that government is a servant of the citizens rather than citizens submitting to government.

Take such actions to secure your community as a Freedom Pod where these rights are the backbone of every decision made by your local government. If you are successful, the idea will get the attention of neighboring communities and another Freedom Pod will be planted there -- and then the next and the next. These are the actions we must take to "flatten the Socialist curve" and take America back! As Winston Churchill said, "Never Give In, Never, Never, Never."

THE GROWING THREAT OF SMART METERS

By Tom DeWeese

Sustainable Development is code for a policy designed to transform human society, essentially eliminating individual life decisions and replacing them with top – down, one-size-fits-all government control. In steady fashion, the agenda for this new policy, designed at the international level, is put into place piece by piece with a new government council here, and new regulation there, each designed to appear as a "local" development program. Like the proverbial frog in the slowly boiling pot, many Americans fail to notice the rise in government heat.

The main course of action to impose the new agenda is through the pretense of environmental protection; "Sorry about your rights, but if we don't save the planet, then we will all perish!" And so with the devastation of a thousand pin pricks, America and its form or government is being changed through the creation of non-elected boards, councils and regional governments, designed to enforce the new regulations and "assure that we protect the environment." A major target is a drive to shut down the coal-based industry based on nothing more than global warming hysteria. As jobs are lost and energy costs soar from this policy, alternative energy (wind and solar), according to the EPA, is the only choice for new sources of power.

In fact, control of energy and water are the two most effective tools in the enforcement of the Sustainable Development agenda. Without energy and water, human society stops. Using strict controls on how, or even if, energy and water can be used provides government with the power to dictate every aspect of society.

However, controlling energy use in individual homes provided a more difficult obstacle than mere taxes or regulations. Government needed to be able to monitor energy use and individual habits in every single home. And so, the Smart Meter was born.

The Smart Meters are being installed in homes across the country, replacing the old style analog meters. The power companies are telling their customers that the Smart Meters will help them save money on electric bills by helping control usage. They also claim that the Smart Meters will help the power companies operate more efficiently by eliminating the need to physically read the meters as they do with analog meters. However, these sales pitches from the power companies hide the real facts behind the push to replace every analog meter in the nation with the Smart Meters.

There are several major problems for homeowners as the Smart Meters are installed. Here are just a few:

- The cost of heating and cooling homes with Smart Meters is going up because of the inefficient alternative energy that is more expensive than coal and nuclear power.

- Homeowners with Smart Meters in place are discovering that they can't heat or cool their homes during peak power usage as the electric companies control the thermostats and automatically cut back on usage.

- Property rights are being violated by Smart Meter installers who come onto property against the will of the owners.

- A 2012 Congressional Report revealed that power companies are able to read data from the meters that expose residents' daily schedules and their personal behavior, the types of appliances they use, even if there are certain types of medical equipment in use in the home. This information can then be sold to private concerns or placed in government files. It can lead to unwarranted government surveillance.

- Evidence is now emerging that the Smart Meters, which operate by emitting electromagnetic signals, have become a health hazard, as thousands of Smart Meters in neighborhoods blast a non-stop signal, creating what is called Electromagnetic Smog. The electromagnetic radiation is dangerous for the elderly, children, pets, and those subject to such disorders as epilepsy, heart disease and more. It can lead to disruptive sleep patterns, chronic fatigue, depression, headaches and much more.

In addition, new evidence is emerging that Smart Meters are actually a danger to national security. In a letter to the Virginia State Corporate Commission, Hugh Montgomery, a member of the Virginia Commission on Energy and Environment, and a national security expert expressed his concerns over the growing danger to our national security through possible cyber attacks on the nation's power grid. Specifically, he cited the growing installation of the "smart grid" power system as a direct threat to U.S. security:

"Contrary to the understanding – and sincere belief – of supporters of the 'smart grid' that such a system is secure from individual hackers or organized terrorist activities, even the most cursory examination at classified levels shows that this is not true. Damage far more severe than hours or days without power can be inflicted from anywhere on the globe by a person with malicious intent, a laptop computer and internet access. Although I regret deeply that this is the case, the smarter the grid becomes, the more vulnerable it becomes – thus the more vulnerable we all become, individually and collectively. And in the case of Dominion Virginia Power, the more vulnerable the corporation becomes to a deliberate externally-induced attack."

Be alert for "Mandatory Safety Inspections." Some utility companies are now attempting to enforce "mandatory" safety inspections of private homes, using the excuse of vague federal laws. In some cases, such inspections have included a team of "inspectors" who actually go through the house, replacing incandescent bulbs with the "green" alternatives – without obtaining permission from the homeowner. They have also made changes in thermostat settings and, of course, installed smart meters. Inspectors sometimes file detailed reports of the "inspections" in a permanent file, detailing such information as how many people live in the house, the type of appliances in use, the kind of windows in the home, and other details that might affect energy use.

As the battle against the Smart Meters grows across the nation, Americans need to understand the issue, the dangers, and the real reasons behind the government's drive to force them on angry and protesting homeowners. Smart Meters are designed to be a major tool for the enforcement of Sustainable Development policy. In addition, they help build the massive power of a central surveillance system that will provide government with detailed information of your energy use, your movements in your home, the way you use your personal private time, and even how many people are in your home at any given time. It is an unconstitutional invasion of your home by government, as set down in the Fourth Amendment to the U.S. Constitution. Every American has a duty to preserve freedom by protesting and stopping the forced installation of these devises.

Colorful Handouts for Public Officials and all Private Citizens

Many people want colorful, easy to grasp data that can be absorbed in less than 2 or 3 minutes. The following flyers pique interests and keep the reader engaged long enough to learn more about Agenda 21 and Sustainable Development.

- "A Sustainable Development Q&A" - A brief single sheet that answers the most common questions regarding Sustainable Development.

- "7 Facts You Should Know About Conservation Easements" - This single sheet offers a quick look at the side of conservation easements most people are not aware of.

- "The Hazards of Conservation Easements" - On two sides, this flyer explains the downsides of conservation easements in more detail. It emphasizes, near the end that all conservation easement contracts are unique, so it is important to read the agreement and ignore the promise made by planners and trusts brokers.

- "The Sustainability Paradox" - On this colorful, one-sided flyer the reader can trace the entire history of Sustainable Development. This sheet contains sources there reader to which readers can refer.

- "The Sustainability Solution" - This two-sided sheet is for use by public officials as it challenges them to take steps to protect individual's property rights above those of the environment. It contains steps officials can take to protect citizen's rights.

- "Sustainable Agriculture, It Sure Sounds G-r-r-eat!" This tri-fold brochure is printable on both sides to create a handout that explains how sustainable agriculture hands control of food production to the government.

A Sustainable Development Q&A

From Plymouth Rock to the Pacific Coast, home owners across America are losing rural land and property rights in alarming numbers.

Willingly or not, they are being crowded into high-density urban living and "walkable" communities in the name of sustainable development, Smart Growth and environmental justice.

■ What is sustainable development?

The United Nations defined the term in a 1987 report as "development that meets the needs of today without compromising the ability of future generations to meet their own needs." A 1992 UN convention, called Agenda 21, codified the report.

■ What is wrong with that?

The "needs" the report refers to are not human needs but those of the planet. It concludes we can only meet them by eliminating or reducing "unsustainable" activities globally. These include property ownership, consumerism, and high meat intake, use of fossil fuels, roadways, automobiles, dams, our legal system, pastures, golf courses and more.

■ How can a United Nation's program affect citizens in the United States?

Three presidents agreed through executive orders to 1. abide by these definitions of sustainable development, 2. reduce the "unsustainable" activities and 3. implement action plans to accomplish this through federal agency regulations.

■ Why have I not heard of this side of sustainable development before?

Because, most see sustainable development as a safe way to protect the planet. The UN and other groups see sustainable development as a political agenda in which it is acceptable to sever personal rights in the name of the environment.

■ How does the UN v ersion of sustainable development enter my community?

Public agencies or planners approach local officials and "stakeholders" (not always residents) with proposals to review Master Plans and conduct surveys to improve living quality and the environment. Frequently, they invoke perceived "crises" such as transportation issues, overpopulation or poor water quality. Grant money often follows, and may include strings that limit property rights. The UN version, while protecting the earth and wildlife, has secondary regard for personal rights.

■ How might sustainable development affect my property rights?

By accepting certain grants and extreme regulations on property usage, owners find their development rights stripped away in favor of bicycle paths, solar farms, open spaces, mixed-use dwellings and controlled property and farming use.

■ The Constitution and local laws protect my property rights, don't they?

Not if you sign them away by agreeing to accept certain grants, surrender them through conservation easements, wetland or endangered species designations, or lose them through eminent domain or specific changes in your town's Master Plan.

■ What can I do?

See pamphlet: The "Sustainability" Solution.

The "Sustainability" Solution

Are individual rights more important than those of the collective community are? Do human rights come before the environment? Public officials must answer these tough questions as sustainable development programs roll across the national landscape.

As green community plans with reassuring names like Smart Growth, open spaces, corridors and multi-use dwellings, transform the American landscape, alert citizens ask if these programs relate to land-grabbing UN initiatives. Planners routinely assure officials their plan is 'pure' and has nothing to do with the UN.

Here is why officials should consider 'pure' as unlikely:

- It is highly unlikely your town's plan does not follow the actions outlined in the 1992 UN Rio Earth Summit (Agenda 21) as they were implemented via the President's Council on Sustainable Development, embedded in every federal agency and state government and are attached to HUD community grants. (Search: UN Agenda 21, Rio Declaration; also: http://clinton4.nara.gov/PCSD/)

- ICLEI, a UN sanctioned Non-Governmental Organization (NGO), has memberships in over 600 US communities for the purpose of implementing Agenda 21, under the name of sustainable development or Smart Growth programs. (Search: ICLEI UN Agenda 21; also http://www.iclei.org/index.php?id=11454)

- Over 2000 NGO's, including the American Planning Association, operate within the US to implement the UN version of sustainable development. (Search: NGO American Planning Association Agenda 21; Go here to see how NGO's work: http://americanpolicy.org/sustainable-development/attack-of-the-ngos.html/)

- Many, if not most planners use the Growing Smart Legislative Guidebook that echoes the UN's Agenda 21 program by using universally acceptable terms and boilerplate solutions. (Search: Growing Smart Legislative Guidebook)

These plans purport to sustain the planet by shifting people from rural areas into high-density urban developments and reducing vehicle use, whether they want to or not.

Plans are generally initiated in response to a presumed and often poorly validated crisis such as "urban sprawl", "farmland development" or "poor water management." Changes to master plans and conservation easements are two methods of implementation. In the process, many citizens lose their property rights. (Search: Global Biodiversity Assessment; wildlands project map)

Here is how public officials can protect citizens' rights and the planet:

- Recognize that citizen's property rights are paramount in America and must be protected first.

- Never assume your plan's initiators know if it is part of a larger global plan; or would share that information if they did.

- Question the validity and source of crises claims such as "wildlife endangerment" or "population explosion in the next 10 years will cause massive overcrowding if we do not act now."

- Do not take grant money unless you check all of the attached strings. There are a lot more than you may think. (See: http://www.hud.gov/offices/adm/grants/nofa10/scrpgsec.pdf Page 11 tells what your new 'livable' community will look like.)

- Refuse federal or state money for new sustainable development or Smart Growth programs that jeopardize rights; and transition out of existing programs.

- Avoid partnerships with the federal government, NGOs, foundations, and corporations that incorporate land-grabbing clauses in their agreements.

- Develop a Property Rights Council (PRC) for reviewing all governmental and intergovernmental activities to protect citizen's rights. (Search: Bonner County Property Rights Council)

- Seek alternative plans and planners who will work with your community to protect individual property rights first, and respect the planet.

- Be certain legislation is in force to repeal any plan that infringes on individual property rights.

Families must not be forced from their homes, nor farmers or citizens forced to surrender property rights to manage our environment.

Hi-density urban housing and 'livable' communities are not for everyone and should be voluntary.

Public officials now assume a new role of protecting the property rights of those who elected them to office as they act responsibly toward the environment.

Read and know all proposed land use regulations and governmental and nongovernmental activities. That is the ultimate "sustainability" solution.

New, updated version!

Agenda 21 In One Easy Lesson

Awareness of Agenda 21 and Sustainable Development is racing across the nation as citizens in community after community are learning what their city planners are actually up to. As awareness grows, I am receiving more and more calls for tools to help activists "fight back. Many complain that elected officials just won't read detailed reports or watch long videos. "Can you give us something that is quick, and easy to read that we can hand out," I'm asked.

So here it is. A one page, quick description of Agenda 21 that "ts on one page. I've also included for the back side of your hand out a list of quotes for the perpetrators of Agenda 21 that should back up my brief descriptions.

A word of caution, use this as a starter kit, but do not allow it to be your only knowledge of this very complex subject. To kill it you have to know the facts. Research, know your details; discover the NGO players in your community; identify who is victimized by the policies and recruit them to your "fight; and then kill Agenda 21. That's how it must be done. The information below is only your first step. Happy hunting.

What is Sustainable Development?

Some think that the planet is in danger of global warming and over consumption.

They really believe that the only way to fix the problem is to control the flow of resources and wealth, which literally means changing human civilization and the way we live.

The problem is, this forced transformation of our society necessarily leads to a thirst for power by some and top-down control by government – and that can eventually lead to tyranny.

According to its authors, the objective of sustainable development is to integrate economic, social and environmental policies in order to achieve reduced consumption, social equity, and the preservation and restoration of biodiversity. Sustainablists insist that every societal decision be
based on environmental impact, focusing on three components; global land use, global education, and global population control and reduction.

Social Equity (Social injustice)

Social justice is described as the right and opportunity of all people "to benefit equally from the resources afforded us by society and the environment." Redistribution of wealth. Private property is a social injustice since not everyone can build wealth from it. National sovereignty is a social injustice. Universal health care is a social injustice. All part of Agenda 21 policy.

Economic Prosperity

Public Private Partnerships (PPP). Special dealings between government and certain, chosen corporations which get tax breaks, grants and the government's power of Eminent Domain to implement sustainable policy. Government-sanctioned monopolies.

Local Sustainable Development policies

Smart Growth, Wildlands Project, Resilient Cities, Regional Visioning Projects, STAR Sustainable Communities, Green jobs, Green Building Codes, "Going Green," Alternative Energy, Local Visioning, facilitators, regional planning, historic preservation, conservation easements, development rights, sustainable farming, comprehensive planning, growth management, consensus.

Who is behind it?

ICLEI – Local Governments for Sustainability (formally, International Council for Local Environmental Initiatives). Communities pay ICLEI dues to provide "local" community plans, software, training, etc. Addition groups include American Planning Council, The Renaissance Planning Group, International City/ County Management Group, aided by US Mayors Conference, National Governors Association, National League of Cities, National Association of County Administrators and many more private organizations and official government agencies. Foundation and government grants drive the process.

Where did it originate?

The term Sustainable Development was first introduced to the world in the pages a 1987 report (Our Common Future) produced by the United Nations World Commission on Environmental and Development, authored by Gro Harlem Brundtland, VP of the World Socialist Party. The term was first offered as official UN policy in 1992, in a document called UN Sustainable Development Agenda 21, issued at the UN's Earth Summit, today referred to simply as Agenda 21.

What gives Agenda 21 Ruling Authority?

More than 178 nations adopted Agenda 21 as official policy during a signing ceremony at the Earth Summit. US president George H.W. Bush signed the document for the US. In signing, each nation pledge to adopt the goals of Agenda 21. In 1995, President Bill Clinton, in compliance with Agenda 21, signed Executive Order #12858 to create the President's Council on Sustainable Development in order to "harmonize" US environmental policy with UN directives as outlined in Agenda 21. The EO directed all agencies of the Federal Government to work with state and local community governments in a joint effort "reinvent" government using the guidelines outlined in Agenda 21. As a result, with the assistance of groups like ICLEI, Sustainable Development is now emerging as government policy in every town, county and state in the nation.

Revealing Quotes From the Planners

"Agenda 21 proposes an array of actions which are intended to be implemented by EVERY person on Earth... it calls for specific changes in the activities of ALL people... Effective execution of Agenda 21 will REQUIRE a profound reorientation of ALL humans, unlike anything the world
has ever experienced... " Agenda 21: the Earth Summit Strategy to Save Our Planet
(Earthpress, 1993).

Urgent to implement – but we don't know what it is!

"The realities of life on our planet dictate that continued economic development as we know it cannot be sustained...Sustainable development, therefore is a program of action for local and global economic reform – a program that has yet to be fully defined." The Local Agenda 21
Planning Guide, published by ICLEI, 1996.

"No one fully understands how or even, if, sustainable development can be achieved; however, there is growing consensus that it must be accomplished at the local level if it is ever to be achieved on a global basis." The Local Agenda 21 Planning Guide, published by ICLEI, 1996.

Agenda 21 and Private Property

"Land...cannot be treated as an ordinary asset, controlled by individuals and subject to the pressures and inefficiencies of the market. Private land ownership is also a principal instrument of accumulation and concentration of wealth, therefore contributes to social injustice." From the report from the 1976 UN's Habitat I Conference.

"Private land use decisions are often driven by strong economic incentives that result in several ecological and aesthetic consequences... The key to overcoming it is through public

policy…" Report from the President's Council on Sustainable Development, page 112.
"Current lifestyles and consumption patterns of the affluent middle class – involving high meat intake, use of fossil fuels, appliances, home and work air conditioning, and suburban housing are not sustainable." Maurice Strong, Secretary General of the UN's Earth Summit, 1992.

Reinvention of Government

"We need a new collaborative decision process that leads to better decisions, more rapid change, and more sensible use of human, natural and financial resources in achieving our goals." Report from the President's Council on Sustainable Development

"Individual rights will have to take a back seat to the collective." Harvey Ruvin, Vice Chairman, ICLEI. The Wildlands Project

"We must make this place an insecure and inhospitable place for Capitalists and their projects – we must reclaim the roads and plowed lands, halt dam construction, tear down existing dams, free shackled rivers and return to wilderness millions of tens of millions of acres or presently settled land." Dave Foreman, Earth First.

What is not sustainable?

Ski runs, grazing of livestock, plowing of soil, building fences, industry, single family homes, paves and tarred roads, logging activities, dams and reservoirs, power line construction, and economic systems that fail to set proper value on the environment." UN's Biodiversity Assessment Report.

Hide Agenda 21's UN roots from the people

"Participating in a UN advocated planning process would very likely bring out many of the conspiracy- oriented groups and individuals in our society… This segment of our society who fear 'one-world government' and a UN invasion of the United States through which our individual freedom would be stripped away would actively work to defeat any elected officials who joined the conspiracy' by undertaking LA21. So we call our process something else, such as comprehensive planning, growth management or smart growth." J. Gary Lawrence, advisor to President Clinton's Council on Sustainable Development.

This sure sounds good — but is it really a win-win situation?

Well, let's take a closer look at the points being raised. After all, there is always more than one side to every issue. The first point actually raises several issues itself:

1. Each community will grow its own food through the use of individual and/or community owned farms.

We need some definitions to understand what this is saying.

"Each community" is of course a reference to a "sustainable community". Washington State University School of Architecture likely has the definitive description of "sustainable community":

"...a sustainable community is one which provides all of its own needs for air, water, land (or food and fiber), and energy resources within the confines of its own site. [1]"

Obviously, creating and maintaining a "sustainable community" has implications that stretch beyond a system of "sustainable agriculture".

Here we have a copy of the University's graphic—it is quite intuitive. The circle around the community is generally referred to as an "Urban Growth Boundary" (UGB) or a "Utility Service Area". Here is an easy to understand definition from the State of Minnesota:

"A UGB is an established line beyond which urban services such as public sewer and water and transportation improvements will not occur. [1a]"

Sounds wonderful until you stop and think about what this will do to property values outside of the UGB. Who would buy property where modern conveniences such as power, road maintenance, etc. will not be permitted? That's right—nobody!

The free market system has been replaced by an official policy that promotes a system of sustainable communities/agriculture. The new system will create a shortage of desirable real estate. As anyone knows, a shortage, created naturally or by government edict, will destroy the average income earner's ability to own a parcel of land.

"Community owned farms" is another point referenced here. The USDA provides an interesting definition. In bureaucratic speak—government doubletalk—a "community owned farm" is CSA—"Community Supported Agriculture".

"In basic terms, CSA consists of a community of individuals who pledge support to a farm operation so that the farmland becomes, either legally or spiritually, the community's farm, with the growers and consumers providing mutual support and sharing the risks and benefits of food production. [2]"

What this means exactly will obviously have to be determined by the bureaucrat who wrote it. But I venture to say that "spiritual ownership" of a private farm is a concept that yearns to be a plot on Twilight Zone.

Another point that must be considered is the concept that farms will form a boundary around the community. This is often referenced as the "foodshed[3]" or "food-circle[4]". The concept is confirmed in the graphic from the Washington State University program. Oh—I forgot to mention the name of their process—it is "A Comprehensive Urban Regenerative Process". Remember EVERYTHING that is consumed in the community is produced in the community. So the concept of a

"foodshed" or "foodcircle" fits right in. Local governments across the country are adopting this concept. The bullseye from Clackamas County Oregon[5] is a fair indicator of its general acceptance. Here the urban center is surrounded by the Metropolitan Foodshed. Food produced in the "foodshed" is intended to be consumed in the "urban center". The outer ring is the Foundation Lands Woodshed and is where "Value-Added Forestry[6]" products will be produced. See the point? A "value added tax" system is being introduced. For instance, the price for agricultural products grown or produced outside of the "foodshed" does not include the full cost of the "food mile". What are those costs? Well, I don't know all of the cost associated with the concept of a "food mile" but see the "food mile" poster above. Footnote 7 provides a link to the information relating to it.

These are some, but not all external costs: transportation, soil degradation, irrigation-related groundwater depletion, and pesticide and fertilizer misuse. [8]"

Ultimately these costs will be calculated by a "governance" system. If you recall, government is not government, it is:

Back to the GOOD OLD

"SUSTAINABLE AGRICULTURE"

As Tony the Tiger says, it sure sounds "G-RR-EAT!! "

You know, we have read glowing reports and articles about "sustainable agriculture." Here are just some of the coming changes to the new agricultural system:

1. Each community will grow its own food through the use of individual and/or community owned farms that form a boundary around the community.

2. All farming will be sustainable and eco-friendly. Organic farming will be certified and monitored by a farm stakeholder committee. This will ensure that food labeled "Organic" is authentic.

3. Constant measurements will be taken to guarantee that the sustainability and eco-friendly parameters [BMPs (best management practices)] are maintained.

4. Organic farming will be productive without the use of pesticides and unnatural fertilizers.

5. Industrial farming will no longer be allowed to damage the earth.

6. Importing foreign food products will be reduced in order to increase local production and thereby help the local economy.

"the framework of rules, institutions, and practices that set limits on the behavior of individuals, organizations and companies[9]"

The "institutions" that sets the "rules" will be a collection of "stakeholders" (those who are recognized as having a degree of responsibility for determining the cost of a "food mile") and local government entities. The true cost after factoring in ecological damage to the earth will include "social justice"[10].

What is "social justice"? Here is a quick run-down. It involves:

- progressive taxation
- income redistribution
- property redistribution
- equality of opportunity, and
- equality of outcome

In summary:

Foodshed Regulations would give these environmental groups and government agencies control over all means of production of the food consumed by the American people. This is pure Marxism (as in control of all means of production through abolition of private property.) In the name of "Social Justice" all food production, distribution and consumption would be controlled by government. Through increased taxation and regulation, American citizens would be stripped of their wealth and property and have all resources redistributed as government sees fit.

When this happened in Russia under Stalin, eleven million people who were seen as resisting socialism were intentionally starved to death. Food (or lack thereof) can become the ultimate weapon, the ultimate control.

Thus far we have only responded to the first item defining "sustainable agriculture." It has consumed most of the space available and has involved a number of rabbit trails we have had to go down.

So that we don't overburden our initial effort, we shall take the advice of a young nine year old nephew we know. He asked his mother a simple question about the birds and bees and she referred him to his father. Well, Dad, being a proper father, was determined to inform his son about things as completely as he could. It was sometime later that Mom asked the boy if his Dad had answered his question. The boy responded, "He sure did! I think I got a lot more than I really wanted to know".

FOOTNOTES

1. www.arch.wsu.edu/09 publications/sustain/modlsust.htm
1a. www.mnplan.state.mn.us/pdf/2000/eqb/ModelOrdWhole.pdf
2. www.nal.usda.gov/afsic/pubs/terms/srb9902terms.shtml
3. ibid
4. ibid
5. http://web12.clackamas.us/alfresco/download/direct/workspace/SpacesStore/fa8597da-c264-11dd-a620-5fa507d8ef06/20080624.pdf
6. http://www.conservationdistrict.org/sheds
7. http://www.hawthornevalleyfarm.org/fep/foodmiles.html
8. http://www.worldchanging.com/archives/009093.html
9. United Nations "Human Development Report" - 1999
10. European Foundation Center

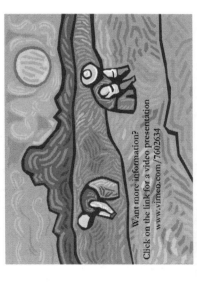

Want more information?
Click on the link for a video presentation
www.vimeo.com/7602634

ALLIANCE FOR CITIZENS RIGHTS
KEN FREEMAN: Chairman 256-498-3802
DON CASEY: Vice-Chairman 205-542-1730
www.keepourrights.org
www.alabamapropertyrights.org

1. Your community is a member of organizations such as ICLEI (International Council for Local Environmental Initiatives), or ICMA (International City/County Management Association) - these organizations promote the creation of sustainable communities in line with United Nations Agenda 21.

2. Your community has a Sustainability Director or Department of Sustainable Development that is in charge of coordinating the planning and implementation of sustainable development policies in your area.

3. Your community has a Vision, Master, or Comprehensive Plan typically created within the past 5-10 years that promotes the three E's of Sustainable Development (Environment, Economy, and Social Equity) also known as the "Triple Bottom Line".

4. Your community supports compact, high density, mixed use, pedestrian and bicycle oriented development patterns, constructed primarily along public transit and rail corridors. This is also known as Smart Growth, New Urbanism, or Resilient Communities. These communities also promote alternative modes of transportation away from the traditional automobile toward policies which endorse and encourage public transit whenever possible to curb fossil fuel usage and lower carbon emissions. This may include the implementation of community wide Biking and Pedestrian plans.

5. Your community is actively promoting healthy communities through sustainable agriculture and community gardens; encouraging a shift away from the current free market driven food system to a new locally-focused, publicly incentivised sustainable food system.

6. Your city or town has established an Urban Growth Boundary beyond which all development including the suburbs is considered SPRAWL and blight and is discouraged through various incentives and regulations.

7. Your town has joined with local regional councils or with the state or federal government to promote Sustainable Communities Planning or to launch new sustainable initiatives.

8. Your community has embraced and is building the infrastructure of the new "green" energy alternatives including solar and wind farms while discouraging the continued use of other forms of energy such as fossil fuel and coal.

9. Your community is placing restrictions on private landowners in the form of increased regulation and changed land use rules in order to promote farmland preservation, environmental protection and conservation of natural resources.

10. Your community is working through state and local mechanisms including NGO's (Non-Governmental Organizations) to gain more and more control over privately owned land in order to secure it in perpetuity as shared, common "green space".

11. You find this or any similar symbol in your community's official government documents:

12. Your community belongs to the Earth Charter, the Sierra Club's Cool Cities Initiative or the Audubon Society's Sustainable Community Initiative or your mayor has signed the U.S. Conference of Mayors' Climate Protection Agreement.

13. Your community leaders accept manmade global warming as fact and begin to endorse policies to mitigate any actions or development that may promote global warming.

14. Your community enacts an energy plan requiring governmentally predetermined efficiency standards in order to lower your community's carbon footprint. This may include utilizing new "green" LEED building and energy code standards for construction and development that include incentives, benchmarks, and retrofitting.

15. Your local leaders begin to refer to your community as a "transition town", a resilient city, or as a "livable community" and begin teaching through local government and institutions a community focus on interdependence with nature, interconnectedness and globalism.

16. Your local government uses the language of Social Equity; such as food justice, economic and environmental justice, fairness, direct democracy, diversity, food deserts, social justice, and wealth redistribution.

17. There is involvement from multiple Non-Governmental Organizations in your city's planning and development initiatives. Any new planning involves these NGO's and many other "stakeholders" in the collaborative, consensus-building, "visioning" process that details the plans for your community's future.

18. Your local school systems begin promoting environmental awareness and sustainable development; with a focus on becoming environmentally literate, good global citizens. Your school may be involved with International Baccalaureate or other UN sponsored education agendas.

19. Your local government authorities begin using and exceeding their constitutionally granted powers alongside private organizations to assist in the promotion of sustainable initiatives through Public-Private Partnerships.

20. You see a focused and significant push toward "social equity" interfaith initiatives that promote a "one world" mentality along with community diversity, multiculturalism, sameness of faiths, social inclusion and environmental stewardship.

21. Your community uses language that calls for "redefining" how we determine progress and prosperity away from traditional wealth and growth measurements like GDP (Gross Domestic Product) toward more philosophical non-specific ideas such as well being and happiness.

21 Signs Agenda 21 is in your Community

The "Hazards" of Conservation Easements

Conservation easements are promoted as a way to gain tax advantages and protect private lands from development. For those who fail to read the fine print, they can be a nightmare of legal proceedings, extreme regulations and the eventual loss of cherished property.

The background:

In a typical conservation easement, a Land Trust purchases some or all of the "bundle" of a property owners' rights. Once signing the agreement, the owner's rights are legally subservient to his new partner, the trust.

Owners make this trade to gain tax benefits, cash payments, protect their property from development or avoid the threat of government land acquisition or regulation.

To receive the benefits the owner agrees among other duties to one or several of the following: protect animals, plants or eco-systems, preserve open spaces for farming, outdoor enjoyment or recreation for the public; historic preservation and to follow best land management practices. The trust enforces the restrictions.

The benefits:

Benefits have the greatest value for wealthy owners. The relief of estate taxes was a primary driver of conservation easements as inheritance laws forced many heirs to sell property to developers to pay the IRS. Conservation easements avoided this sell-off.

Today, trusts sell easement programs to lower income owners who may gain little from tax benefits. Instead, trusts promote cash payments, assurances land will not be sold to developers, safety for heirs and good environmental stewardship. In this way, trusts, collaborating with public agencies, gain control of vast amounts of private property in perpetuity as part of an ecological initiative.

- The property owner receives charitable deductions on federal taxes based on the difference between the values of the land before and after granting the easement.
- The property owner receives relief from federal estate or inheritance taxes.
- Many states provide income tax credits and property tax relief for conservation easements.
- Owner receives a payment for development rights.
- Property usage and development is strictly controlled.

The hazards:

- Under a conservation easement, the owner sells his development rights and therefore no longer has controlling interest in his or her property.
- Trusts often re-sell the easement to government agencies, which alter best management practices, driving up compliance costs. Eventually, these cost increases can force owners to sell their land at a reduced price.

LAND FOR SALE

- Third party trusts, non-profit organizations or government agencies can attack or enforce your easement restrictions even if your trust does not.
- By law, conservation easements can be challenged by third parties, but only if the party can issue conservation easements. Therefore, there can be no third party challenge by the landowner or even a supporter of the landowner.
- Because the ownership rights are muddled between taxes, restrictions and best practices requirements, it can be difficult to find a buyer willing to pay a fair market price for the land *or* the tax deductions. Further, it will be hard to find a lender or to get full title insurance.
- The IRS demands the easement remains in perpetuity. This ignores changes in science, nature and even the definition of what is ecologically beneficial over time.
- The cozy promises of a friendly working partnership between the landowner and the trust prior to the contract have no bearing in a court of law. The Ninth Federal Circuit Court of Appeals has ruled pre-contract discussions unenforceable.
- Land Trusts are in the sales business. They are under no legal obligation to disclose information detrimental to closing the sale.
- Often land trusts "flip" your easement to a public agency to make a "pre-acquisition" profit. (In one example, The Nature Conservancy paid $1.2 million for an easement and promptly sold it to the Bureau of Land Management for $1.4 million. This enabled a non-scrutinized transfer of private property to the federal government while avoiding publicity, regulations, zoning changes or eminent domain.)
- Through "mitigation banking," and "habitat protection" your property can be condemned and used to offset damage, loss of endangered species, wetlands or proposed development to another ecosystem or habitat; it can be allocated to complete a contiguous wildlife habitat.

> - *According to a Gulf of Maine Times article, "The Maine Coast Heritage Trust has sold more than 700 of its 850 easements and acquisitions to federal and state agencies."*
> - *Additionally, more than 2/3 of The Nature Conservancy's operating budget is to purchase private lands that are then sold to federal and state agencies, says American Enterprise.*

What you can do:

- Think twice before selling anyone your property development rights.
- Be aware that federal, state and local governments collaborate with Land Trusts every day for the purpose of acquiring private land through conservation easements. Arguably, this is to protect the environment. Practically, it forever severs your personal property rights, which are the foundation of freedom.

- Know that once you sell your development rights you have sold the control of your property for you and your heirs. Your remaining rights will likely decrease in value.
- Remember, nothing the land trust representative or the government representative says; nor anything manuals or brochures depict, prior to signing the contract, is binding or legal. The only words that matter are those in the contract.
- Be aware that you can protect the environment without surrendering your property rights.
- Before signing any documents, discuss your wants, needs and expectations with your family. Read every document.
- Hire an unbiased attorney of your choosing, not the land trust's, government's or broker's. Choose one who will place your rights above all else to review each document before entering into any agreements.

Sources:
- Uniform Conservation Easement Act - National Conference of Commissioners on Uniform State Laws, Approved by the ABA
- Big Meadows, Big Mistake - American Land Foundation
- Colorado Landowners Burned By Conservation Easements - Fred Grant
- Conservation Easements and Title Insurance - L.M.Schwartz
- Conservation Easements: The Good, the Bad, and the Ugly - National Center for Public Policy Research
- Environmental Protection Agency Website - Mitigation Banking Factsheet

Unraveling the "Sustainability" Paradox

The word "sustainability" flashes images of fresh air, clean water and revitalized resources. Yet, Americans are discovering it also means lost property rights and value, reduced mobility and the surrender of family land. Because of "sustainable development":

- Mike Sackett faces $100s of thousands in EPA fines for building his dream home on his own ID property.
- Planners in Carver County, MA force citizens to accept solar farms few want.
- In Dade County, Florida, the local government is forcing 1500 homeowners from their property.
- In King County, WA, 17,000 residents filed court complaints attempting to win back lost property rights.

Here is why a good idea like sustainability has such destructive outcomes:

Locally, most see sustainable development (SD) as a reasonable way to protect the environment. Globally, SD is much different. *It is a social, political and economic action plan that forces boilerplate solutions for real or perceived environmental crises on willing and unwilling participants.*

Most citizens and public officials are not aware their local sustainable plan derives from the coercive global one. Here is how it happened:

- The term Sustainable Development came from a 1987 UN report called "Our Common Future" which concluded that developed nations, such as the US, were responsible for global warming and poverty, which in turn created an unsustainable planet. The solution was to limit property ownership and growth in the US, and transfer consumer wealth to developing nations. (Read, "Our Common Future" - Amazon)

- The 1992 UN Rio Earth Summit in Brazil codified the report, created a worldwide action plan called Agenda 21, and was signed onto by 178 nations including the US. (Search: "UN Agenda 21 Rio," "Rio Declaration")

- A 1993 executive order bypassed Congress to create the President's Council on Sustainable Development (PCSD) whose stated purpose was to "implement UN Agenda 21 in the US" via regulatory agencies. (Search: EO 12852; State Dep't. submission to the 5th Session of the Commission on Sustainable Development, April 1997)

- In 1998, J. Gary Lawrence, an advisor to the PCSD, recommended the term Agenda 21 and UN references be dropped to more easily implement SD in the US. Agencies and planners changed their terminology to Smart Growth and other environmentally friendly terms. (Search: "The Future of Local Agenda 21 in the New Millennium" p.5)

- By 2001, Sustainable Development/Smart Growth was part of the regulatory makeup of every federal agency and signed onto by the US Conference of Mayors, The National Governor's Association and several Leagues of Municipalities. It is now in your hometown. (Search: your town, state, and sustainable development)

- In 2002, HUD and other federal agencies funded the American Planning Association's, Growing Smart Legislative Guidebook 2 to incorporate Agenda 21 principles. This is now the standard planning apparatus throughout US communities. (Search for guidebook by name)

Now you know the problem. For what to do read, The "Sustainability" Solution.

MEET ICLEI

Many Americans ask how dangerous international policies can suddenly turn up instate and local government, all seemingly uniform to those in communities across the nation and around the globe. The answer – Meet ICLEI, one of the original authors of Agenda 21. It's a non-profit, private foundation and UN NGO that has made its mission to bring Agenda 21 policy into every community in the world.

Originally known as the International Council for Local Environmental Initiatives (ICLEI), today the groups has removed the word "International,: to call itself simply, "ICLEI – Local Governments for Sustainability."

In 1992, ICLEI was one of the main groups instrumental in creating Agenda 21. Today, ICLEI is used as one of the mechanisms to undo the political recognition of unalienable rights. The group's mission is to push local communities to implement Agenda 21 policy that restructures our representative form of government through global and non-elected regional government. Of course, ICLEI uses global warming and environmental protection as the reason for the need for these policies.

First, ICLEI approaches local government and promise to bring in all the tools they need to implement the plans. In return the communities pay dues to ICLEI, which now takes control to assure that the mayors, city councils, and county commissions keep their promises and meet their goals. Specifically, when a community signs an agreement with ICLEI, they are agreeing to impose Sustainable Development as official community policy.

Here are just some of the programs ICLEI pushes into the community agenda in the name of "community services" and environmental protection: When ICLEI takes over a town, it organizes like a well-oiled machine, using access to a network of "Green" experts, newsletters, conferences and workshops. To assure the proper indoctrination of city employees is complete so that their entire planning process is based on sustainable policy, ICLEI provides Toolkits, online resources, case studies, fact sheets, policy and practice manuals, and blueprints use by other communities, just to assure them that they are not alone in implementing these policies. This is how your local government officials begin to believe that all of this is the proper role of government. And of course, there's notification of relevant grant opportunities – this is the important one – money – with severe strings attached.

And some of the ways to implement those regulations can get downright silly. For example, ICLEI's program called "Green Power Government," creates legislation to guarantee homeowners and businesses access to sunlight by establishing a hypothetical "solar fence" that limits the amount of shade cast by new construction sites.

ICLEI recommends that the community hire a full time "sustainability manager" who, even in small towns, can devote 100% of his time to assure that every nook and corner of the government is on message and under control. Increased taxes, fees, regulations, and restrictions are all part of ICLEI's game. It's all part of a successful agenda for imposing Sustainable Development policy resulting in the creation of a "soviet" system of non-elected boards, councils, and regional governments in which local residents have little or no ability to question or oppose government actions.

A few years ago, more than 650 American cities were dues-paying members of ICLEI. However, the American Policy Center has successfully used the attached petition to raise awareness of ICLEI and call on those cities to rescind that membership. As a result, over 150 of those cities did just that. ICLEI was shocked and has never fully recovered. Use this petition and this information to expose ICLEI in your city!

Remove ICLEI - Restore the Republic!

PETITION TO THE MAYOR AND CITY COUNCIL

Whereas: under your leadership, this community is imposing the policies of Sustainable Development, and

Whereas: under your leadership, this community is paying dues to an international organization called "ICLEI - Local Governments for Sustainability," for the express purpose of creating and imposing Sustainable Development programs based in large part on the theory of global warming, and

Whereas: ICLEI works in secret, violating transparency of government and the public's right to know, and

Whereas: it is the duty of every elected representative to provide full disclosure and open discussion and debate on policies that affect private property rights, community development, water use and restrictions, restrictions on auto use and parking, open space restrictions, building codes and restrictions, restrictions on types of materials to be used in building, taxes designed to restrict development and auto use, and many more policies that have a damaging effect on the rights of citizens and the economy of the community, and

Whereas: Sustainable Development, based on the unproven and disputed theory of Global Warming, is the driving force behind these policies now being imposed on all the citizens of this community, created, discussed and decided in private meetings rather than before the full community, with ICLEI as the guiding force, now,

Therefore, I the undersigned citizen of this community demand:

A. That all citizens be allowed to openly discuss and debate these Sustainable Development restrictions on our economy, our property and our way of life, and

B. That there be a full disclosure to the citizens of this community concerning the financial association with ICLEI and its involvement with these Sustainable Development policies, and finally,

C. That such contract with ICLEI be immediately terminated and the community have no further dealings with this international organization.

Signed _____ Date _____

Commissioner's Letter on the Dangers of Agenda 21

Following is an actual letter written by County Commissioner Roger Nutt, of Spartanburg, SC to other county commissions alerting them to the dangers of Agenda 21 in their community.

It may be reproduced as is to pass out at local government meetings; used by other county commissioners; used by activists to alert their own commissioners; even used as a basis for a letter to the editor.

Spartanburg County Council
Roger A. Nutt, P.E.
District 6 Representative

July 4th, 2011

Hamilton County Commissioners
401 Courthouse
625 Georgia Ave.
Chattanooga, TN 37402

Fellow Commissioners,

I am writing to you today to offer some peer background information on a movement that should be very concerning to all of us that have taken an oath to protect the freedoms of our citizens. If you are like me, you probably cringe every time you hear from those that are bringing you the latest conspiracy. I understand that there are far too many real problems to deal with to be spending any time on the perceived ones. From the research I've done on this topic myself, however, I am convinced that this is something that is worth the time of all of us as elected representatives.

As a civil engineer working specifically as a land designer and consultant, I have been aware for decades that there has been a very strong and specific push to encourage government to place more and more controls on land use. This push has come from the EPA, the State Department of Environmental Control, local environmental groups and many others - all under the umbrella of being for the 'public good'. As you are aware, some government regulation is not only a good idea, but necessary in a civilized society for the people to have peaceful enjoyment of their property. The problem with land use controls, as with most government regulations, is finding a balance between the public good and an individual's rights and freedoms. It is my strong belief that the founders of this country strongly favored the individual freedoms over government regulations in every case - including government control of land.

The movement going around the country has to do with the buzz word 'sustainability'. No doubt Chattanooga, like many other cities or counties around the country, is dealing with groups and consultants touting the 'sustainable communities' initiative. Most likely your county is also involved with the international group ICLEI (International Coalition for Local Environmental Initiatives) that highlights its mission to promote global environmental programs by enlisting local governments to implement their sustainability agenda. The agenda that they overtly promote in conjunction with your local environmental groups is taken from what's called The UN Sustainable Development Agenda 21. I encourage you to look over Agenda 21 as I have done and reach your own conclusion about what place it has in our free market society. Although certainly some good can come from developing a more 'sustainable' community, the part that particularly should concern us is land use (Chapter 10). It is the belief of ICLEI and these local environmental groups that government should, and actually must, exercise control of land to ensure that it is being utilized for its 'best use'. This concept taken to its logical conclusion truly flies in the face of the principle of private property rights given to us by our constitution.

One of the problems with this movement is trying to figure out just what 'sustainable' really means. We have sustainable advisory committees here and they spent the first meeting or so in utter frustration just trying to define it. ICLEI classifies items such as cars, paved roads, private property, and suburban housing as 'unsustainable'. From their own videos (see their YouTube page) you'll find that they do feel, however, that the infamous slums in India (over 1M+ in population) are considered 'sustainable' and are models of such. You don't have to engage in extensive research to see just where they stand on these issues. In order to show our taxpayers that we were serious about protecting their rights and freedoms, Spartanburg County Council unanimously voted to end its membership with ICLEI in May of this year.

Over the years, we have all seen subtle pushes for our governments to enact more stringent land use controls. Many counties and cities have some type of Zoning ordinance in place (we have so far avoided such here in Spartanburg) and, as is true with most things, it works better in some areas than in others. The new 'Sustainable Development' movement however is not so subtle. In this movement you will certainly hear talk of directing people to live in certain areas - namely the urban areas. Some will call for the Urban Growth Boundaries where little or no development will be allowed outside the circle. You may hear that you (the government) should control the land so that farm land stays that way, and that infrastructure should only be provided in certain areas that are designated. All of this is an attempt to dictate - for the satisfaction of this ideology - where people can live and what they can and can't do with the property that they purchased with their hard earned money. We all know from experience that when controls like these are put in place, only the big money wins. Even with Zoning, if a company comes in with enough money and resources, typically the property will be rezoned. As our constitution tells us, we are not here to pick winners nor losers, but to ensure that all rights are protected - including the right to own, enjoy and use our personal property.

Today there are many who abhor 'cul-de-sac type' neighborhoods. They label them 'unsustainable' and 'sprawl'. The argument you hear is that people are leaving them in droves to move into the city because they desire a more 'walkable community'. As commissioners you have to ask yourself the logical question : "If that is the case, won't the free market take care of itself?" With people moving out, more developers will move to the city and less development will take place in the rural areas. The sustainable development group is satisfied and you didn't have to infringe on anyone's property rights. So if it's that easy, why the great push? Obviously there's a push (and developers still build these neighborhoods) because that's where many of us <u>choose </u>to live - maybe even you or your fellow commissioners. Is it our duty to limit or eliminate that choice for our citizens or provide the services to them in support of that choice?

Every county and city in this country must decide for themselves how they will govern and how they will grow. I certainly don't hold myself up as an expert or one who has any place in giving other officials advice. My goal was just to share my thoughts and concerns about a movement I see invading our local governments. We all owe it to our constituents and ourselves to be informed and proactive in the defense of all our rights and freedoms.

I appreciate your time and your service. Please don't hesitate to contact me if you have any questions.

Sincerely,

Roger A. Nutt, P.E.
District 6 Representative, Spartanburg County Council

The CRDINATION
STRATEGY

EVERYTHING passed in Washington D.C. must be implemented in your community to take effect. There has been little we can do to affect the policies that hurt our communities... **UNTIL NOW!**

CURRENT

OUR STRATEGY
Restoring Local Control

1. Congress Passes Law

2. Agency Designated to Impliment Law

3. Agency Enforces Law on Local Communities Affecting Economy and Way of Life

3. Before an Agency Can Implement a Law it Must Coordinate with Local Governments, Protecting the Community's Economy and Way of Life

The answer is restoring local control across America by making the government agencies coordinate with you. This is where we step in. Through the strategies we teach, communities are protecting their local economy, restoring productive use of their land, and preserving their way of life.

THE COORDINATION PRIMER

Federal and state statutes require administrative agencies to work coordinately with local government -- to "coordinate" with local government in developing and implementing plans, policies and management actions.

The statutes create a process through which local government has an equal position at the negotiating table with federal and state government agencies. They create a process which mandates agencies to work with local government on a government-to-government basis. Implicit in the mandate of coordination is the duty of the governmental representatives to work together in an effective relationship to seek to reach agreement on consistency between federal, state and local plans and policies.

The coordination process is the most effective method for protection of the rights of citizens to own and use property. It provides a process through which local government can bring administrative agencies to the negotiating table on issues related to the community's economic stability and social and cultural cohesiveness.

Citizens are limited in their ability to influence the decisions of government agencies. Their only participation, as individuals in the decision making-process, is through offering written or oral comments as to the agency's proposal. Most always, their oral remarks are limited to three minutes maximum. The agency's only responsibility is to summarize the public comments; they are under no obligation to negotiate any alteration of plans, policies or actions based on public input.

In federal actions where the National Environmental Policy Act requires an environmental assessment or an environmental impact statement, the agencies have only the duty to summarize public comments in the assessment or statement.

When local government represents its constituents' positions through coordination, the agencies have much broader duties. The agencies must listen to the local input, must analyze the local position to determine whether there is conflict between the proposed agency action and the local plan or policy and must use good faith effort to resolve any existing conflict to achieve consistency between the proposed plan, policy or action and the local plan or policy.

When Congress or the state legislature orders agencies to coordinate their activities with local government, they require the agencies to go to the negotiating table on an equal footing with local government. The word "coordinate" is a word of common usage, a word of daily usage in general public communication. It is not a term of art or a term of scientific and special meaning.

DEFINITION : (DE-Fə-NI-SHəN)

Federal and state courts have said repeatedly that when the legislative body uses a word of common, everyday usage without specific definition it is presumed that the legislative intent was to use the word as it is commonly defined for public use.

The common dictionary definition of "coordinate" shows that a person or party operating in "coordinate" fashion is operating as a party *of equal importance, rank or degree, not subordinate."* (Webster's New International Dictionary)

a number used in specifying the spatial arrangement of the constituent groups of **co·or·di·na·tion** \ (koh-awr-dn-ey-shuh) *n.* **1.** of equal importance, rank or degree, not subordinate, **2.** one that is equal in importance, rank, or degree, **3.** to harmonize in a common action or effort, **4.** to work together harmoniously, **5.** the act of coordinating; the state of being coordinate; harmonious adjustment or

The American Heritage Dictionary defines "coordinate" as "one that is equal in importance, rank, or degree." It also states that as a verb the term means "to harmonize in a common action or effort," "to work together harmoniously." It defines the term "coordination" as "the act of coordinating; the state of being coordinate; harmonious adjustment or interaction."

The Courts which have been put to the task of defining the meaning of the term have gone to the dictionary definitions. In *California Native Plant Society v. City of Rancho Cordova*, 172 Cal. App. 4th 603, 91 Cal. Rpr. 3d. 571 (Third App. Dist. 2009) the Court said this of "coordinate":

"... the concept of 'coordination' means more than trying to work together with someone else. Even under the City's definition of the word 'coordination' means negotiating with others in order to work together effectively. To 'coordinate' is 'to bring into a common action, movement, or condition'; it is synonymous with 'harmonize." (Merriam-Webster's Collegiate Dictionary. Supra, at p. 275, col. 1) Indeed, the very dictionary the City cites for the definition of the word 'coordinate' defines the word 'coordination' as 'cooperative effort resulting in an effective relationship.' (New Oxford Dict., supra, at p. 378, col.3)
*"Although the city suggests 'coordination' is synonymous with 'consultation' -- and therefore, the city satisfied its 'coordination' obligation under the general plan at the same time it satisfied 'consultation' obligation under the plan -- that is not true. While the City could 'consult' with the Service [Fish and Wildlife] by soliciting and considering the Service's comments on the draft EIR, the City could not 'coordinate' with the Service by simply doing those things. . . . by definition 'coordination' implies some measure of cooperation that is not achieved merely by asking for and considering input or **trying** to work together."*

The California case involved interpretation of a city General Plan relating to land use restrictions and zoning requirements. The plaintiff urged the court to set aside two city actions approving residential and commercial development on the ground that the city had not followed the General Plan's requirement that mitigation of the impact of such developments be set in "coordination" with the United States Fish and Wildlife Service.

The city argued that all coordination requires is soliciting input, carefully considering the input and responding to comments by the inputting party. Thus, the city argued that by soliciting input from the Fish and Wildlife Service, by considering the input and responding to, it "tried" to work together with the service and satisfied the "coordinate" requirement of its General Plan. As seen above, the Court repudiated the argument, holding that "coordination" requires far more than just seeking, considering and responding to input comments.

Within the accepted dictionary definitions relied on by the California Court, when local government asserts the coordination authority granted to it by statute, it can and should expect to approach the negotiating table on an even par with the state or federal agency involved. It can and should expect that the state or federal agency will enter negotiations prepared to work effectively toward resolution of conflicts which may exist between local and state or federal policy, plan or action.

In the state of Texas, when the Eastern Central Texas Sub-Regional Planning Commission was formed and asserted its authority to coordinate with the Texas Department of Transportation, as provided by Section 391 of the Local Government Code of Texas, it relied on the "equal, not subordinate" definition of the word. The Texas Court of Civil Appeals referred to the dictionary definition when defining the term "coordination" in *Empire Ins. Co. of Texas v. Cooper.* (138 S.W.2nd 159 (1940))

It is patently obvious that when a legislature uses the word "coordinate" or "coordination" it means more than "cooperate" or "consult". As the California court reasoned in *Native Plant Society*, supra, if the legislature intended mere cooperation or consultation, it could and would have said so.

CONGRESSIONAL MANDATE

The first land use statute on the federal level that required coordination with local government was the Federal Land Policy and Management Act passed in 1976. Congress defined the term "coordination" by specifying exactly how the federal agency should negotiate with local government. 43 United States Code Section 1712 orders that the Bureau of Land Management coordinate its "land use inventory, planning and management actions with...any local government..." Congress directs that the agency implement this requirement by doing the following:

1. Keep apprised of State, local and tribal land use plans;
2. Assure that consideration is given to local plans when developing a federal plan, policy or management action;
3. Provide early notification (prior to public notice) to local government of development of any plan, policy or action;
4. Provide opportunity for meaningful input by local government into development of the plan, policy or action; and
5. Make all practical effort to resolve conflicts between federal and local policy, and reach consistency.

The National Forest Management Act requires the Forest Service to coordinate with local government; in 16 United States Code Section 1604, Congress ordered the Service to "develop, maintain, and, as appropriate revise land use resource management plans. . .coordinated with the land and resource management planning processes of State and local governments and other Federal agencies."

Both the Bureau of Land Management and the Forest Service issued rules for implementation of "coordination" and the rules reflect the statutory mandate of seeking consistency between federal and local plans, policies and actions.

The "coordination" mandate is included in every other natural resource management statute which Congress has passed since 1976. Even in the Homeland Security Act, Congress directs that coordination exist with local government AND with local officials.

The most recent Congressional direction that coordination take place is in the Owyhee Public Lands Management Act of 2009, in which the Secretary of Interior is directed to implement the act in coordination with the County, State and Tribes.

Given the dictionary definition of the term and concept of "coordination," given the actions which the agencies must take under FLPMA, it is apparent that Congress intended to require equal base negotiations to reach consistency.

In 1982, the Secretary of Agriculture issued the first rules to define coordination as required by the National Forest Management Act. Those rules required Forest Service line officers to take the same steps as those required of Bureau of Land Management officers by FLPMA. The bottom line for compliance with the 1982 rules is to reach consistency.

The 1982 rules are significant and relevant because they are the only Forest Service rules issued in the last three decades that have passed judicial muster, and thus are still applicable. All successor planning rules have been declared invalid because of NEPA violations in the rule making process.

When a unit of local government -- any unit of local government that is a political subdivision under state law -- exercises its statutory authority to "coordinate," it can and should expect the federal or state agency to negotiate with it on an equal footing, making a good faith effort to reach consistency between federal/state and local plan, policy or action.

Congressional Criteria

The agency shall:
1. Keep apprised of State, local and tribal land use plans;
2. Assure that consideration is given to local plans when developing a federal plan, policy or management action;
3. Provide early notification (prior to public notice) to local government of development of any plan, policy or action;
4. Provide opportunity for meaningful input by local government into development of the plan, policy or action; and
5. Make all practical effort to resolve conflicts between federal and local policy, and reach consistency.

COORDINATION IS NOT...

We have set forth clearly what coordination is in "The Coordination Primer." The parameters of the meaning are prescribed clearly by considering what Coordination is not.

COORDINATION IS NOT COOPERATION

Coordination is much more than cooperation. It is not "cooperation," "cooperate" or "cooperating." The word "cooperate" is defined as "to act or work with one another" or "to associate with another or others for mutual benefit." The word "cooperation" means "common effort… for common benefit." (Merriam-Webster Dictionary)

a number used in specifying the spatial arrangement of the constituent groups of **co·op·er·a·tion** \ (kō-ä-pə-ˈrā-shən) *n*. **1**. to associate with another or others for mutual benefit, **2**. assistance or willingness to assist, **3**. The association of persons or businesses for common, usually economic, benefit, **4**. The act or practice of cooperating, **5**. more or less active assistance from a person, organization, etc.: *We sought the cooperation*

No version of the word "cooperate" carries any connotation of equal parties striving for harmonious result as does coordinate and coordination. A superior party can cooperate with an inferior party. By the act of cooperation, the inferior party does not become equal to the superior. Unequal parties can "cooperate" by working together to accomplish their unequal goals. But, by

dictionary definition and under the definition set forth in the *California Native Plant Society v. City of Rancho Cordova*, 172 Cal. App. 4th 603, 91 Cal. Rpr. 3d. 571 (Third App. Dist. 2009) only equal parties coordinate.

The federal agencies, particularly the Forest Service, seek to lure local government into a "cooperating agency" role. As such "cooperating agency," the local government sits at the planning table with the federal interdisciplinary planning team. The agency can provide input into the planning activity, and the federal team listens. But, then most often, the local input is ignored and never referred to in the planning document that emerges from the meetings.

There is no requirement that the federal agency use the local input, refer to the local input, describe how it has used the input or describe why it has not used the input. Often, as in the case of Fremont County, Wyoming, the input of the County was ignored. The Fremont County Commissioners explained to the Forest Supervisor when deciding to "coordinate" instead of "cooperate," "we talk, you appear to listen, but we never see any further reference to what we say; what we say is never discussed and it doesn't appear anywhere in your planning product."

As a cooperating agency, the local government can be assigned planning tasks, which it is expected to finance and perform. Yet, there is no obligation on the agency to make any meaningful use of the task result.

The 1982 Forest Planning Rules, the Forest Travel Management Plan Rules, and the BLM Planning Rules all require that the agency coordinate by being apprised of local plans and policies, noting conflicts between federal and local plans and policies, reporting the interactive impacts of the federal and local plans and policies, and establishing alternatives for dealing with the impacts, i.e., resolving conflicts. There are no such requirements related to the cooperating local government.

Two parties can "cooperate" by sitting together and discussing an issue simply for the purpose of understanding each other's position. It is to their mutual benefit to understand their competing positions, even though there is no resolution of the conflict that exists. They each describe their position; they listen to each other and decide that they cannot reconcile their differences. They have "cooperated." They have not "coordinated."

COORDINATION IS NOT CONSULTATION

The term "consultation" means deliberating together, discussing with each other. The word "consult" means "to ask the advice or opinion of another" or to "deliberate together." In effect, an agency can consult with local government simply by talking to the governing board of the government, and listening to its advice or opinion.

Again, in the act of consultation, there is no obligation on the part of the agency to determine whether there is a conflict between the federal plan and policy and the local plan and policy or to attempt to resolve the conflict. An agency can "consult" with local government by doing no more than listening to the local government's governing board. As determined by *California Native Plant Association*, merely listening, i.e., consultation, does not constitute "coordination."

to seek advice or information from; ask guidance from: *Consult your lawyer before signing*
con·sul·ta·tion \ (kon-suhl-tey-shuh) *n.* **1.** the act of consulting; conference, **2.** a meeting for deliberation, discussion, or decision, **3.** to ask the advice or opinion of another, **4.** to deliberate together, **5.** a meeting of physicians to evaluate a patient's case and treatment, **6.** to deliberate together,

A superior officer can consult with a junior officer with regard to who should be promoted. That means he speaks to the junior about the promotion and listens to his opinion. Suppose the junior officer recommends "x" for the promotion. After listening, the senior officer promotes "y" and does not bother to explain why he did not follow the junior's advice. The senior officer has consulted with the junior officer, but he has not coordinated with him.

COORDINATION IS NOT SUPREMACY

In the early days of local government's foray into the coordination concept established in the Federal Land Policy Management Act, local government urged that it had supremacy over the federal agency with regard to land lying within the boundaries of the unit of local government. The "county supremacy" doctrine was based not only on the language of FLPMA, but on the historical and traditional place of the county in the hierarchy of government.

The counties which urged the existence of supremacy contended that the federal agency had to manage in accordance with local policies and plans, had to acquire county approval for entry into the county to conduct its management duties, and had to obey the county land use plan and policy. Boundary County, Idaho enacted an ordinance in 1991, which required all federal and state agencies to comply with its land use policy and plan. It based its ordinance on "local custom and culture." The County simply followed the lead of Catron County, New Mexico, which acted on the ill-conceived argument that the custom and culture of local government gave the county a supremacy position with regard to land use control over federal lands.

How much the "supremacy" of local custom and culture was influenced by the ill-fated Nye County, Nevada resolutions that the county owned all federal lands, is not clear. But, the Nevada notion was stricken down in *United States v. Nye County*, 920 F. Supp. 1108. Catron County rescinded its ordinance before it could be stricken by a court, leaving Boundary County to be the scapegoat. The Idaho Supreme Court declared the ordinance invalid in *Boundary Backpackers v. Boundary County*, 128 Idaho 371, holding that it violated the supremacy clause of the Constitution. The Court held that Congress' power under the property clause is exclusive, without limitation, and free from state interference.

Therein lies the difference between coordination and supremacy. Congress does have exclusive power over the federal lands. In the exercise of that exclusive power, Congress has mandated that the Bureau of Land Management and the Forest Service "coordinate" their planning and management processes with local government. The coordination mandate is found in the Federal Land Policy Management Act and the National Forest Management Act. Both are federal statutes passed in accordance with Congress' constitutional power, thus they are the supreme law of the land.

Therefore, the coordination requirement is the supreme law of the land which must be obeyed by the agencies.

Coordination is a process for reconciliation of conflicts between federal and local policies. It does not provide local government with any type of supremacy. It does provide local government with an equal seat at the negotiating table. It does require the federal agencies to negotiate in good faith to resolve conflicts.

As Lois J. Schiffer, Assistant Attorney General for the Environment Division of the Department of Justice said on July 28, 1995: "We welcome local participation in land management decisions." She made the statement as she and Peter Coppelman, Deputy Assistant Attorney General for the Environment and Natural Resources Division asked the District Court in Las Vegas to set aside Nye County's resolution of supremacy. Coppelman later authored an opinion in the American Judicature Society Journal that while local government was not supreme, it did have the authority to use the coordination process set forth in FLPMA.

SUMMARY

Coordination is a process far stronger than either cooperation or consultation. It is not supremacy and does not carry with it any type of veto or control over federal management. It does, however, authorize local government to come to the negotiation table on an equal basis with the federal management agency, which has the obligation to use good faith in trying to resolve conflicts between local and federal policies and plans.

THE COORDINATION PROCESS

The coordination process is simple to initiate; implementation is a simple processing job, but effective coordination requires hard work. Victories, like the big win in Texas, do not just "happen," they require that folks roll up their sleeves and work. There must be commitment to make the process work. Almost assuredly, the agency will not help you provide the energy or the will needed to make the process work.

There is no set process for implementing the coordination requirement, but the following outline is a good guide. Whatever the process or outcome, coordination facilitates solutions to local issues and is the embodiment and implementation of local control.

1. IDENTIFY THE LOCAL GOVERNMENT TO EXERCISE COORDINATION

Coordination is performed by local units of government. These normally include counties, incorporated cities, water districts, school districts, or any legislatively, statutorily created government entity with local planning, taxing, enforcement, or regulatory authority.

If local officials haven't initiated coordination on their own, begin by identifying which local unit of government will serve your interests best.

a. **Educate Yourself:** Begin by developing a good working understanding of the process. Reading this pamphlet is a good start. Read through the statutory language applicable to the agency at issue found in the Coordination Workbook and online at www.americanstewards.us. Read through the case studies and letters that have been written by local governments and received from state and federal agencies in the coordination process, also found in the workbook. Attending workshops where you can visit one-on-one with those who have used this process successfully is also very helpful. Call American Stewards with your questions. You do not need to be an expert on coordination, but should be knowledgeable on how this process can help your local governments consider this approach.

b. **Identify the Local Government Unit:** Local politics can easily get in the way of implementing good ideas such as the coordination process. If you do not already know the people on the various governing boards in your community gather as much information as you can on your leaders. Consider their positions on different issues. Visit with the elected officials to get a more personal understanding of their perspective. Look at the board's decisions to see where they align. Through this research, it may become clear which unit of government would be most likely to utilize coordination. If not, then start by focusing on your county. They have responsibility over all issues in the county and are formally structured with regular meetings.

c. **Meet One-on-One with Local Leaders:** Begin with the County Judge, Chairman, Mayor, or President of the Board you have selected (or someone you already know personally on the board). Ask for a meeting to visit with them about a process you've heard other local governments using to preserve their economy and way of life. Bring copies of materials, such as this pamphlet or the coordination workbook for them to study after you leave. Tell them why you believe the local government needs to be involved in this. Discuss the issues that can be resolved through this government-to-government process by having a seat at the table with the agencies. If they are interested in moving forward, ask for time on their agenda to present the idea and then begin meeting individually with the other board members so they have time to consider this and ask questions as well. Remember to keep your discussion focused on local issues, not national problems. Your local governments cannot fix problems in Washington D.C., but they can fix problems at home. Stay focused on the issues that need to be resolved locally.

d. **Navigating Potential Opposition:** Depending upon the political climate of your area, you may meet resistance from advocacy groups or even elected officials. In this case, you need to assess whether you should work publicly or quietly to get the local government committed to coordinate. Identifying these people before you begin making the effort public is critical to your success. You need to understand the political mine fields upfront, or your entire effort can be derailed. The one-on-one conversations with the elected leaders whom you know will be friendly are very important to determining whether you should work to get the public behind the process first or whether you should work quietly to get the local government on board. If there is going to be major opposition from board members, give strong consideration to choosing a different local government unit. Key to successful coordination is a committed and unified board, one that cannot be swayed by agency pressure or politically split because there is no unified consensus.

e. **Execute Simple Resolution:** Once a local government unit has agreed to utilize coordination, all that is needed to begin the process is the adoption of a simple resolution by the local unit of government setting forth the following: 1) You are the duly elected governing body of your unit of government; 2) It is your duty to care for the public health, safety and welfare of your constituents, which includes a stable economy, productive industry and healthy environment; and, 3) Set forth that you are asserting the coordination authority to request the agency to coordinate with you as required by federal and/or state statute. The resolution shows the unity of the board, to show that it is board action, and not one member's action, that authorized utilizing coordination with the agencies.

2. INITIATING THE PROCESS

a. **Decide Policy or Plan:** You need to establish a clear agenda of what you wish to achieve through coordination. Some refer to this as setting priorities. What are the priority issues that must be resolved? What is the outcome that would solve the problem for your community? Discuss fully the issues you are having with an agency or several agencies; include in the discussion the federal or state agency action, plan, or policy that is harming your community or you think will harm you in the future. Decide what you would like to see substituted for the government policy or plan, and formulate your local policy or plan to deal with the resource, economic or social issues discussed below. Your local unit of government can choose to adopt a detailed plan, but these take much longer and are much more difficult to arrive at any kind of consensus. Normally, it is better to start simple and deal, at most, with one or two issues.

b. **Factors in Deciding Policy or Plan:** In developing a plan or policy, keep the following concerns in the forefront of all your choices: What are the economic, environmental, social and public safety concerns that directly affect your local community. For economic include the protection of your tax base, economic stability of your citizens and local businesses, resource revenue from farming, ranching, timber, mining, and all other resource extractions that benefit your local economy, protection of private property; for environment consider protection of natural resources, land improvement, wildlife protection, water and air quality; for social consider the welfare of your local school system and how your volunteer fire department and ambulance services are funded and maintained, recreational and tourism opportunities, and all elements of the cultural structure of the community; and for public safety consider law enforcement and public hazards. Remember, health, safety, and welfare of the community should always take precedence in your thought process.

Sample Policy: If a Travel Management Plan is being prepared, your policy could be "All open trails and roads should be designated as open. Full open access should be made available to the public lands for local purposes such as safety, health, economics, and use of recreation as assured by Executive Order of the President. No road or trail should be closed unless public safety or health demands its closing. No RS 2477 right of way should be closed." In Texas, it was as simple as: "No Trans-Texas Corridor shall be built through our jurisdiction."

c. **People Resources:** As you begin, it is desirable to gather together people who will become resources from which you can depend on for research, expertise, advocacy, and support. These are called various things depending on how formal or informal the group is to the coordination process. You can either have a simple working group or an advisory council or committee and it can be a formal or informal group. If formal, have the elected body appoint the members. Select a chair, vice-chair, and secretary, hold regular meetings that coincide with and function as a support group to the coordination process, and take minutes. Remember, local units of government and their elected representatives are the ones who will perform the coordination process with federal and state agencies. Your job as a support group is to serve if asked, make presentations if called upon during coordination meetings, and provide support with research and documents that help further the cause and focus the efforts of the coordination process. These groups can include various industries of the area, affected individuals, landowners, businesses, and organizations that have a vested interest in the process. If there is no such group, you don't need to recruit one. If there is such a group, they can be invaluable to you as advisors on policy and strategy. If you have such a group, name them as an advisory committee or a work group and let them help you set local policy.

d. **Write, Sign, and Send Letter:** To begin the formal process of coordination with the agency a letter needs to be sent to the local head of the federal or state agency explaining that you have asserted your coordination status and that you would like to meet with him/her to begin coordination discussions. If you have decided on a priority issue or two that you are ready to meet about, then schedule a meeting and inform the agency of your desire to begin coordination over your priorities/issues.

Sample Letter: "We would like to meet with you on _____or_____ at 2pm in _____

_____. Please call our clerk by (normally give them 30 days to respond) and advise us of the date convenient to you. If neither of these dates is available, please arrange with her/him a date available to both you and the Board." If you have decided to discuss a specific issue then list the issue you wish to discuss. The letter should contain a brief statement of the authority giving you the right to assert coordination.

In most instances, the agencies first reaction will be to ignore or reject your coordination request. Never give up. This will likely be their first introduction into the process. On the other hand, local agency personnel may understand the requirements and try to neutralize your effort by convincing your elected officials to "coordinate" as a "cooperating agency." These efforts must be resisted if you are to successfully focus the agency on your local issues. If the agency resists real government-to-government coordination, the local unit of government should send a second or third letter to the next level up the chain of command until you reach the head of the federal or state agency. You may also eventually notify the Department of Justice as your final effort, so that they can clarify the coordination requirements to the agency.

3. IMPLEMENTING THE COORDINATION PROCESS

a. **Coordination Agenda:** After the meeting is scheduled, you should send an agenda labeled "Coordination Agenda for _____," state your agenda and then ask for the agency to add anything to the agenda they would like to discuss. State that this will be a "government-to-government coordination meeting." It will be an open meeting so that the public can attend, but there will be no public comment because of the government-to-government nature of the meeting." The Agenda should be sent at least ten days prior to the meeting date. If they respond and even add to the agenda, then they have tacitly agreed to coordination.

b. **Post Notice of Meeting:** Each meeting should follow all Open Meeting laws and be posted normally 72 hours prior to each coordination meeting. The agenda should represent all the business that will occur and should be posted the normal way all other meetings are posted for the county, city or local unit of government.

c. **Be Prepared: Prepare well for the first meeting.** The agency will be checking you out to see whether you are serious about this process or whether they can just let you slide and you will go away. Be prepared on your facts. Use your work group to help get prepared for the meeting. Study the agencies statutes and regulations so you can ask specific questions that they aren't prepared to answer. You want to be able to keep them on the defensive, which is why you need to know your facts. For instance, if the meeting involves open trails or roads, be prepared to discuss some of the roads and trails you know are used and be able to tell them what the public safety, health, or economy issues are by keeping that road or trail open (always think public safety, health and economy). Be prepared with the latest agency map, that you are aware of, so that they can show you what they are up to; let them know that you expect a map on which they are currently working. You may have all or some of the advisory committee at the table with you as advisors. If someone has specific knowledge about a road, let them describe the road and ask questions regarding its use.

4. The Meeting

a. Welcoming Statement: As the local government body who called the meeting the chairman (head) of your local government is in charge of running the agenda. Welcome the agency and introduce your commissioners or special district directors and advisory committee members who may have a special part in your meeting. Make sure you welcome them to a "coordination meeting," then let the agency head introduce staff he or she has brought.

b. Opening Statement: Next, make an opening statement that says "this is a government-to-government coordination meeting made possible by federal and/or state statute. It is an open meeting at which the public may attend and listen, but there will be no public comment period since it is a government-to-government meeting. If any member of the public has a comment, you can make it at the public comment period provided at our next regular meeting." Once finished, you can ask the agency head if he/she would like to make an opening statement. Do not let this become an opportunity for the agency to monopolize the time. Keep this brief and on point.

c. Proceed with Agenda: Begin to work through the agenda items. The purpose of the meeting is to have an open discussion with the agency about the issues of concern. Present your issues first to make sure that your concerns are delivered and time is not absorbed by agency officials discussing irrelevant issues. Your concerns are the focus of the meeting. Have each one of your elected officials prepared to ask questions on different topics so that the time is productive for both you and the agency. For the more detailed issues, you can have someone (associate, consultant, committee member) prepared to address that issue in greater detail if necessary, depending upon the direction the discussion takes.

d. Identify Issues: As the meeting ends, identify the issues that were not decided and that need more discussion or more information from the agency or from you (the new maps the agency is working from for example), and make a list of them. Make a list of things the agency needs from you. Then ask the agency head for a date for the follow up meeting at which the new information can be reviewed and discussed. Agree on a date for the next meeting before ending the meeting.

e. Record Meeting: If possible, purchase a digital recorder preferably with an attachable microphone so everyone around the table can be heard and recorded. After the meeting, have your recording secretary transcribe the discussion attributing each statement to the person speaking so they can be identified as to who said what. The secretary also needs to draft the minutes of the meeting to be signed by the members of the  local unit of government and placed in the official record book of the coordination group. All correspondence from and to the local unit of government should be placed in the "Official Record Book."

5. AFTER MEETING

a. Debriefing: After the meeting, have a debriefing session with your members and the working group or advisory committee members that were allowed to participate in the coordination meeting. Get their ideas as to how the meeting went and begin to develop your goals for the next meeting. *Remember, in this baby step process, if the agency agreed to come to the second meeting, progress was made.*

b. Press Release: If the press was not present, get a press release about your first coordination meeting with the agency to the local newspaper (s), and arrange to speak to an announcer on local radio programs about the meeting. It is important that your constituents know that you are meeting with the agency. Keeping the public aware of what you are doing is almost as important as the fact that you are doing it. We live in a land of people who are sick and tired of doing nothing; they want action taken.

c. Letter to Agency: Write a letter to the agency thanking them for attending the meeting and reminding them of the material you requested, and either provide information you promised or at least tell them that you will get it to them rapidly.

d. Gain Support/Allies: Locate and contact either in writing or in person with organizations in your community that have issues with the agency and tell them about your first meeting with the agency. Explain what coordination is, and ask them to advise you of any issues they are currently having with the agency. Tell them about your next meeting, explain that it is an open meeting, but it is government-to-government with no public comment period. Gain their trust the best you can and get them to help with research and/or to support the coordination process and the local elected officials who are performing the task. This gets the public involved and keeps the elected officials focused and enthusiastic about the process.

e. All Follow-up Meetings: For all subsequent meetings, follow the same preparation and presentation for the first. Be working constantly to develop the strategy you will use with the agency regarding each issue. Begin to prepare local policy for each of the issues you identified in the beginning stages of coordination. Strategy is an on-going process -- coordination is a process run by strategy. Always have your strategy in mind before you go into a meeting. Each meeting you will learn something new. If you have multiple meetings with multiple agencies, you will learn something from each that can be used to your advantage. You will be told something that the other agency won't want you to know. Use it to your advantage. This is why you need to record and transcribe your meetings so you can review and study what was said in response to your questioning.

6. THE PLAN

Is a formal plan necessary? No. What is necessary is that you have a definite local policy, in writing, through resolution or a motion by the board, that shows the position you expect the agency to take. As you develop policies, it is useful to put them in a "Plan" document so that you have proof in quickly readable form of your policy, and so that your constituents know your policy regarding resource issues. The Plan, as a document, can be amended through additions of policies with background explanations of the policy. Normally, you want to follow the KISS doctrine (keep it simple stupid). Starting with one or two policies is much easier than developing an entire plan for your community.

7. SUPPORT

Remember, coordination is a process. Victories come after long hours of work, research, meetings with the agencies, discovery, and diligence. Perseverance is a virtue. If you prepare and realize victories can be small or large, you will succeed at this. Set your goals, work extremely hard to achieve your goals and watch how the coordination process produces miraculous results.

If you get to a place where you need advice, call our offices and we will help you through the next step. We can arrange to meet by teleconference with your local leaders if necessary to help answer questions. In some cases, we can also visit your area and work with your elected officials, committee members and others who will be vital to your success to help develop your specific strategies. Our goal is to educate and train you and your key people to be able to handle all the issues you may face today and in the future.

Activists seeking to cut communities ties with ICLEI should keep in mind that they don't have to be a member of ICLEI to be affected by Agenda 21/ICLEI polices. Around the nation ICLEI partners with other, established organizations, like the American Planning Association (APA), and the International City/County Management Association (ICMA), and the Renaissance Planning Group, to name a very few.

These groups and hundreds like them work hand in had with groups like the U.S. Conference of Mayors, the National Governors Association, the National League of Cities, the National Association of County Administrators, and more that locally-elected officials probably belong to.

It is now being discovered that, while ICLEI is a convenient target because of its obvious ties to the UN, the American Planning Association may be the more dangerous player in the game. That's because the APA is in literally every city. Trusted as a legitimate, non-controversial, established organization with nothing to tie it to an international UN conspiracy – or so we are told. In reality, the policies APA advocates for its member communities are directly tied to Agenda 21. In 2011, the APA issued it latest planning guide, shipped to nearly every community in the nation. A quick look through it finds references to social justice; smart growth; stopping "urban sprawl; promotion of "affordable" housing (a euphemism for mixing low income, government housing into wealthier neighborhoods); combating climate change; energy preservation; and provisions for child care – all out of the social justice plank of Agenda 21.

The American Planning Association

The American Planning Association (APA) is one of the largest planning groups in the United State, with chapters in at least 47 states and 100,000 members and over 16,000 certified planners operating in nearly every American city.

From its early urban planning roots, the APA transformed itself into one of the nation's leading proponents of Smart Growth and Sustainable Development. HUD and other federal agencies paid the APA to create the, "Growing Smart Legislative Guidebook." is a massive1500 page compilation of boilerplate legislation and planning practices that operationalizes the principles of United Nations Agenda 21 as implemented though the now disbanded President's Council on Sustainable Development. Today, the APA is one of the main forces in the nation to implement Agenda 21 policies through what it calls "local planning."

The American Planning Association and its "Faulty" Handbook
by Tom DeWeese

With great fanfare, the American Planning Association (APA) reported results of a recent survey the group conducted, ("Planning America: Perceptions and Priorities") showing that the anti- Agenda 21 "crowd is slim." Said the report, only 6% of those surveyed expressed opposition to Agenda 21, while 9% expressed support for Agenda 21 and 85%, "the vast majority of respondents, don't know about Agenda 21."

Typically, APA is using the survey to formulate the image that opponents to Agenda 21/ Sustainable Development are just a lunatic fringe with no standing and of no consequence in the "real" world. !ey continue

The APA- Professional Planners or *Anti-Capitalist Political Advocacy?*

APA embraces ICLEI Programme(s)
1.1 "The built environment is a primary contributor to climate change" ...Business as usual will not suffice"
1.3 Social Equity and Climate Change (& Environmental Justice)
2.4 #6: "Should reduce reliance on coal..."
2.4 #10: Grow food for local consumption (starve the world?)
2.4 #14: Reduce VMT (Vehicle Miles Traveled)
2.4 #15: Cap & Trade for carbon ... needed.
Land Use#15: Create city-funded housing repair programs
Transportation #4: Increase CAFÉ standards

to portray Agenda 21 as simply a 20 year old idea, and just a suggestion that planners and local governments might consider.

However, a closer look at the full survey, plus some additional APA reports reveal some interesting, and in some cases, astounding facts.

First the survey:

It was designed to show support for "Planning." It has become an obsession with the "planning community" because Agenda 21 and Sustainable Development have become the center of protests by property owners and those who feel government has grown too big and powerful. So the APA has launched a series of efforts to fight back. These include conducting a "boot camp" to train their legions of planners across the nation on how to deal with anti-Agenda 21 protestors.

PlannersNetwork.org

- **STATEMENT OF PRINCIPLES:** *"We believe planning should be a tool for allocating resources... and eliminating the great inequalities of wealth and power in our society... because the free market has proven incapable of doing this."*

According to the APA, the "ndings of the Survey reveal that: Only one-third believe their communities are doing enough to address economic situations; Very few Americans believe that market forces alone (the free market) improve the economy or encourage job growth; 84 % feel that their community is getting worse or staying the same; Community planning is seen as needed by a wide majority of all demographics; and of course, that 85% of Americans just don't know enough to hold an opinion about Agenda 21.

Those are pretty astounding findings. Looks like these "honest" planners have their fingers on the pulse of the nation. And as the APA constantly reminds us in their materials, "there is no hidden agenda," (as in Agenda 21). Astounding perhaps, until you look at the actual questions asked in the survey. For example, Finding #4: Community planning is seen as needed by a wide majority of all demographics (79% agree; 9% disagree; and 12% don't know). Wow!

But here is the actual question that was asked: "Generally, do you agree or disagree that your community could benefit from a community plan as defined above?" The definition provided in order to answer the question was this: "Community planning is a process that seeks to engage all members of a community to create more prosperous, convenient, equitable, healthy and attractive places for present and future generations."

Asking the question in that manner is akin to holding up a picture of Marilyn Monroe along with one of Rosy O'Donnell and asking which one would they want to date. Give me the pretty one please – says 79%. In fact, in some actual planning meetings they do just that – hold up a picture of downtown depicting decaying, dreary buildings verses one of a shining, beautiful utopia, and they literally say, "which one do you want?" If the answer is (of course) the pretty one, then, YES, the community supports planning! Talk about a "dumbed down" process.

Moreover, as the American Planning Association adamantly denies any connection to the United Nations' policy of Agenda 21 and its planning programs, how strange it is then, that the APA definition of planning is almost identical to the definition used by the UN to define Sustainable Development. Compare: UN Definition: "Development that meets the needs of today without compromising the ability of future generations to meet their own needs." The UN further defines Agenda 21: "Effective execution of Agenda 21 will require a profound reorientation of all human society, unlike anything the world has ever experienced." Such a forced policy would certainly "engage all members of a community" whether they want to be or not. The UN calls it a "redeployment of human resources."

Other than semantics, there is no difference in the APA's and the UN's definitions of planning." The planners' definition uses an interesting term, "equitable." The UN also uses such a term in describing Agenda 21 – "Social Equity." And that is translated into another term: "Social Justice." It means "redistribution of wealth." Is that what the "local" planners have in mind for their community development?

It's obvious that the APA is playing word games with its surveys and definitions of planning. No wonder such an overwhelming majority answer in the affirmative to such questions.

And, yes, maybe a lot of Americans don't know what Agenda 21 really is. However, if the APA asked real questions that gave a solid clue as to the planning they actually have in mind, I'm quite sure they would get a much different response – whether the person answering had ever heard of Agenda 21 or not. For example, here are some sample questions that could help the APA take the real pulse of the community – if they wanted to be honest:

Real questions planners should ask:
- How do the citizens feel about planning policy that dictates the size of their yard and forces high density developments where one practically sits on top of their neighbors? Do they still support such "Planning?"
- How do the citizens feel about planning that enforces the creation of public transportation with a limited number of riders – yet could cost taxpayers so much money that it would be literally cheaper to buy each potential rider a brand new Rolls Royce, even when the chau#eur is thrown in for good measure? Do they still support such "Planning?
- How do they feel about planning that enforces limits on energy use and forces up energy costs? What if that included forcing residents to replace their appliances with more energy e%cient ones to meet "Planning Standards?" Do they still support such "Planning?"
- How do the citizens feel about Planning that forces cars to "share the road" with bicycles and foot tra%c, even as Planners narrow the streets, deliberately making it harder to drive? Do they still support such "Planning?"
- How do the citizens feel about Planning that forces tax payers to pay for plug-in stations for electric cars that hardly anyone wants or uses, for the specific purpose of forcing people to buy them? Do they still support such "Planning?"
- How do the citizens feel about Planning that creates non-elected boards, councils and regional governments to enforce their policies, which actually diminish the power of the officials they elected, severely reducing citizen input into policy? Do they still support such "Planning?"

Ask the questions in this manner instead of trying to whitewash them into sounding like innocent, non-intrusive local ideas for community development. Ask the questions so that they reflect the consequences of the plans, and then see if the 85% now are so eager to ignore the effects of Agenda 21.

The reality is that Americans across the nation are now openly protesting such policies as they are being enforced in communities everywhere. They are directly tied to the stated goals of Sustainable Development, the social policy of Agenda 21. And that is why a twenty year old "suggestion" has become the focal point of attacks on "local" planning.

Planners are shocked that people are opposed to such attacks on their private property and their pocketbooks, and they are doing everything possible to label such Americans as "fringe conspiracy theorists." The survey is part of that effort.

In fact, the APA survey follows a barrage of news articles, obviously contrived by the public relations firm hired by APA, to again, paint its image as just a group of honest planners trying to do their jobs while being unjustly attacked by fringe radicals. Such convenient reports have suddenly appeared on the front page of the New York Times, Washington Post, Wisconsin Watch, Mother Jones and the Southern Poverty Law Center, to name a few. It's interesting to note that most of these stories name me as the perpetrator.

As mentioned, the APA has organized a boot camp to train their planners how to combat we nasty protestors. Through its new training, the APA downplays revealing details of the plan, instead, suggesting ways to make their presentations merely "conversations with the community," using empathy, and terms that are non-technical." Obviously APA believes the protestors are just simpleminded and unable to see their wisdom. One shouldn't be so upset over losing control of their property, their business or their farm. There's a higher good at stake here, after all.

And so, to accomplish that task of dumbed- down "planning," (and in fact, hiding its real purpose) the APA is going to great lengths to change the words. For example, the APA has issued to its members a "Glossary for the Public" that suggests what words should no longer be used in public meetings when discussing planning, because they make the opposition see "red." So the planners should not use words like collaboration and consensus, or public visioning, or even "Smart Growth."

The Glossary provides speci"c language and tactics to be used to defuse protests. "Stay on message," it says. "!e following phrases may be useful to help you frame your message in a way that is positive and inclusive, when transitioning to a local example, or to stay on message during public meetings where critics may attempt to distract from the agenda or topic at hand." And here is the language they suggest: "Plans and planning are time-tested ways for communities and neighborhoods to create more options and choices for their residents..." In other words, we've always had planning, so what's the problem?"

Such "public" meetings that the APA is so worried about being disrupted are not public at all. !ey are "consensus" meetings, run by professional facilitators, trained in psychology to use stealth to direct the audience into a pre-determined direction for a pre- determined outcome. Anyone asking questions outside the well-controlled box is labeled a protestor. And yes, we are protesting that! It is not how things are to be done in a free society, especially when your own property is at stake.

Yes, there has been planning throughout the history of America. Many communities have come up with e%cient ways to deal with water use and waste disposal, and to assure that factories weren't built next door to private homes, and so forth. And no one is protesting that!

Our "ght is with "planning" that is speci"cally designed to curtail energy use, drive up costs, control private property and development and building – literally dictating a change in our lives and even changing the very structure of our system of government.

One of the tools the APA uses to enforce planning is through the International Code Council (ICC), an international set of standards based on a one size "ts all set of regulations. !e ICC also develops the International Energy Conservation Code, a model for energy e%ciency code. And it develops a standard for Accessible And Usable Building Facilities. Each of these codes is aimed at cutting back energy use, controlling private property use, and, in short, enforcing sustainable development. Where was the concept of sustainable development "rst introduced and perfected as an agenda for development? Oh yes, in Agenda 21. !ere is no room for discussion, reason or consideration for exceptional local situations. !e APA brings these codes and others into the community planning as a pre- packaged deal in&icting the community with (yes) foreign regulations. And yes, dedicated Americans protest that this is not local government or planning, but the enforcement of an international (UN) agenda.

We further "nd similar pre-packaged regulations coming from federal agencies, including the EPA (which openly admits that some of its grant programs are designed to impose Agenda 21) the Forest Service (which admits that its policies on forest conservation are coming from the UN's Brundtland Commission on Global Governance), as well as polices from the Department of Housing and Urban Development (HUD), and the Department of Transportation, to name a few.
And so it goes. Government in the U.S., at all levels, is happily moving forward with such plans, using the ground troops supplied by the American Planning Association in every community. It's happening fast, and is all-pervasive. And as people are being run over by such plans, some are trying to slow down the runaway freight train by standing in the tracks and yelling stop! !ey of course are the ones labeled as fringe nuts.

However, as the APA does everything it can to so label our movement, a shocking new report provides new evidence that the sustainable polices advocated by APA in the cities – the policy known as Smart Growth – is wrong headed and really pretty dumb. And where does such a report appear? Here's the real shocker. It was published in the Journal of the American Planning Association in an article entitled "Does Urban Form Really Matter." It is an analysis of Smart Growth polices in the United Kingdom which shows that the "compact city" controls don't work.

Says the report, "!e current planning policy strategies for land use and transportation have virtually no impact on the major long-term increases in resource and energy consumption. !ey will generally tend to increase costs and reduce economic competitiveness." Continues the report, "Claims of compaction will make cities more sustainable have been debated for some time, but they lack conclusive supporting evidence as to the environmental and, particularly, economic and social e#ects."

There you have it. Right out of the pages of the APA's own Journal, the very policies that they are forcing on communities across the nation, are wrong. Forcing mass migration into cities where people are to live in high density buildings, or homes on lots so close together that the dog can't squeeze between houses, have no e#ect on the environment. But as I have stated in articles and speeches across the nation, such "planning" creates an arti"cial shortage of land, causing housing costs to go up. It doesn't cut down on energy use or protect the environment. It's a useless intrusion in the lives of honest Americas.

And that is exactly why we are protesting Agenda 21. It is wrong. !e premise is wrong.
!e facts as presented by the APA and other planners, are wrong. It is wrong for our nation. Wrong for property owners. Wrong for future generations.

In the 1970s, author Richard Bach, who wrote the classic book, Jonathan Livingston Seagull, also wrote a second book entitled, "Illusions: The Adventures of a Reluctant Messiah." In the book, a Messiah, forced to come up with answers to the problems of life, consulted the "Messiah's Handbook." All he had to do was open the book and it would miraculously open to the very page containing the answer he sought. He stumbled through his adventures, following the handbook. But finally, in the end, as he consulted it a final time, the page read simply, "Everything in this book may be wrong.

There is only one right approach for a community to come together to discuss and solve common problem: open discussion, honest debates and votes, and above all, a full concentration on the protection of private property rights as the ultimate decider. The American Planning Association needs a new handbook!

Glossary for the Public   Stealth from the American Planning Association

What follows is an exact copy of the American Planning Association's "Glossary for the Public," which it distributed to its members to teach them how to use different words to hide the true intent of their planning programs. Of special interest, take a good look at the opening line in which the APA tells its people – BE CAREFUL WHAT YOU SAY TO THE PUBLIC!

Read this document carefully. It is raw evidence of the evil that is slithering into your local government. It exposes the new language and tactics you will face. Use it openly. Expose it. Here's a legitimate question for your fellow citizens, even if they don't agree with your opposition to Agenda 21: Do you trust a government and its policies that are enforced through lies and stealth? Is that how you want your government to run? This document proves that is what they are doing. What is wrong with Sustainable Development if they have to hide it from the "public?"

When people reject absolute truth, they lose their standards for reality. They will believe anything in their search for something.

Glossary for the Public

Introduction

Given the heightened scrutiny of planners by some members of the public, what is said — or not said — is especially important in building support for planning.

These suggestions are designed to help planners frame what they say in positive terms; use examples that people can identify with and relate to; avoid jargon and technical words; and turn allies and elected officials into strong and articulate champions of planning.

When talking about planning and its value to the community, keep in mind the messages APA developed several years ago that emphasize value, choice, and engagement:

APA members help create communities of lasting value.

Good planning helps create communities that offer better choices for where and how people work and live.

Planning enables civic leaders, business interests, and citizens to play a meaningful role in creating communities that enrich people's lives.

Frame your message

Certain words in the planning lexicon have been seized upon by some planning opponents and critics to be "code" for top-down, government-controlled policies and approaches that interfere with individual choices and freedoms. Some opponents of planning argue in blogs that, for example, sustainable development, including its definition and implementation, adversely affects not only an individual's rights and freedoms, but also true local control. Given such a perspective, it is imperative that planners frame discussions about sustainability, regionalism, livability and the like (see trigger words below) in a way that emphasizes the economic value, long-lasting benefits and positive outcomes that result from good planning and plan implementation.

A Fall 2010 Ford Foundation national poll found overwhelming public support (79 percent) for sustainable development when defined as *"An urban, suburban or rural community that has more housing and transportation choices, is closer to jobs, shops or schools, is more energy independent and helps protect clean air and water."* This finding underscores the importance of discussing sustainability and planning in terms of generating more jobs, lowering housing and transportation costs, and using limited public funds more wisely.

APA Chief Executive Officer Paul Farmer, FAICP, likens good plans to stories and planning to conversations with the community. To have meaning, plans and planning need to be relevant and meaningful to the everyday lives, hopes and aspirations of residents, community leaders, business interests and elected officials. This guide offers suggestions about how to define and discuss planning terms and concepts in ways that are understandable and non-technical, and that resonate with your audience's concerns, priorities and goals.

Critics see red
The following are examples of words and phrases that have become highly politicized and generate suspicion among some citizens:

Affordable; Agenda 21 *(see Communications Boot Camp How-To Guide #1, "Agenda 21 & Planning: Myths & Facts")*

Collaboration, Consensus

Delphi technique

Density

Livable; Localized planning; Long-term, region-wide planning

Organize and facilitate

Public visioning; Public-Private Partnerships

Regional, regionalism, regional planning

Smart growth; Stakeholders; Sustainability

Walkable

Make it meaningful, relevant, memorable
This list includes examples of terms and phrases that planners use every day that, depending on the audience and situation, may exacerbate misunderstandings. *These are not words to avoid, but are singled out to help you think about how to describe plans and planning to non-professional audiences, or to elected officials and other decision makers in the public planning process so they are meaningful, relevant and memorable.*

Remember people are most interested in themselves and things that affect them directly, so you will get and hold a person's attention when talking about plans and planning in ways to which they can relate. Always focus on the outcomes of good planning and meaningful public engagement as opposed to planning process.

Business improvement district, Central business district — Some may find the words "district" or "central" to be an indication of a "top down" or "Big Brother" process. Using the common word "downtown" or "business area" may be more neutral and preferable.

Charrettes — "Meeting" or "workshop" are simpler and don't require definitions, or provide the opportunity for others to seize upon the French origins of the word to accuse you of trying to make American cities more European.

Code enforcement, design review, design review standards — Avoid talking about or linking plans and planning with regulatory matters. While code enforcement, code violations and design review may be among the responsibilities of your department or office, these are separate issues from plans and planning. Don't mix them with conversations about plans and planning.

Comprehensive plan, master plan, general plan, plan update, etc. — To some critics, words describing any kind of "plan" may be met with disagreement and skepticism. In such situations, it may be more productive to not focus on the plan itself, but the tangible benefits and outcomes to the neighborhood, community, etc. from a plan. For example, plans are a way for residents to talk about what is important to them not just today, but tomorrow. Plans give residents an opportunity to talk about what is important to them over the long term and to see if their priorities and preferences have changed since the last time they had a chance to look at (and the city approved) the last plan.

Councils of governments (COGs), metropolitan planning organizations (MPOs), regional planning agencies, etc. — Some problems or issues facing one's community (or neighborhood for that matter) cannot be adequately addressed alone. Watershed protection, for instance, involves many communities working together. Focus on the benefits and what an individual community stands to gain by not "going it alone."

Density, cluster development, infill development — Any discussion of density may cause alarm bells to ring among some audiences who are concerned about the location of multi-family dwellings in areas where single-family homes predominate. Density is also context-dependent. Use these discussions as an opportunity to talk about the cost of shared services (sewer service, roads, schools, fire protection, etc.), what residents like about their community, and the benefits that can result from changes to the number and type of available housing. Listening to concerns and identifying shared values are important parts of reasoned discussion about density and related issues.

Eminent domain, police powers, taking, condemnation, land assembly — Used only as a tool of last resort, discussions about plans and eminent domain should be site- and case- specific, and underscore the multiple benefits that result and the lack of other options or alternatives. Extreme public opposition may be an indication that the use of eminent domain in this instance is not appropriate or that not enough time was spent securing public support for a project requiring the use of condemnation.

Green infrastructure — Discuss in terms of protecting clean air and water and the plants, animals and environments people are familiar with — trees, streams, lakes, forests, soil, rain water, etc.

Moratorium, building moratorium — Any discussion needs to include the reasons, time-limited nature of moratoria, benefits, and value to a community at a particular time and place. Critics may cite it as an example of government restricting individual freedoms and rights.

Mixed-use development, live-work units — Seen by some as an example of "smart growth" being forced upon a community. There is a long tradition of mixed uses in U.S. cities, especially during the early history of the country. When discussing this type of development, point out the benefits to residents and the local economy and what makes this type of development especially attractive to the community at this time (attracts new residents, helps keep community vibrant and prosperous, infrastructure cost savings, etc.).

Overlay plan, overlay zone, overlay district — Discuss in terms of the benefits to property owners and positive outcomes that result when taking a more focused or concentrated approach to a specific area. Consider using an analogy (similar to rebuilding an older property) to help explain the thinking and reasons additional planning tools and resources are needed for the particular area.

Smart growth, sustainability — Consider using the term "quality growth" instead (used by the Envision Utah plan developed for the Greater Salt Lake City metropolitan area), growth that will help ensure the long-term health and productivity of our local economy.

Tax increment financing (TIF), tax increment financing district — Discuss in terms generating new investment, creating new jobs for the community, and cost-effective development incentives. Discuss in terms of the tangible benefits and outcomes that will result from this method of attracting new investment to the community.

Transportation corridor — Describe in terms of transportation routes and location of roads, highways, public transit, etc. Some may view the term "corridors" with suspicion simply because it is "planner speak." If critics are alarmed by this term, listen to them describe what negative outcomes or concerns they associate with the word.

Urban growth boundary, urban service area — Discuss in terms of minimizing the cost of services used by the entire community, and protecting existing land use outside of the boundary or service area. Recognize that these terms can generate much controversy and disagreement. Given nature of discussion, it may be more productive to listen to critics and gain a better understanding of their concerns and fears about such terms.

Zoning, conditional zoning, Euclidean zoning, pyramidal zoning, Zoning Board of Adjustment, form-based zoning, inclusionary zoning, exclusionary zoning — Focus on the benefits zoning provides property owners and the role it plays in protecting property values. Listen and learn from objections being raised to better understand what it is about zoning that has people concerned, worried, etc.

Stay on message

The following phrases may be useful to help you frame your message in a way that is positive and inclusive, when transitioning to a local example, or to stay on message during public meetings where critics may attempt to distract from the agenda or topic at hand.

Plans and planning are time-tested ways for communities and neighborhoods to create more options and choices for their residents. Let me give you an example ...

Plans produce tangible results. Take _____, for instance, which came about because of the plan the community developed.

Local choice and control is important, and planning is a way our community can choose its future. When it comes to making investments in our community, planning can lead to a return on public investments many times over. Let me give you a couple of examples ...

Planning is a way to exercise democracy and our country's constitutional form of government. The founders of this country, going back to the 1600s and 1700s, planned their towns and rural areas this same way we are today. There is a long tradition of planning in America. It is the way we protect what we love and fix what we don't love about our communities.

Protecting and improving property values over the long term is one of the ways plans benefit property owners. Plans provide certainty, which gives people confidence to invest in our community for the long term.

We have a responsibility to think through the long-term consequences of our decisions. Planning enables us to do that. Take _____, for example.

We need to understand together how to make sure our local community and our local economy are strong enough for our children to grow up and have a good life here. Planning helps us do that.

We need to make decisions that are careful, cost effective, efficient, and fair to everybody. That is the purpose of this meeting. There is no hidden agenda.

There is no hidden agenda. But there is a responsibility to make wise, long-term decisions and this meeting has been set up to make sure all points of view are heard and are equally important. All points of view will be part of the permanent record and copies of the permanent record will be available to the public.

Remember big picture

As planning and planners have become targets of suspicion and mistrust, it is more important than ever to avoid polarizing jargon, to focus on outcomes important to local citizens, and to maintain a fair, open, and transparent process in which even opponents of planning have the opportunity to express their desires for their communities. Also, the book *Planning in Plain English* by Natalie Macris (APA Planners Press, 2000) may be useful. It is available at www.planning.org/apastore/Search/Default.aspx?p=1867.

American Planning Association

Making Great Communities Happen

SAMPLE LEGISLATION

AND THE

FIVE BILL PACKAGE TO

REDUCE THE

Size, Cost, Reach, And Power

OF GOVERNMENT

SCRAP

New Hampshire Bill to Protect Property Rights: HB 514

This proposed bill prevents any person, whether or not authorized by federal, state or local agencies or nongovernmental organizations from entering private property or gathering information while on that property without a warrant or prior written permission of the property owner. This is a direct response to Agenda 21/Sustainable Development practices of entering and monitoring private properties.

HB 514 – AS AMENDED BY THE HOUSE

18Jan2012... 0254h

2011 SESSION

11-0336

06/03

HOUSE BILL *514*

AN ACT relative to entry on private land.

SPONSORS: Rep. Weyler, Rock 8; Sen. Barnes, Jr., Dist 17

COMMITTEE: Judiciary

ANALYSIS

This bill prohibits certain entry on private property for data gathering without a warrant or the written consent of the landowner.

. . . .

Explanation: Matter added to current law appears in ***bold italics.***

Matter removed from current law appears [in brackets and struckthrough.]

Matter which is either (a) all new or (b) repealed and reenacted appears in regular type.

18Jan2012... 0254h

11-0336

06/03

STATE OF NEW HAMPSHIRE

In the Year of Our Lord Two Thousand Eleven

AN ACT relative to entry on private land.

Be it Enacted by the Senate and House of Representatives in General Court convened:

1 New Chapter; Entry on Private Property. Amend RSA by inserting after chapter 7-B the following new chapter:

CHAPTER 7-C

ENTRY ON PRIVATE PROPERTY

7-C:1 Entry on Private Property.

I. Absent a lawfully issued warrant, no person shall enter private property to gather data about the property, whether or not authorized by federal, state, or municipal agencies, boards, or commissions, or any nongovernmental organization, without first giving written notice to the property owner and obtaining the prior written permission of the property owner.

II. No information gathered by entering private property without permission or a lawfully issued warrant shall be recorded, made public, or used for studies or grants, including information gathered without property owner permission prior to enactment of this section.

III. Information gathered on the property with permission may only be used for the specific purpose stated in the notification.

7-C:2 Notification Requirements. Notice required by RSA 7-C:1, I to the landowner shall include:

I. The purpose of the data gathering.

II. The date and duration of the data gathering.

III. The specific land and features of the land that will be evaluated.

IV. The manner in which the person gathering the data will record and retain the information.

V. The method by which the person gathering the data will share the information, and who the person gathering the data will share the information with.

VI. A full disclosure of the potential restrictions that may be placed on the property, and on abutters, as a consequence of such information being recorded.

7-C:3 Property Owner Response. If written permission is not received from the property owner within 15 days of the notice, permission to enter the property shall be deemed denied.

7-C:4 Effect on Land Use Board Decisions. No state or municipal agency, board, or commission, or other governmental entity shall use data from abutting land as a factor in the denial of any permit or approval.

7-C:5 Exemptions.

I. The requirements of this chapter shall not apply to:

(a) State officials acting under statutory authority explicitly authorizing entry upon private property without permission; however written notification shall be sent to the property owner prior to entry upon the private property.

(b) State, county, or local officials for the purpose of perambulation; however written notification shall be sent to the property owner prior to entry upon private property.

(c) Federal, state, or local officials conducting inspections related to permits, licenses, or certifications applied for by the property owner.

(d) Federal, state, or local law enforcement responding to an emergency, or who have been called to the property, or who are inquiring about a report of activity on the property.

(e) Land surveyors conducting standard property surveys of abutting property.

(f) Emergency responders responding to an emergent public health threat or who have been called to the property.

(g) Municipal assessing officials.

(h) Public utility workers in the course of their normal duties or when responding to an emergency.

II. The exemptions in paragraph I shall not be construed to expand any authority to enter onto the property of another without first obtaining either the permission of the property owner or a court order.

7-C:6 Remedies.

I. If any public body or public agency or officer, employee, or other official thereof, violates any provisions of this chapter, such public body or public agency shall be liable for reasonable attorney's fees and costs incurred in a lawsuit under this chapter, provided that the court finds that such lawsuit was necessary in order to enforce compliance with the provisions of this chapter or to rectify a purposeful violation of this chapter. Fees shall not be awarded unless the court finds that the public body, public agency, or person knew or should have known that the conduct engaged in was in violation of this chapter or if the parties, by agreement, provide that no such fees shall be paid.

II. The court may award attorney's fees to a public body or public agency or employee or member thereof, for having to defend against a lawsuit under the provisions of this chapter, when the court finds that the lawsuit is in bad faith, frivolous, unjust, vexatious, wanton, or oppressive.

III. The court may invalidate an action of a public body or public agency taken in part due to data gathered in violation of this chapter.

IV. If the court finds that an officer, employee, or other official of a public body or public agency has knowingly violated any provision of this chapter, the court shall impose against such person a civil penalty of not less than $250 and not more than $2,000. Upon such finding, such person or persons shall also be required to reimburse the public body or public agency for any attorney's fees or costs it paid pursuant to paragraph I.

V. The court may also enjoin future violations of this chapter, and may require any officer, employee, or other official of a public body or public agency found to have violated the provisions of this chapter to undergo appropriate remedial training, at such person or person's expense.

2 Effective Date. This act shall take effect 60 days after its passage.

SMART GROWTH

Most people, when observing the use of the word SMART in reference to community planning, or as an attached label to power meters and home appliances, believe it refers to "intelligent," Unique," or "Scientific" new ideas for protecting the environment and cutting our carbon footprint. In fact, the use of the word SMART is actually engineering lingo meaning:

S- Specific
M-Measurable
A- Achievable
R –Relevant
T-Time Oriented

In other words, use of the acronym SMART means a controlled outcome in a specific period of time.

Agenda 21, Agenda 2030, Green New Deal = S.M.A.R.T.!

New Hampshire Bill Prohibits Joining ICLEI: HB 1634

This bill prohibits the state, counties, towns, and cities from implementing programs of, expending money for, receiving funding from, or contracting with the International Council for Local Environmental Initiatives.

HB 1634 – AS INTRODUCED

2012 SESSION

12-2669

10/03

HOUSE BILL *1634*

AN ACT prohibiting the state, counties, towns, and cities from implementing programs of, expending money for, receiving funding from, or contracting with the International Council for Local Environmental Initiatives.

SPONSORS: Rep. Cartwright, Ches 2; Rep. Pettengill, Carr 1; Rep. L. Vita, Straf 3; Rep. S. Tremblay, Rock 3

COMMITTEE: Executive Departments and Administration

ANALYSIS

This bill prohibits the state and political subdivisions from implementing programs of, funding, receiving funding from, or contracting with, the International Council for Local Environmental Initiatives (ICLEI).

- -
- - - - - -

Explanation: Matter added to current law appears in *bold italics.*

Matter removed from current law appears [in brackets and struckthrough.]

Matter which is either (a) all new or (b) repealed and reenacted appears in regular type.

12-2669

10/03

STATE OF NEW HAMPSHIRE

In the Year of Our Lord Two Thousand Twelve

AN ACT prohibiting the state, counties, towns, and cities from implementing programs of, expending money for, receiving funding from, or contracting with the International Council for Local Environmental Initiatives.

Be it Enacted by the Senate and House of Representatives in General Court convened:

1 New Section; Towns and Cities; Prohibition Added. Amend RSA 31 by inserting after section 8-a the following new section:

31:8-b International Council for Local Environmental Initiatives; Contracts; Expenditures Prohibited. No town or city shall implement programs of, expend any sum for, be a member of, receive funding from, contract for services from, or give financial or other forms of aid to the International Council for Local Environmental Initiatives (ICLEI) in furtherance of the United Nations program known as Agenda 21.

2 New Section; State Budget; Prohibition Added. Amend RSA 9 by inserting after section 28 the following new section:

9:29 International Council for Local Environmental Initiatives; Contracts; Expenditures Prohibited. No agency or department of the state shall implement programs of, expend any sum for, be a member of, receive funding from, contract for services from, or give financial or other forms of aid to the International Council for Local Environmental Initiatives (ICLEI) in furtherance of the United Nations program known as Agenda 21.

3 New Section; Counties; Prohibition Added. Amend RSA 23 by inserting after section 1-a the following new section:

23:1-b International Council for Local Environmental Initiatives; Contracts; Expenditures Prohibited. No county nor any department thereof shall implement programs of, expend any sum for, be a member of, receive funding from, contract for services from, or give financial or other forms of aid to the International Council for Local Environmental Initiatives (ICLEI) in furtherance of the United Nations program known as Agenda 21.

4 Effective Date. This act shall take effect 60 days after its passage.

"No one fully understands how, or even if, sustainable development can be achieved. However, there is growing consensus that it must be accomplished at the local level if it is ever to be achieved on a global basis." The Local Agenda 21 Planning Guide, published by ICLEI, 1996.

The Five Bill Package

Bill #1 Prohibits International Law Over Property Rights

This bill prohibits the use of international law to infringe on property rights. This includes the 1972 Earth Summit, the 1973 Convention on International Trade in Endangered Species, the 1973 UN Environmental Program (UNEP), the 1976 Conference on Human Settlements (Habitat I), and numerous other terrible international laws, including the 1992 UN Commission on Sustainable Development.

AN ACT Relating to prohibiting the use of international law to infringe on property rights; adding new sections to 04 adding a new section to adding a new section to and creating a new section.

BE IT ENACTED BY THE LEGISLATURE OF THE STATE OF

NEW SECTION. **Sec. 1.** The legislature finds that for more than forty years international interests have worked to systematically erode the property rights of our citizens. Among the most egregious examples of this can be seen in the material and documents produced through the 1971 Ramsar treaty on wetlands, the 1972 earth summit,
1 the 1973 convention on international trade in endangered species, the
2 1973 united nations environment program, the 1975 Belgrade charter,
3 the 1976 conference on human settlements, the 1982 world charter for
4 nature, the 1983 world commission on environment and development, the
1988 global forum on human survival, the 1990 international council
5 for environmental initiatives, the 1992 united nations commission on
sustainable development, the 1994 united nations conference on
6 population and development, the 1995 commission on sustainable
7 development, the 1996 conference on human settlements, and approval
8 of the earth charter in 2000.

1   Many of these forums produced documents which called for the
2   government to control population according to resources, government
3   control of land use in order to achieve equitable distribution of
4   resources, government control of land use through zoning and
5   planning, government control of excessive profits from land use,
6   government control of urban and rural land through public land
7   ownership, and government authorities holding development rights
8   using taxpayers' dollars. The legislature finds implementation of
9   many of these international accords result in the physical and
10 regulatory taking of private property and constitutes a violation of
11 the natural rights of citizens to own and enjoy private property.

12 <u>NEW SECTION.</u> **Sec. 2.**A new section is added to chapter
13 RCW to read as follows:
14   It is the policy of the state of to prohibit the
15 adoption, development, or implementation of community development
16 policies based on international accords that infringe or restrict
17 private property rights. The expenditure of public funds in
18 furtherance of any international accords that endanger a citizen's
19 private property rights is prohibited.

20 <u>NEW SECTION.</u> **Sec. 3.** A new section is added to
21   to read as follows:
22   (1) As used in this section, "political subdivision" means the
23 state, any county, incorporated city, unincorporated city, public
24 local entity, special purpose district, public-private partnership,
25 and any other public entity of the state, a county, or city.
26   (2) The state of and all political subdivisions may not adopt
27 or implement policy recommendations that deliberately or
28 inadvertently infringe or restrict private property rights without
29 due process as may be required by policy recommendations originating
30 in or traceable to international law, international accord, or
31 ancillary plan of action that contravenes the Constitution of the
32 United States or the Constitution of the state of .
33   (3) The state of and all political subdivisions may
34 not enter into any agreement, expend any sum of money, or receive
35 funds contracting services or giving financial aid to or from
36 nongovernmental, nonprofit, or intergovernmental organizations for
37 the implementation of policy recommendations originating in or
38   traceable to international law, international accord, or ancillary

1 plans of action that contravene the Constitutions of the United
2 States and state.

3   NEW SECTION. **Sec. 4.** A new section is added to to read as
4 follows:
5   In addition to other remedies provided by law, any person
6 aggrieved or adversely affected by the failure of the state of
7 Washington or any political subdivision to abide by the prohibition
8 set forth in sections 2 and 3 of this act may apply to the superior
9 court of the county where the agency is located or to the superior
10 court of Thurston county if the defendant is a state agency. The
11 superior court has jurisdiction to hold a prompt hearing where
12 petitioners may show cause that the state of or political
13 subdivision has failed to adhere to the requirements of this act and
14 adopted, implemented, or expended money in the implementation of
15 policy recommendations in violation of this chapter. The court may
16 issue a temporary or permanent injunction restraining any person,
17 agency, or all agencies from further violations of this chapter.

18   NEW SECTION. **Sec. 5.** A new section is added to to read as
19 follows:
20   Sections 1 through 4 of this act apply to all actions required by
21 or taken under the authority of this chapter.

22   NEW SECTION. **Sec. 6.** A new section is added to to read as
23 follows:
24   Sections 1 through 4 of this act apply to all actions required by
25 or taken under the authority of this chapter.

                    --- **END** ---

"Land…cannot be treated as an ordinary asset, controlled by individuals and subject to the pressures and inefficiencies of the market. Private land ownership is also a principle instrument of accumulation and concentration of wealth, therefore contributes to social injustice." From the 1976 report of the UN's Habitat 1 conference.

"What's been hardest is the way our legal system is structured to favor private property. I think people all over this city, of every background, would like to have the city government be able to determine which building goes where, how high it will be, who gets to live in it, what the rent will be." New York Mayor Bill deBlasio, 2017 Interview with New York Magazine

Bill #2   Stop Eminent Domain for Private Economic Development

This bill states that private property may be taken only for public use and the taking of private property by any public entity for economic development does not constitute a public use. No public entity may take property for the purpose of economic development.

```
 1      AN ACT Relating to prohibiting the use of eminent domain for
 2   economic development; amending and adding a new chapter
 3
     BE IT ENACTED BY THE LEGISLATURE OF THE STATE OF
 4
 5      NEW SECTION.   Sec. 1.   The definitions in this section apply
 6   throughout this chapter unless the context clearly requires
 7   otherwise.
 8      140.
 9      (2) "Economic development" means any activity to increase tax
10   revenue, tax base, employment, or general economic health, when that
11   activity does not result in:
12      (a) The transfer of property to public possession, occupation,
13   and enjoyment;
14      (b) The transfer of property to a private entity that is a public
15   service company, consumer-owned utility, or common carrier;
16
17      (c) The use of eminent domain:
18      (i)(A) To remove a public nuisance;
19      (B) To remove a structure that is beyond repair or unfit for
20   human habitation or use; or
21      (C) To acquire abandoned property; and
```

1   (ii) To eliminate a direct threat to public health and safety
2 caused by the property in its current condition; or
3   (d) The transfer of property to private entities that occupy an
4 incidental area within a publicly owned and occupied project.
5   "Economic development" does not include the transfer of property
6 to a public service company, a consumer-owned utility, or a common
7 carrier for the purpose of constructing, operating, or maintaining
8 generation, transmission, or distribution facilities. "Economic
9 development" also does not include port districts' activities under
10 Title "Economic development" also does not include highway
11 projects.
12   (3) "Public service company" has the same meaning as defined in
13 80.04.010.
14   (4)(a) "Public use" means:
15   (i) The possession, occupation, and enjoyment of the property by
16 the general public, or by public agencies;
17   (ii) The use of property for the creation or functioning of
18 public service companies, a consumer-owned utility, or common
19 carriers; or
20   (iii) Where the use of eminent domain:
21   (A)(I) Removes a public nuisance;
22   (II) Removes a structure that is beyond repair or unfit for human
23 habitation or use; or
24   (III) Is used to acquire abandoned property; and
25   (B) Eliminates a direct threat to public health and safety caused
26 by the property in its current condition.
27   (b) The public benefits of economic development, including an
28 increase in tax base, tax revenues, employment, and general economic
29 health, may not constitute a public use.

30   NEW SECTION. **Sec. 2.** Private property may be taken only for
31 public use and the taking of private property by any public entity
32 for economic development does not constitute a public use. No public
33 entity may take property for the purpose of economic development.

34   NEW SECTION. **Sec. 3.** In an action to establish or challenge the
35 asserted public use of a taking of private property, the taking of
36 private property shall be deemed for economic development, and not a
37 proper basis for eminent domain, if the court determines that the
38   taking of the private property does not result in any of the

1 exceptions to economic development set forth in section 1(2) of this
2 act, and economic development was a substantial factor in the
3 governmental body's decision to take the property.

4   as follows:
5   A municipality shall have the right to acquire by condemnation,
6 in accordance with the procedure provided for condemnation by such
7 municipality for other purposes, any interest in real property, which
8 it may deem necessary for a community renewal project under this
9 chapter after the adoption by the local governing body of a
10 resolution declaring that the acquisition of the real property
11 described therein is necessary for such purpose. Condemnation for
12 community renewal of blighted areas is declared to be a public use,
13 and property already devoted to any other public use or acquired by
14 the owner or a predecessor in interest by eminent domain may be
15 condemned for the purposes of this chapter. Condemnation of property
16 in blighted areas for economic development, as defined in section 1
17 of this act, is not a public use.
18   The award of compensation for real property taken for such a
19 project shall not be increased by reason of any increase in the value
20 of the real property caused by the assembly, clearance, or
21 reconstruction, or proposed assembly, clearance, or reconstruction in
22 the project area. No allowance shall be made for the improvements
23 begun on real property after notice to the owner of such property of
24 the institution of proceedings to condemn such property. Evidence
25 shall be admissible bearing upon the insanitary, unsafe, or
26 substandard condition of the premises, or the unlawful use thereof.
27

28   NEW SECTION. **Sec. 5.** Sections 1 through 3 of this act
29 constitute a new chapter in

--- **END** ---

"Check your premise – All is not as it seems."

Bill #3   If Government Takes it, Government Pays For It

This bill requires government authorities to provide just compensation to property owners whenever land use ordinances, regulations, or policies adopted require the property owner to alter their property in any of numerous ways from placing signage, making an expenditure for the protection of riparian areas, or grant easements for public access on the property.

AN ACT Relating to technology-enhanced government surveillance; adding new sections creating a new section; and prescribing penalties.

BE IT ENACTED BY THE LEGISLATURE OF THE STATE OF

NEW SECTION.   **Sec. 1.**   The legislature finds that technological advances have provided new, unique equipment that may be utilized for surveillance purposes.   These technological advances often outpace statutory protections and can lead to inconsistent or contradictory interpretations between jurisdictions.   The legislature finds that

1 regardless of application or size, the use of these extraordinary
2 surveillance technologies, without public debate or clear legal
3 authority, creates uncertainty for citizens and agencies throughout
   state.   The legislature finds that extraordinary surveillance
4 technologies do present a substantial privacy risk potentially
   contrary to the strong privacy protections enshrined in Article I,
5 section 7 of the state Constitution that reads "No person shall be
6 disturbed in his private affairs, or his home invaded, without
7 authority of law." The legislature further finds that the lack of
8 clear statutory authority for the use of extraordinary
9
10
11
12
13
14
15
16
17
18
19

1   surveillance technologies may increase liability to state and local
2   jurisdictions. It is the intent of the legislature to provide clear
3   standards for the lawful use of extraordinary surveillance technologies
4   by state and local jurisdictions.

5   <u>NEW SECTION.</u> **Sec. 2.** The definitions in this section apply
6   throughout this section and sections 3 through 13 of this act unless
7   the context clearly requires otherwise.
8   (1)(a) "Agency" means the state of , its agencies, and political
9   subdivisions.
10   (b) "Agency" also includes any entity, whether public or private,
11   with which any of the entities identified in (a) of this subsection has
12   entered into a contractual relationship for the operation of a system
13   of personal information or unmanned aircraft system to accomplish an
14   agency function.
15   (2) "Biometric identification system" is a system that collects
16   unique physical and behavioral characteristics including, but not
17   limited to, biographical data, facial photographs, fingerprints, and
18   iris scans to identify individuals.
19   (3) "Court of competent jurisdiction" means any district court of
20   the United States or any United States court of appeals that has
21   jurisdiction over the offense being investigated or is located in a
22   district in which surveillance with the assistance of the extraordinary
23   sensing device will be conducted, or a court of general jurisdiction
24   authorized by the state of to issue search warrants.
25   (4) "Extraordinary sensing device" means an unmanned aircraft
26   system.
27   (5) "Personal information" means all information that:
28   (a) Describes, locates, or indexes anything about a person
29   including, but not limited to, the person's social security number,
30   driver's license number, agency-issued identification number, student
31   identification number, real or personal property holdings derived from
32   tax returns, and the person's education, financial transactions,
33   medical history, ancestry, religion, political ideology, or criminal or
34   employment record;
35   (b) Affords a basis for inferring personal characteristics, such as
36   finger and voice prints, photographs, or things done by or to such

1   person; and the record of the person's presence, registration, or

2   membership in an organization or activity, or admission to an

3   institution; or

4   (c) Describes, locates, or indexes anything about a person

5   including, but not limited to, intellectual property, trade secrets,

6   proprietary information, or operational information.

7   (6)(a) "Sensing device" means a device capable of remotely

8   acquiring personal information from its surroundings, using any

9   frequency of the electromagnetic spectrum.

10   (b) "Sensing device" does not include equipment whose sole function

11 is to provide information directly necessary for safe air navigation or

12 operation of a vehicle.

13   (7) "Unmanned aircraft system" means an aircraft that is operated

14 without the possibility of human intervention from within or on the

15 aircraft, together with associated elements, including communication

16 links and components that control the unmanned aircraft that are

17 required for the pilot in command to operate safely and efficiently in

18 the national airspace system.

19   NEW SECTION. **Sec. 3.**   (1) Agency procurement and use of

20 extraordinary sensing devices for surveillance purposes must be

21 conducted in a transparent manner that is open to public scrutiny, as

22 provided in this section.

23   (2)(a) For the purposes of this section, "governing body" means the

24 council, commission, board, or other controlling body in which

25 legislative powers are vested, except as provided in (b) of this

26 subsection.

27   (b) For a state agency in which there is no governing body other

28 than the state legislature, "governing body" means the chief executive

29 officer responsible for the governance of the agency.

30   (3) An agency may not procure an extraordinary sensing device for

31 surveillance purposes without first obtaining explicit approval from

32 the agency's governing body.

33   (4) The governing body shall develop and make publicly available

34 written policies and procedures for the use of any extraordinary

35 sensing device procured, and provide notice and opportunity for public

36 comment prior to adoption of the written policies and procedures.

1   NEW SECTION. **Sec. 4.** All operations of an extraordinary sensing
2   device or disclosure of personal information about any person acquired
3   through the operation of an extraordinary sensing device must be
4   conducted in such a way as to minimize the collection and disclosure of
5   personal information not authorized under this chapter.

6   NEW SECTION. **Sec. 5.** (1) An extraordinary sensing device may be
7   operated and personal information from such operation disclosed in
8   order to collect personal information pursuant to a search warrant
9   issued by a court of competent jurisdiction as provided in this
10   section.
11   (2) Each petition for a search warrant from a judicial officer to
12   permit the use of an extraordinary sensing device and personal
13   information collected from such operation must be made in writing, upon
14   oath or affirmation, to a judicial officer in a court of competent
15   jurisdiction for the geographic area in which an extraordinary sensing
16   device is to be operated or where there is probable cause to believe
17   the offense for which the extraordinary sensing device is sought has
18   been committed, is being committed, or will be committed.
19   (3) The law enforcement officer shall submit an affidavit that
20   includes:
21   (a) The identity of the applicant and the identity of the agency
22   conducting the investigation;
23   (b) The identity of the individual and area for which use of the
24   extraordinary sensing device is being sought;
25   (c) Specific and articulable facts demonstrating probable cause to
26   believe that there has been, is, or will be criminal activity and that
27   the operation of the extraordinary sensing device system will uncover
28   evidence of such activity or facts to support the finding that there is
29   probable cause for issuance of a search warrant pursuant to applicable
30   requirements; and
31   (d) A statement that other methods of data collection have been
32   investigated and found to be either cost prohibitive or pose an
33   unacceptable safety risk to a law enforcement officer or to the public.
34   (4) If the judicial officer finds, based on the affidavit
35   submitted, there is probable cause to believe a crime has been
36   committed, is being committed, or will be committed and there is
37   probable cause to believe the personal information likely to be

1   obtained from the use of the extraordinary sensing device will be
2   evidence of the commission of such offense, the judicial officer may
3   issue a search warrant authorizing the use of the extraordinary sensing
4   device. The search warrant must authorize the collection of personal
5   information contained in or obtained from the extraordinary sensing
6   device, but must not authorize the use of a biometric identification
7   system.

8   (5) Warrants may not be issued for a period greater than ten days.
9   Extensions may be granted, but no longer than the authorizing judicial
10 officer deems necessary to achieve the purposes for which it was
11 granted and in no event for longer than thirty days.

12   (6) Within ten days of the execution of a search warrant, the
13 officer executing the warrant must serve a copy of the warrant upon the
14 target of the warrant, except if notice is delayed pursuant to section
15 6 of this act.

16   NEW SECTION. **Sec. 6.** (1) A governmental entity acting under this
17 section may, when a warrant is sought, include in the petition a
18 request, which the court shall grant, for an order delaying the
19 notification required under section 5(6) of this act for a period not
20 to exceed ninety days if the court determines that there is a reason to
21 believe that notification of the existence of the warrant may have an
22 adverse result.

23   (2) An adverse result for the purposes of this section is:
24   (a) Placing the life or physical safety of an individual in danger;
25   (b) Causing a person to flee from prosecution;
26   (c) Causing the destruction of or tampering with evidence;
27   (d) Causing the intimidation of potential witnesses; or
28   (e) Jeopardizing an investigation or unduly delaying a trial.

29   (3) The governmental entity shall maintain a copy of certification.

30   (4) Extension of the delay of notification of up to ninety days
31 each may be granted by the court upon application or by certification
32 by a governmental entity.

33   (5) Upon expiration of the period of delay of notification under
34 subsection (2) or (4) of this section, the governmental entity shall
35 serve a copy of the warrant upon, or deliver it by registered or first-
36 class mail to, the target of the warrant, together with notice that:

1   (a) States with reasonable specificity the nature of the law
2   enforcement inquiry; and
3   (b) Informs the target of the warrant: (i) That notification was
4   delayed; (ii) what governmental entity or court made the certification
5   or determination pursuant to which that delay was made; and (iii) which
6   provision of this section allowed such delay.

7   <u>NEW SECTION.</u> **Sec. 7.** (1) It is lawful under this section for any
8   law enforcement officer or other public official to operate an
9   extraordinary sensing device and disclose personal information from
10 such operation if such officer reasonably determines that an emergency
11 situation exists that involves criminal activity and presents immediate
12 danger of death or serious physical injury to any person and:
13 (a) Requires operation of an extraordinary sensing device before a
14 warrant authorizing such interception can, with due diligence, be
15 obtained;
16 (b) There are grounds upon which such a warrant could be entered to
17 authorize such operation; and
18 (c) An application for a warrant providing such operation is made
19 within forty-eight hours after the operation has occurred or begins to
20 occur.
21 (2) In the absence of a warrant, an operation of an extraordinary
22 sensing device carried out under this section must immediately
23 terminate when the personal information sought is obtained or when the
24 application for the warrant is denied, whichever is earlier.
25 (3) In the event such application for approval is denied, the
26 personal information obtained from the operation of a device must be
27 treated as having been obtained in violation of this chapter, except
28 for purposes of section 12 of this act, and an inventory must be served
29 on the person named in the application.

30 <u>NEW SECTION.</u> **Sec. 8.** (1) It is lawful under this section for a
31 law enforcement officer, agency employee, or authorized agent to
32 operate an extraordinary sensing device and disclose personal
33 information from such operation if:
34 (a) An officer, employee, or agent reasonably determines that an
35 emergency situation exists that:
36 (i) Does not involve criminal activity;

1   (ii) Presents immediate danger of death or serious physical injury

2   to any person; and

3   (iii) Requires operation of an extraordinary sensing device to

4   reduce the danger of death or serious physical injury;

5   (b) An officer, employee, or agent reasonably determines that the

6   operation does not intend to collect personal information and is

7   unlikely to accidentally collect personal information, and such

8   operation is not for purposes of regulatory enforcement including, but

9   not limited to:

10 (i) Monitoring to discover, locate, observe, and prevent forest

11 fires;

12 (ii) Monitoring an environmental or weather-related catastrophe or

13 damage from such an event;

14 (iii) Surveying for wildlife management, habitat preservation, or

15 environmental damage; and

16 (iv) Surveying for the assessment and evaluation of environmental

17 or weather-related damage, erosion, flood, or contamination;

18 (c) The operation is part of a training exercise conducted on a

19 military base and the extraordinary sensing device does not collect

20 personal information on persons located outside the military base;

21 (d) The operation is for training and testing purposes by an agency

22 and does not collect personal information; or

23 (e) The operation is part of the response to an emergency or

24 disaster for which the governor has proclaimed a state of emergency

25 under

26 (2) Upon completion of the operation of an extraordinary sensing

27 device pursuant to this section, any personal information obtained must

28 be treated as information collected on an individual other than a

29 target for purposes of section 11 of this act.

30 NEW SECTION.   **Sec. 9.**   An unmanned aircraft system may not be

31 utilized for the purposes of investigation or enforcement of regulatory

32 violations or noncompliance until the legislature has adopted

33 legislation specifically permitting such use.

34 NEW SECTION.   **Sec. 10.**   Whenever any personal information from an

35 extraordinary sensing device has been acquired, no part of such

36 personal information and no evidence derived therefrom may be received

1   in evidence in any trial, hearing, or other proceeding in or before any
2   court, grand jury, department, officer, agency, regulatory body,
3   legislative committee, or other authority of the state or a political
4   subdivision thereof if the collection or disclosure of that personal
5   information would be in violation of this chapter.

6   NEW SECTION. **Sec. 11.** Personal information collected during the
7   operation of an extraordinary sensing device authorized by and
8   consistent with this chapter may not be used, copied, or disclosed for
9   any purpose after conclusion of the operation, unless there is probable
10 cause that the personal information is evidence of criminal activity.
11 Personal information must be deleted as soon as possible after there is
12 no longer probable cause that the personal information is evidence of
13 criminal activity; this must be within thirty days if the personal
14 information was collected on the target of a warrant authorizing the
15 operation of the extraordinary sensing device, and within ten days for
16 other personal information collected incidentally to the operation of
17 an extraordinary sensing device otherwise authorized by and consistent
18 with this chapter. There is a presumption that personal information is
19 not evidence of criminal activity if that personal information is not
20 used in a criminal prosecution within one year of collection.

21   NEW SECTION. **Sec. 12.** Any person who knowingly violates this
22 chapter is subject to legal action for damages, to be brought by any
23 other person claiming that a violation of this chapter has injured his
24 or her business, his or her person, or his or her reputation. A person
25 so injured is entitled to actual damages and reasonable attorneys' fees
26 and other costs of litigation.

27   NEW SECTION. **Sec. 13.** (1) For any calendar year in which an
28 agency has procured or used an extraordinary sensing device, the agency
29 must prepare an annual report. The report must be made publicly
30 available electronically and must, at a minimum, include the following:
31   (a) The types of extraordinary sensing devices procured and used,
32 the purposes for which each type of extraordinary sensing device was
33 procured and used, the circumstances under which use was authorized,
34 and the name of the officer or official who authorized the use;
35   (b) Whether deployment of the device was perceptible to the public;

1   (c)   The   specific   kinds   of   personal   information   that   the
2   extraordinary sensing device collected;
3   (d) The length of time for which any personal information collected
4   by the extraordinary sensing device was retained;
5   (e)   The   specific   steps   taken   to   mitigate   the   impact   on   an
6   individual's privacy, including protections against unauthorized use
7   and disclosure and adoption of a data minimization protocol; and
8   (f)   An   individual   point   of   contact   for   citizen   complaints   and
9   concerns.
10   (2)(a) Each agency, except as provided in (b) of this subsection,
11   must submit to the agency's governing body the annual report for the
12   previous calendar year by March 1st, beginning in
13   (b) In the case of state agencies with no governing body other than
14   the legislature, the annual reports must be filed electronically with
15   the office of financial management, who must compile the results and
16   submit them electronically to the legislature by September 1st of each
17   year, beginning in

18   NEW SECTION. **Sec. 14.**   Sections 2 through 13 of this act are each
19   added to chapter 9.73 RCW and codified with the subchapter heading of
20   "extraordinary sensing devices."

21   NEW SECTION.   **Sec. 15.**   If any provision of this act or its
22   application   to   any   person   or   circumstance   is   held   invalid,   the
23   remainder of the act or the application of the provision to other
24   persons or circumstances is not affected.

--- END ---

Bill #4 No Developer Entry without Property Owners Permission

This bill makes it illegal to make entry onto private property to collect resource data without legal authorization.

```
1       AN ACT Relating to unlawful entry onto private property; adding a
2   new section to  and prescribing penalties.

3   BE IT ENACTED BY THE LEGISLATURE OF THE STATE OF :

4       NEW SECTION.   Sec. 1.   A new section is added  to read as
5   follows:
6       (1) A person is guilty of trespassing to unlawfully collect
7   resource data from private land if he or she:
8       (a) Enters onto private land for the purpose of collecting
9   resource data; and
10      (b) Does not have: (i) An ownership interest in the real property
11  or statutory, contractual, or other legal authorization to enter the
12  private land to collect the specified resource data; or (ii) written
13  or verbal permission of the owner, lessee, or agent of the owner to
14  enter the private land to collect the specified resource data.
15      (2) A person is guilty of unlawfully collecting resource data if
16  he or she enters onto private land and collects resource data from
17  private land without:
18      (a) An ownership interest in the real property or statutory,
19  contractual, or other legal authorization to enter the private land
20  to collect the specified resource data; or
```

1   (b) Written or verbal permission of the owner, lessee, or agent
2   of the owner to enter the private land to collect the specified
3   resource data.

4   (3) A person is guilty of trespassing to access adjacent or
5   proximate land if he or she:

6   (a) Crosses private land to access adjacent or proximate land
7   where he or she collects resource data; and

8   (b) Does not have: (i) An ownership interest in the real property
9   or statutory, contractual, or other legal authorization to cross the
10   private land; or (ii) written or verbal permission of the owner,
11   lessee, or agent of the owner to cross the private land.

12   (4)(a) Except as provided in (b) of this subsection, a violation
13   of subsection (1), (2), or (3) of this section is a misdemeanor
14   punishable under

15   (b) A second or subsequent violation of this section is a gross
16   misdemeanor punishable under

17   (c) A person who commits multiple violations of this section may
18   be prosecuted and punished for each violation separately.

19   (5) For the purposes of this section:

20   (a) "Collect" means to take a sample of material, acquire,
21   gather, photograph, or otherwise preserve information in any form,
22   and the recording of a legal description or geographical coordinates
23   of the location of the collection;

24   (b) "Peace officer" means a general authority peace
25   officeror a limited authority peace officer as those
26   terms are defined in

27   (c) "Resource data" means data relating to land or land use
28   including, but not limited to, data regarding agriculture, minerals,
29   geology, history, cultural artifacts, archaeology, air, water, soil,
30   conservation, habitat, vegetation, or animal species. "Resource data"
31   does not include data: (i) For surveying to determine property
32   boundaries or the location of survey monuments; (ii) used by a state
33   or local governmental entity to assess property values; or (iii)
34   collected or intended to be collected by a peace officer while
35   engaged in the lawful performance of his or her official duties.

36   (6) No resource data collected on private land in violation of
37   this section is admissible in evidence in any civil, criminal, or
38   administrative proceeding, other than a prosecution for violation of
39   this section or a civil action against the violator.

```
1        (7) Resource data collected on private land in violation of this
2     section in the possession of any state or local governmental entity
3     shall be destroyed by the entity from all files and databases, and it
4     shall not be considered in determining any agency action.
```

--- END ---

PRIVATE PROPERTY RIGHTS DEFINED

Experts have left a clear understanding of what property means:

"The moment the idea is admitted into society that property is not as sacred as the law of God, and that there is not a force of law and public justice to protect it, anarchy and tyranny commence." President, John Adams

"Ultimately, property rights and personal rights are the same thing." President Calvin Coolidge

"If you don't have the right to own and control property then you are property." Wayne Hage, Rancher

Private Property Rights Means:

• That local, city, county, state, and federal governments are prohibited from exercising eminent domain for the sole purpose of acquiring legally purchased/deeded private property so as to resell to a private interest or generate revenues;

• That no local, city, county, state, or federal government has the authority to impose directives, ordinances, fees, or fines regarding aesthetic landscaping, color selections, tree and plant preservation, or open spaces on legally purchased/deeded private property;

• That no local, city, county, state or federal government shall implement a land use plan that requires any part of legally purchased/deeded private property be set aside for public use or for a Natural Resource Protection Area directing that no construction or disturbance may occur;

• That no local, city, county, state, or federal government shall alter or impose zoning restrictions or regulations that will devalue or limit the ability to sell legally purchased/deeded private property;

• That no local, city, county, state, or federal government shall limit profitable or productive agriculture activities by mandating and controlling what crops and livestock are grown on legally purchased/deeded private property;

• That no local, city, county, state, or federal government representatives or their assigned agents may enter private property without the written permission of the property owner or is in possession of a lawful warrant from a legitimate court of law. This includes invasion of property rights and privacy by government use of unmanned drone flights.

Bill #5   Clear Standards and Guidelines for Drone Use Over Private Property

Because technological advances have provided new, unique equipment that may be utilized for surveillance purposes (i.e. drones, etc.), and because these advances often outpace statutory protections, the legislature finds that regardless of application or size, the use of unmanned aerial vehicles, without public debate or clear legal authority, this creates uncertainty for both citizens and agencies. The lack of clear statutory authority for their use may increase liability to state and local jurisdictions. Therefore, clear standards need to be provided.

1
2
3
4
5
6
7
8
9
10
11
12
13
14
15
16
17
18
19

   AN ACT Relating to protecting   citizens from warrantless
surveillance, reducing liability, and establishing clear standards
under which agencies may utilize unmanned aerial vehicles;
prescribing penalties; and declaring an emergency.

BE IT ENACTED BY THE LEGISLATURE OF THE STATE OF

   <u>NEW SECTION.</u> **Sec. 1.** The legislature finds that technological
advances have provided new, unique equipment that may be utilized for
surveillance purposes.   These technological advances often outpace
statutory protections and can lead to inconsistent or contradictory
interpretations between jurisdictions.   The legislature finds that
regardless of application or size, the use of unmanned aerial vehicles,
without public debate or clear legal authority, creates uncertainty for
citizens and agencies throughout   state.   As stated in the
congressional research service report entitled 'Integration of Drones
into Domestic Airspace,' "the extent of their potential domestic
application is bound only by human ingenuity. . .the full-scale
introduction of drones into U.S. skies will inevitably generate a host
of legal issues. . .With the ability to house high-powered cameras,

1   infrared sensors, facial recognition technology, and license plate
2   readers, some argue that drones present a substantial privacy risk."
3   The legislature finds that drones do present a substantial privacy risk
4   potentially contrary to the strong privacy protections enshrined in
5   section state Constitution that reads "No person shall be disturbed
6   in his private affairs, or his home invaded, without authority of
7   law."

8   The legislature further finds that the lack of clear statutory
9   authority for the use of unmanned aerial vehicles may increase
10   liability to state and local jurisdictions. It is the intent of the
11   legislature to provide clear standards for the lawful use of unmanned
12   aerial vehicles by state and local jurisdictions.

13   <u>NEW SECTION.</u> **Sec. 2.** The definitions in this section apply
14   throughout this chapter unless the context clearly requires otherwise.
15   (1) "Agency" means any agency, authority, board, department,
16   division, commission, institution, bureau, or like governmental entity
17   of the state or of any unit of local government including counties,
18   cities, towns, regional governments, and the departments thereof, and
19   includes constitutional officers, except as otherwise expressly
20   provided by law. "Agency" also means each component part of the
21   legislative, executive, or judicial branches of state and local
22   government, including each office, department, authority, post,
23   commission, committee, and each institution or board created by law to
24   exercise some regulatory or sovereign power or duty as distinguished
25   from purely advisory powers or duties. "Agency" also includes any
26   entity, whether public or private, with which any of the foregoing has
27   entered into a contractual relationship for the operation of a system
28   of personal information to accomplish an agency function.
29   (2) "Biometric identification system" is a system that collects
30   unique physical and behavioral characteristics including, but not
31   limited to, biographical data, facial photographs, fingerprints, and
32   iris scans to identify individuals.
33   (3) "Court of competent jurisdiction" includes any district court
34   of the United States or any United States court of appeals that has
35   jurisdiction over the offense being investigated; is in a district in
36   which the public unmanned aircraft will conduct a search or a court of

general jurisdiction authorized by the state of   to issue search warrants.

(4) "Inspection warrant" is an order in writing, made in the name of the state, signed by any judge of the court whose territorial jurisdiction encompasses the property or premises to be inspected or entered, and directed to a state or local official, commanding him or her to enter and to conduct any inspection, testing, or collection of samples for testing required or authorized by state or local law or regulation.

(5) "Judicial officer" means a judge, magistrate, or other person authorized to issue a criminal, inspection, or administrative search warrant.

(6) "Law enforcement officer" means any general authority, limited authority, or specially commissioned   peace officer or federal peace officer as those terms are defined

(7) "Person" includes any individual, corporation, partnership, association, cooperative, limited liability company, trust, joint venture, government, political subdivision, or any other legal or commercial entity and any successor, representative, agent, agency, or instrumentality thereof.

(8) "Personal information" means all information that (a) describes, locates, or indexes anything about a person including, but not limited to, his or her social security number, driver's license number, agency-issued identification number, student identification number, real or personal property holdings derived from tax returns, and his or her education, financial transactions, medical history, ancestry, religion, political ideology, or criminal or employment record; (b) affords a basis for inferring personal characteristics, such as finger and voice prints, photographs, or things done by or to such person; and the record of his or her presence, registration, or membership in an organization or activity, or admission to an institution; or (c) describes, locates, or indexes anything about a person including, but not limited to, intellectual property, trade secrets, proprietary information, or operational information.

(9) "Public unmanned aircraft system" means an unmanned aircraft and associated elements, including communications links, sensing devices, and the components that control the unmanned aircraft,

2   agency.

3   (10) "Sensing device" means a device capable of acquiring data

4   information from its surroundings including, but not limited t

5   cameras using visible, ultraviolet, or infrared frequencie

6   microphones, thermal detectors, chemical detectors, radiation gauge

7   and wireless receivers in any frequency.

8   (11) "Trade secrets" means all forms and types of financia

9   business, scientific, technical, economic, or engineering informatio

10   including patterns, plans, compilations, program devices, formula

11   designs, prototypes, methods, techniques, processes, procedure

12   programs, or codes whether tangible or intangible, and whether or h

13   stored, compiled, or memorialized physically, electronicall

14   graphically, photographically, or in writing, which the owner has tal

15   reasonable measures to protect and has an independent economic value.

16   (12) "Unmanned aircraft" means an aircraft that is operated witho

17   the possibility of human intervention from within or on the aircraft.

18   (13) "Unmanned aircraft system" means an unmanned aircraft a

19   associated elements, including communication links and components th

20   control the unmanned aircraft that are required for the pilot

21   command to operate safely and efficiently in the national airspa

22   system.

23   NEW SECTION. **Sec. 3.** Except as otherwise specifically authoriz

24   in this chapter, it shall be unlawful to operate a public unmanr

25   aircraft system or disclose personal information about any pers

26   acquired through the operation of a public unmanned aircraft system.

27   NEW SECTION. **Sec. 4.** (1) No state agency or organization havi

28   jurisdiction over criminal law enforcement or regulatory violati

29   including, but not limited to, the state patrol, shall procur

30   public unmanned aircraft system without the approval of

31   legislature.

32   (2) No department of law enforcement of any city, county, or to

33   or any local agency having jurisdiction over criminal law enforceme

34   or regulatory violations shall procure a public unmanned aircra

35   system without the approval of the governing body of such locality.

1   NEW SECTION. **Sec. 5.** All operations of a public unmanned aircraft
2   system or disclosure of personal information about any person acquired
3   through the operation of a public unmanned aircraft system shall be
4   conducted in such a way as to minimize the collection and disclosure of
5   personal information not authorized under this chapter.

6   NEW SECTION. **Sec. 6.** A public unmanned aircraft system may be
7   operated and personal information from such operation disclosed in
8   order to collect personal information only pursuant to a criminal
9   warrant issued by a court of competent jurisdiction or as otherwise
10   provided in this section.
11   (1) Each petition for a search warrant from a judicial officer to
12   permit the use of a public unmanned aircraft system and personal
13   information collected from such operation shall be made in writing,
14   upon oath or affirmation, to a judicial officer in a court of competent
15   jurisdiction for the geographic area in which a public unmanned
16   aircraft system is to be operated or where there is probable cause to
17   believe the offense for which the public unmanned aircraft system is
18   sought has been committed, is being committed, or will be committed.
19   (2) The law enforcement officer shall submit an affidavit that
20   shall include:
21   (a) The identity of the applicant and the identity of the agency
22   conducting the investigation;
23   (b) The identity of the individual and jurisdictional area for
24   which use of the public unmanned aircraft is being sought;
25   (c) Specific and articulable facts demonstrating probable cause to
26   believe that there is criminal activity and that the operation of the
27   public unmanned aircraft system will uncover evidence of such activity
28   or facts to support the finding that there is probable cause for
29   issuance of an administrative search warrant pursuant to applicable
30   requirements; and
31   (d) The name of the county or city where there is probable cause to
32   believe the offense for which use of the unmanned public aircraft
33   system is sought has been committed, is being committed, or will be
34   committed.
35   (3) If the judicial officer finds, based on the affidavit
36   submitted, that there is probable cause to believe that a crime has
37   been committed, is being committed, or will be committed and that there

1 is probable cause to believe the personal information likely to be
2 obtained from the use of the public unmanned aircraft system will be
3 evidence of the commission of such offense, the judicial officer may
4 issue a search warrant authorizing the use of the public unmanned
5 aircraft system. The search warrant shall authorize the collection of
6 personal information contained in or obtained from the public unmanned
7 aircraft system but shall not authorize the use of a biometric
8 identification system.

9   (4) Warrants shall not be issued for a period greater than forty-
10 eight hours. Extensions may be granted but shall be no longer than the
11 authorizing judicial officer deems necessary to achieve the purposes
12 for which it was granted and in no event for longer than thirty days.

13   (5) Within ten days of the execution of a search warrant, the
14 officer executing the warrant must serve a copy of the warrant upon the
15 person or persons upon whom personal information was collected except
16 notice may be delayed under section 7 of this act.

17   NEW SECTION. Sec. 7. A governmental entity acting under this
18 section may, when a warrant is sought, include in the petition a
19 request, which the court shall grant, for an order delaying the
20 notification required under section 6(5) of this act for a period not
21 to exceed ninety days if the court determines that there is a reason to
22 believe that notification of the existence of the warrant may have an
23 adverse result.

24   (1) An adverse result for the purposes of this section is:
25   (a) Placing the life or physical safety of an individual in danger;
26   (b) Causing a person to flee from prosecution;
27   (c) Causing the destruction of or tampering with evidence;
28   (d) Causing the intimidation of potential witnesses; or
29   (e) Jeopardizing an investigation or unduly delaying a trial.
30   (2) The governmental entity shall maintain a copy of certification.
31   (3) Extension of the delay of notification of up to ninety days
32 each may be granted by the court upon application or by certification
33 by a governmental entity.
34   (4) Upon expiration of the period of delay of notification under
35 subsection (1) or (3) of this section, the governmental entity shall
36 serve a copy of the warrant upon, or deliver it by registered or first-

1   class mail to, the person or persons upon whom personal information was
2   collected together with notice that:
3   (a) States with reasonable specificity the nature of the law
4   enforcement inquiry; and
5   (b) Informs the person or persons upon whom personal information
6   was collected (i) that notification was delayed; (ii) what governmental
7   entity or court made the certification or determination pursuant to
8   which that delay was made; and (iii) which provision of this section
9   allowed such delay.

10   NEW SECTION.   **Sec. 8.**   It shall be lawful under this section for
11 any law enforcement officer or other public official to operate a
12 public unmanned aircraft system and disclose personal information from
13 such operation if:
14   (1) Such officer reasonably determines that an emergency situation
15 exists that involves immediate danger of death or serious physical
16 injury to any person and:
17   (a) Requires operation of a public unmanned aircraft system before
18 a warrant authorizing such interception can, with due diligence, be
19 obtained;
20   (b) There are grounds upon which such a warrant could be entered to
21 authorize such operation; and
22   (c) An application for a warrant providing such operation is made
23 within forty-eight hours after the operation has occurred or begins to
24 occur.
25   (2) In the absence of a warrant, an operation of a public unmanned
26 aircraft system carried out under this subsection shall immediately
27 terminate when the personal information sought is obtained or when the
28 application for the warrant is denied, whichever is earlier.
29   (3) In the event such application for approval is denied, the
30 personal information obtained from the operation of a device shall be
31 treated as having been obtained in violation of this section and an
32 inventory shall be served on the person named in the application.

33   NEW SECTION.   **Sec. 9.**   A public unmanned aircraft system may be
34 operated and personal information from such operation disclosed in
35 order to collect information pursuant to administrative search warrant
36 or inspection warrant issued by a court of competent jurisdiction by

1   any judicial officer having authority to issue such warrants whose
2   territorial jurisdiction encompasses the area to be inspected or
3   entered or as otherwise provided in this section.
4   (1) Each petition for a warrant from a judicial officer to permit
5   the use of a public unmanned aircraft system and information collected
6   from such operation shall be made in writing, upon oath or affirmation,
7   to a judicial officer in a court of competent jurisdiction for the
8   geographic area in which a public unmanned aircraft system is to be
9   operated or where there is probable cause, supported by affidavit,
10 particularly describing the place, property, things, or persons to be
11 inspected, tested, or information collected and the purpose for which
12 the inspection, testing, or collection of information is to be made.
13   (2) Probable cause shall be deemed to exist if either:
14   (a) Reasonable legislative or administrative standards for
15 conducting such inspection, testing, or information collected are
16 satisfied with respect to the particular place, property, thing, or
17 person; or
18   (b) There is cause to believe that there is such a condition,
19 object, activity, or circumstance that legally justifies such
20 inspection, testing, or collection of information.
21   (3) The agency official shall submit an affidavit that shall
22 include the identity of the applicant and the identity of the agency
23 conducting the inspection.
24   (4) The supporting affidavit shall contain either a statement that
25 consent to the search and collection of information has been sought and
26 refused or facts or circumstances reasonably justifying the failure to
27 seek such consent in order to enforce effectively the safety and health
28 laws, regulations, or standards of the warrant based on legislative or
29 administrative standards for inspection.
30   (5) The affidavit shall contain factual allegations sufficient to
31 justify an independent determination by a judge that the search is
32 based on reasonable standards and the standards are being applied to a
33 particular area in a neutral and fair manner.
34   (6) The issuing judicial officer may examine the affiant under oath
35 or affirmation to verify the accuracy of any matter in the affidavit.
36   (7) Any warrant issued shall be effective for the time specified
37 therein, but not for a period of more than fifteen days unless extended
38 or renewed by the judicial officer who signed and issued the original

1 warrant. The warrant shall be executed and shall be returned to the
2 judicial officer by whom it was issued within the time specified in the
3 warrant or within the extended or renewed time. The return shall list
4 the information collected pursuant to the warrant. After the
5 expiration of such time, the warrant, unless executed, shall be void.

6   (8) No warrant shall be executed in the absence of the owner,
7 tenant, operator, or custodian of the premises unless the issuing
8 judicial official specifically authorizes that such authority is
9 reasonably necessary to affect the purposes of the law or regulation.
10 Entry pursuant to such a warrant shall not be made forcibly. The
11 issuing officer may authorize a forcible entry where the facts (a)
12 create a reasonable suspicion of immediate threat to the health or
13 safety of persons or to the environment or (b) establish that
14 reasonable attempts to serve a previous warrant have been unsuccessful.
15 If forcible entry is authorized, the warrant shall be issued jointly to
16 the applicant agency and a law enforcement officer shall accompany the
17 agency official during the execution of the warrant.

18   (9) No court of the state shall have jurisdiction to hear a
19 challenge to the warrant prior to its return to the issuing judicial
20 officer, except as a defense in a contempt proceeding or if the owner
21 or custodian of the place to be inspected submits a substantial
22 preliminary showing by affidavit and accompanied by proof that (a) a
23 statement included by the affiant in his or her affidavit for the
24 administrative search warrant was false and made knowingly and
25 intentionally or with reckless disregard for the truth and (b) the
26 false statement was necessary to the finding of probable cause. The
27 court may conduct in camera review as appropriate.

28   (10) After the warrant has been executed and returned to the
29 issuing judicial officer, the validity of the warrant may be reviewed
30 either as a defense to any notice of violation or by declaratory
31 judgment action brought in court. The review shall be confined to the
32 face of the warrant, affidavits, and supporting materials presented to
33 the issuing judicial officer. If the owner or custodian of the place
34 inspected submits a substantial showing by affidavit and accompanied by
35 proof that (a) a statement included in the warrant was false and made
36 knowingly and intentionally or with reckless disregard for the truth
37 and (b) the false statement was necessary to the finding of probable

1   cause, the reviewing court shall limit its inquiry to whether there is
2   substantial evidence in the record supporting the issuance of the
3   warrant and may conduct a de novo determination of probable cause.

4   NEW SECTION. **Sec. 10.** Whenever any personal information from a
5   public unmanned aircraft system has been acquired, no part of such
6   personal information and no evidence derived therefrom may be received
7   in evidence in any trial, hearing, or other proceeding in or before any
8   court, grand jury, department, officer, agency, regulatory body,
9   legislative committee, or other authority of the state or a political
10   subdivision thereof if the collection or disclosure of that personal
11   information would be in violation of this chapter.

12   NEW SECTION. **Sec. 11.** No personal information collected on an
13   individual or area other than the target that justified the issuance of
14   a search warrant may be used, copied, or disclosed for any purpose.
15   Such personal information shall be deleted as soon as possible, and in
16   no event later than twenty-four hours after collection.

17   NEW SECTION. **Sec. 12.** Personal information collected on any
18   individual or area specified in the warrant shall be deleted within
19   thirty days unless there is a reasonable belief that the personal
20   information is evidence of criminal activity or civil liability related
21   to the reason that allowed the use of the unmanned public aircraft
22   system.

23   NEW SECTION. **Sec. 13.** The disclosure or publication, without
24   authorization of a court, by a court officer, law enforcement officer,
25   or other person responsible for the administration of this section of
26   the existence of a search warrant issued pursuant to this section,
27   application for such search warrant, any affidavit filed in support of
28   such warrant, or any personal information obtained as a result of such
29   search warrant is punishable as a class C felony.

30   NEW SECTION. **Sec. 14.** Any use of unmanned aircraft systems shall
31   fully comply with all federal aviation administration requirements and
32   guidelines.

1   <u>NEW SECTION.</u>   **Sec. 15.** By July 1st of each year, any judicial

2   officer who has authorized the issuance of a search warrant or

3   extension of a public unmanned aircraft system that expired during the

4   preceding year or who has denied approval during that year shall report

5   to the chief justice of the supreme court or his or her designee

6   the following information:

7   (1) The fact that a warrant or extension was applied for;

8   (2) The kind of warrant or extension applied for;

9   (3) The fact that the warrant or extension was granted as applied

10   for, was modified, or was denied;

11   (4) The period of interceptions authorized by the order, and the

12   number and duration of any extensions of the order;

13   (5) The offense or purpose specified in the petition and the

14   probable cause giving rise to such warrant or extension of such

15   warrant; and

16   (6) The identity of the applying state agency applicant or law

17   enforcement officer, the agency making the application, and the

18   judicial officer authorizing the petition.

19   <u>NEW SECTION.</u>   **Sec. 16.** By July 1st of each year, any law

20   enforcement agency who applied for a criminal search warrant for the

21   use of a public unmanned aircraft system shall report to the chief of

22   the state patrol or his or her designee the following

23   information:

24   (1) The information required by section 15 of this act with respect

25   to each application for a search warrant or extension made during the

26   preceding calendar year;

27   (2) The general description of the information gathered under such

28   search warrant or extension including:

29   (a) The approximate nature and frequency of incriminating conduct

30   gathered;

31   (b) The approximate number of persons upon whom information was

32   gathered; and

33   (c) The approximate nature, amount, and cost of the manpower and

34   other resources used in the collection;

35   (3) The number of arrests resulting from information gathered under

36   such search warrant or extension and the offenses for which arrests

37   were made;

1   (4) The number of trials resulting from such information;

2   (5) The number of motions to suppress made with respect to such

3   information and the number granted or denied;

4   (6) The number of convictions resulting from such information and

5   the offenses for which the convictions were obtained and a general

6   assessment of the importance of the information; and

7   (7) The information required by section 15 of this act with respect

8   to search warrants or extensions obtained in the preceding calendar

9   year.

10   NEW SECTION. **Sec. 17.** By July 1st of each year, each state agency

11   that applied for an administrative search warrant or inspection warrant

12   or extension of a public unmanned aircraft system shall report to the

13   governor or his or her designee the following information:

14   (1) The fact that such a warrant or extension was applied for;

15   (2) The kind of order or extension applied for;

16   (3) The fact that the order or extension was granted as applied

17   for, was modified, or denied;

18   (4) The period of interceptions authorized by the order and the

19   number and duration of any extensions of the order;

20   (5) The identity of the applicant and state agency making the

21   petition and the judicial officer authorizing the petition;

22   (6) The probable cause giving rise to the issuance of the

23   administrative search warrant or inspection warrant in the petition or

24   extension of such warrant, including the conditions, object, activity,

25   or circumstance that legally justified such inspection, testing, or

26   collection of information;

27   (7) The general description of the information gathered under such

28   warrant or extension, including:

29   (a) The approximate nature and frequency of the information

30   gathered, collected, or inspected from such place, property, things, or

31   persons;

32   (b) The approximate number of persons upon whom personal

33   information was gathered; and

34   (c) The approximate nature, amount, and cost of the manpower and

35   other resources used in the collection or inspection; and

36   (8) If applicable, the identity of the judicial officer authorizing

1   forcible entry, the identity of the law enforcement officer who
2   assisted the agency official, and information justifying the issuance
3   of the forcible entry order.

4   NEW SECTION. **Sec. 18.** By December 1st of each year, the chief
5   justice of the supreme court or his or her designee, the chief of
6   the state patrol or his or her designee, and the governor or his or
7   her designee shall transmit to the legislature a full and complete
8   report concerning the number of applications for search warrants
9   authorizing or approving operation of a public unmanned aircraft system
10 or disclosure of information or data from the operation of a public
11 unmanned aircraft system pursuant to this section and the number of
12 search warrants and extensions granted or denied pursuant to this
13 section during the preceding calendar year. Such report shall
14 include a summary and analysis of all the data required to be filed
15 with the supreme court, the Washington state patrol, and the governor.
16

17   NEW SECTION. **Sec. 19.** Excluding personally identifiable
17 information, records required by sections 15 through 18 of this act
18 shall be open to public disclosure under the Washington public records
19 act, chapter 42.56 RCW.
20

21   NEW SECTION. **Sec. 20.** The governing body of any locality
21 permitting the use of public unmanned aircraft systems shall publish
22 publicly available written policies and procedures for the use of
23 public unmanned aircraft systems by the law enforcement agencies of
24 such locality.
25

26   NEW SECTION. **Sec. 21.** The governing body of any locality
26 permitting the use of public unmanned aircraft systems shall, by
27 ordinance, require the law enforcement agency of such locality
28 operating a public unmanned aircraft system to maintain records of each
29 use of a public unmanned aircraft system, including the date, time,
30 location of use, target of data collection, type of data collected, the
31 justification for the use, the operator of the public unmanned aircraft
32 system, and the person who authorized the use.
33

1   NEW SECTION.   **Sec. 22.**   The governing body of any locality
2   permitting the use of a public unmanned aircraft system shall conduct
3   an annual comprehensive audit on the operation of all public unmanned
4   aircraft systems, including the law enforcement log book, corresponding
5   emergency telephone calls, warrants, and other documentation of the
6   justification for use and data collected. The audit shall be publicly
7   available. The audit shall include:
8   (1) The number of uses of a public unmanned aircraft system
9   organized by types of incidents and types of justification for use;
10   (2) The number of crime investigations aided by the use and how the
11   use was helpful to the investigation;
12   (3) The number of uses of a public unmanned aircraft system for
13   reasons other than criminal investigations and how the use was helpful;
14   (4) The frequency and type of data collected for individuals or
15   areas other than targets;
16   (5) The total cost of the public unmanned aircraft system; and
17   (6) Additional information and analysis the governing body deems
18   useful.

19   NEW SECTION.   **Sec. 23.**   The governing body of any locality
20   permitting the use of a public unmanned aircraft system shall, upon
21   completion of the publicly available annual audit on the use of public
22   unmanned aircraft systems, review the use of public unmanned aircraft
23   systems and consider both the benefits and risks to privacy before
24   authorizing the continued operation of a public unmanned aircraft
25   system in such locality.

26   NEW SECTION.   **Sec. 24.**   Sections 1 through 23 of this act
27   constitute a new chapter in Title 10 RCW.

28   NEW SECTION.   **Sec. 25.**   This act is necessary for the immediate
29   preservation of the public peace, health, or safety, or support of the
30   state government and its existing public institutions, and takes effect
31   immediately.

--- **END** ---